2007–2008 Annual Supplement to

THE PIANO BOOK

BUYING & OWNING A NEW OR USED PIANO

LARRY FINE

BROOKSIDE PRESS • BOSTON, MASSACHUSETTS

Brookside Press
P.O. Box 300168, Jamaica Plain, Massachusetts 02130
(617) 522-7182
(800) 888-4741 (orders: Independent Publishers Group)

info@pianobook.com
www.pianobook.com

2007–2008 Annual Supplement to The Piano Book copyright © 2007 by Lawrence Fine
All rights reserved

Printed in the United States of America

Distributed to the book trade by Independent Publishers Group,
814 North Franklin St., Chicago, IL 60610
(800) 888-4741 or (312) 337-0747

No part of this book may be reproduced in any form whatsoever without prior written permission of the publisher, except for brief quotations embodied in critical articles and book reviews.

ISBN 1-929145-21-7 (print edition)
ISBN 1-929145-22-5 (electronic edition)

NOTICE

Reasonable efforts have been made to secure accurate information for this publication. Due in part to the fact that manufacturers and distributors will not always willingly make this information available, however, some indirect sources have been relied upon.

Neither the author nor publisher make any guarantees with respect to the accuracy of the information contained herein and will not be liable for damages—incidental, consequential, or otherwise—resulting from the use of the information.

INTRODUCTION

Given the long time span between new editions of *The Piano Book,* it's impractical to provide in the book itself the detailed model and price data that piano shoppers increasingly seek. Similarly, updated information about manufacturers and products is needed in a timely manner. This *Annual Supplement to The Piano Book,* published each summer, is designed to fill that information gap. I hope this modest companion volume will effectively extend the "shelf life" of *The Piano Book* as a valuable reference work, and serve as an additional information resource for piano buyers and piano lovers.

Larry Fine
June 2007

CONTENTS

MANUFACTURER and PRODUCT UPDATE 5
   Trends 5
   Summary of Brands and Ratings 11
   Brand Listings 20
MODEL and PRICING GUIDE 113

For more assistance:

- **New Piano Pricing Guide Service**
- **Phone Consultation with the Author**

See www.pianobook.com

MANUFACTURER and PRODUCT UPDATE

This section contains brief reviews of most brands of new piano distributed nationwide in the United States. The reviews contain (often verbatim) material from the fourth edition of *The Piano Book* where still relevant and accurate, accumulated changes from past *Supplements*, and new material gleaned from interviews with manufacturers, distributors, dealers, technicians, and other sources. Most manufacturers had an opportunity to see, comment upon, and correct for factual accuracy the reviews of their products.

This year's *Supplement* differs from those of past years in that the reviews are written as complete, standalone pieces of writing, rather than as an accumulation of changes that must be integrated by the reader into the main reviews in *The Piano Book*. To keep the size manageable, however, much historical and technical information was abbreviated or omitted, including information on older, discontinued models and on problems or defects that have long since been rectified. Although the information in this *Supplement* will usually be sufficient to help guide you in purchasing a new piano, you may wish, at your leisure, to peruse *The Piano Book* for additional commentary on the brands you are considering. Just be aware that, particularly where it conflicts with information in this *Supplement*, *The Piano Book* may no longer be accurate. In most cases, brands included in *The Piano Book* but not in the *Supplement* are either out of business or no longer being distributed in the United States.

As in *The Piano Book*, the reviews here are a bit quirky—that is, they vary in their length and in the thoroughness with which they treat their subjects. Some companies have more interesting history, some instruments have more unusual technical features, some brands have more controversial issues associated with them, and some manufacturers were more helpful than others in providing access to interesting material. The reviews are more descriptive than evaluative, preferring the perspective of the piano technician to the vague, flowery (and, in my opinion, unhelpful) descriptions of piano tone sometimes found in instrument reviews. For a "road map" depicting how I think the different brands stack up against each other, see the "Summary of Brands and Ratings" on page 11.

Be sure to read *The Piano Book* for basic information on buying a piano, understanding technical features, and negotiating the best deal.

Trends

Pianos made in China continue to dominate the North American market. By some estimates, about one-third of all new pianos sold in the U.S. are made in China. As recently as 2001, most pianos from China, though technically acceptable, were not musically desirable. Over the past few years, however, the musical qualities have taken a big leap forward. The jury is still out as to whether these pianos will hold up over the long term and in demanding climates and situations. Reports suggest less consistency than with pianos from most other countries, and the need for thorough pre-sale preparation by the dealer (and sometimes the dealer needs to weed out the bad ones and return them to the factory), but otherwise few major problems. Prices are so low, however, that for many entry-level buyers these pianos are an excellent value despite some uncertainty about their longevity. At least as short-term investments, and in milder climates and less demanding situations, they are probably fine.

The first piano factory in China is said to have been established in 1895 in Shanghai (perhaps by the British?). During the 1950s, the Communists consolidated the country's piano manufacturing into four government-owned factories: Shanghai, Beijing, and Dongbei (means "northeast") in the northern part of the country, and Guangzhou Pearl River in the south. Piano making, though industrial, remained primitive well into the 1990s. In that decade, the government of China began to open the country's economy to foreign investment, first only to partnerships with the government, later to completely private concerns.

As the economy has opened up, the rising Chinese middle and upper classes have created a sharp increase in demand for pianos. Tempted by the enormous potential Chinese domestic market, as well as by the lure of cheap goods for the West, foreign interests have built new piano factories in China, bought existing factories, or contracted with existing factories for the manufacture of pianos. The government has also poured money into its own factories to accommodate the growing demand and to make the factories more competitive.

Except for the government involvement, the piano making scene in China today is reminiscent of that in the United States a hundred years ago: Hundreds of small firms assemble pianos from parts or subassemblies obtained from dozens of suppliers and sell them on a mostly regional basis. The government factories and a few large foreign ones sell nationally. Most of the pianos sold in the Chinese domestic market are still primitive by Western standards. Primarily where foreign technical assistance or investment has been involved has the quality markedly improved, and only those pianos are good enough to be sold in the West.

Although the government factories have long had a monopoly on sales in China through piano dealers, that hold is gradually being eroded, and the government entities are experiencing great competitive pressure from all the smaller players. Combined with the inefficiencies and debt inherent in government operations, the current competitive situation is probably making the government think twice about continuing to subsidize the piano industry. Already, one of its factories, Dongbei, has announced its impending privatization by way of sale to the Baldwin Piano Company.

For the first half of this decade, most sales of Chinese pianos in the United States were based on the idea of luring customers into the store to buy the least expensive piano possible. Dealers that staked their business on this approach often lost it. A growing trend now is to manufacture and sell somewhat higher-priced pianos that have added value in the form of better components, often imported from Europe and the U.S., but still taking advantage of the low cost of Chinese labor. The best ones are not just a collection of parts, however, but also have improved designs developed with foreign technical assistance, and sufficient oversight to make sure the designs are properly executed.

The oversight is especially important. Chinese piano manufacturers have been quite aggressive at acquiring piano-making knowledge, and are happy to use their alliances with Western distributors to that end. However, the distributors frequently complain that agreements as to technical specifications, quality, and exclusivity of relationship are routinely disregarded by their Chinese business partners. Once the Western inspectors leave the factory, the Chinese managers do whatever they feel is in their own best interest, which often amounts to maximizing production at the expense of quality. The distributors have gradually discovered that the only way to overcome this problem is to own the factory themselves, to maintain a constant presence at the factory, or to constitute such a large percentage of the Chinese company's business that they (the Westerners) can control production. Alternatively, a Western company can examine all the pianos in its home country before sending them on to dealers, but this is less satisfactory than stopping problems at the source. Western distributors of Korean pianos used to complain of a similar problem with Korean piano factory managers during the height of that country's piano industry in the 1980s and '90s.

For the consumer, there are two lessons to take from this. First, although the average quality is quite reasonable, depending on how well the distributor handles the quality-control issue, and how well the dealer examines and prepares the pianos, you may find a fair amount of variation among Chinese-made pianos as you shop (this is in addition to whatever variation naturally exists between brands). Therefore, it may be in your best interest to hire a piano technician to examine one of these pianos before purchase. Second, statements by salespeople as to particular specifications or exclusivity of relationship ("Of all the brands that ZYX Piano Company makes, this is the only one with a graduated calibrator") should not be relied upon as true in every case, even though such statements may be made in good faith. Buy what you can see with your eyes and hear with your ears.

There has been an explosion of different brand names under which Chinese-made pianos are being marketed, there now being about a dozen Chinese manufacturers making pianos for export to the U.S. Piano shoppers should keep in mind, however, that cosmetics aside, if two brands of piano originate in the same factory, they are often very similar, sometimes identical. (Exceptions to this are usually noted in the brand reviews.)

On the other end of the price spectrum, European piano makers seem to be in a race to redesign their pianos for better sound projection and sustain, à la Steinway. While the European piano market is languishing, the U.S. market for high-end pianos, relatively speaking, is thriving, and for a number of companies, Steinway is the principal competitor. Considering how tradition-bound these companies are, this degree of activity is unusual. Some of the redesigns—new models from Seiler and Schimmel come to mind—have been terrific musical successes. My only worry is that the palette of available piano tonal qualities is becoming smaller and more homogeneous as the old-world sounds pass away.

Changes in China and in Europe, and their far-reaching consequences, are causing a paradigm shift in the piano industry that is making it more difficult to give advice to piano shoppers. (A paradigm is a theoretical framework from which generalizations are formulated.) For many years, the paradigm for piano quality has been an international pecking order with pianos from Russia and China (and, more recently, Indonesia) at the bottom, followed by Korea, Japan, Eastern Europe, and finally Western Europe (mostly Germany) at the top, with pianos from the United States scattered here and there depending on the brand. While this pecking order has never been foolproof, it has served its purpose as a generalization well enough for use by a generation of piano buyers.

Now these distinctions are being blurred by globalization. Unable to escape the high cost of doing business at home, some Western European manufacturers are developing satellite operations and more affordable second product lines in Eastern Europe and third product lines in China. Some makers of high-end instruments are also quietly beginning to source parts and subassemblies from Asia and elsewhere. To the extent they can afford it, they are also investing in high-tech equipment to reduce the expense and inconsistency of hand labor, even while continuing to tout their status as makers of "hand-made" instruments. Some Korean and Chinese manufacturers, on the other hand, are importing parts and technology from Germany and Japan, producing instruments that when well prepared by the dealer rival the performance qualities of far more expensive pianos from Japan and, occasionally, Europe. The most we can say is that their longevity is unknown, an argument that, while true, becomes weaker with each passing year. In addition, global alliances are sure to bring new products to the market that are more hybridized than anything we've seen before. Although the old paradigm still has validity, the number of nonconforming situations is increasing, all of which will cause temporary confusion in the marketplace until such time as a new paradigm emerges.

At the same time that quality differences between low-end and high-end instruments are becoming narrower, price differences are greater than they've ever been, bringing issues of "value" into greater prominence. Eastern European quality in some cases now closely approaches that of Western Europe, but at a price comparable to that of Japan. Some of the better pianos from China, Korea, and Indonesia have specifications equal to almost anything from Japan, and workmanship nearly as good, at a fraction of the price. Caught in the middle, the Japanese are gradually being squeezed out of the piano market despite their perennially good quality.

Another consequence of globalization has been the diminishing number of independent suppliers of parts and materials (actions, hammers, pinblocks, soundboards, keys, plates, etc.) to the piano industry. (Actually, the enormous Chinese piano industry has numerous parts suppliers, but most of these supply parts only for pianos sold in the domestic Chinese market, not internationally.) At one time there were large differences in quality between suppliers, but globalization has reduced and sometimes eliminated those differences. For example, as recently as a few years ago, Detoa (Czech) actions were markedly inferior to Renner (German) actions, and Chinese-made actions were terrible. Now there is at most only a small difference in quality between Detoa and Renner, virtually all Chinese actions are acceptable, and one Chinese supplier, Ningbo Orient, is producing very good-looking knockoffs of Renner actions.

At the same time, many manufacturers continue to use a "recipe" approach to differentiating differently-priced piano lines: Choose an action (Renner, Detoa, Chinese), combine it with a hammer (Renner, Abel, Imadegawa), add a pinblock (Delignit, Dehonit, Bolduc), and so forth, to produce a piano at a particular price. But with fewer suppliers to choose from, and less difference between them, the implied difference in quality at different price points is threatening to become more a matter of image than actuality.

The above notwithstanding, differences still do exist. The most important is that between performance-grade pianos on the one hand (Groups 1 and 2 in *The Piano Book* rating system) and consumer-grade pianos on the other (Groups 3, 4, and 5). There have been some fairly successful attempts by makers to bridge this gap (e.g., some high-end Japanese pianos), but for the most part, the two different types of manufacturers still live in two different worlds. The difference between the two worlds is less than it used to be, but still exists in the form of selection, drying, and use of wood; final regulation and voicing; and attention to technical and cosmetic detail; in other words, the difference is more than just the "recipe."

Theoretically, it would be possible for, say, a Chinese company to duplicate the finest pianos. But the market for these instruments is small, and some have unique and idiosyncratic designs that are not amenable to mass production. Therefore, it is always likely to be more of a niche market entered into by those whose profit-seeking is mixed with a love for the instrument and perhaps a desire to carry on a family business. At this point in time, such businesses are more likely to be Western than Asian, but who knows . . . that may one day change.

As I mentioned, globalization means more than just Chinese pianos, and in general it should not be feared. A German company making pianos or parts in a Czech or Polish factory it owns or controls is not much different from an Ohio company sourcing parts from a factory over the border in Kentucky. These days, among the countries of Europe, there is enough of a commonality of business practices, laws, culture, and attitudes toward quality that geographic differences carry little meaning, except as to labor costs, where the savings may be great. (In fact, it's not unusual for an Eastern European piano manufacturer to make parts for its Western European competitors.) When a Japanese or Korean piano maker sets up shop in China or Indonesia, it tends to transplant the entire culture of its home factory to the new one, including machinery, managers, and quality standards. After a short period of start-up issues, the quality will usually be comparable to what is produced at home.

The phenomenon of Western makers of high-end pianos sourcing parts in China may be inevitable, but it does trouble me a little more than the other manifestations of globalization. I'm especially concerned about action parts, which get tremendous use and abuse over the life of the piano and are especially sensitive to microscopic imperfections, climate changes, and so forth. Piano makers are seeking out alternatives because of the high price of Renner parts from Germany and the danger of relying too heavily on one supplier. This certainly makes sense for lower-cost pianos. But when a customer is laying out tens of thousands of dollars for a high-end piano, he or she expects that the manufacturer will use only the most time-tested components. I don't want to be alarmist about this because I know that several manufacturers have tested the Chinese parts and are convinced they are as good as the genuine Renner parts. However, experience has shown, especially with regard to action parts, that there are a myriad of opportunities for things to go wrong, and some may be ones that do not show up in tests other than the test of time. In fact, some may not show up as "problems" at all, but rather as a subtle difference in musical expressiveness or as slightly greater wear and tear over the long term. The risk is theoretical at this point, as no substantial issues have been reported with these parts to date. But purchasers of high-end European and American pianos probably do not expect Chinese-made components in their instruments, and the pianos are certainly not advertised that way. My feeling is that customers should be notified in an appropriate way of substantial "alternative" content in high-end pianos so they can make a risk/benefit analysis according to their own values.

SUMMARY OF BRANDS AND RATINGS

People absorb information in different ways. For newcomers to the piano market, just reading brand reviews is usually not sufficient to orient them to how the market is organized. Rather, a simple, visual summary is also needed. The charts and commentary that follow are intended to provide that summary in the form of a "road map" to how the brands compare to one another in quality. This chart is much simpler than the one in the fourth edition of *The Piano Book*. That one contains a great deal more information, but too often readers skip the explanations and end up misunderstanding or misusing the chart. This one, on the other hand, though more up-to-date, is simple to the point of being simplistic, so I've added commentary to provide some additional context.

The ratings take into account musical design, workmanship, durability, quality control, and the perceived dependability of the company in honoring the warranty. For the purposes of this simple chart, many generalizations have had to be made, as there can be great differences in quality even within a single model line. For a few newer brands that I have not yet even seen, mostly from China, I have estimated the quality based on what I know about the maker, materials, specifications, and so on. However, for some brands, I have not felt comfortable even estimating, so I have omitted them. No negative inference should be drawn from this.

It has never been my intention to set myself up as the ultimate judge of pianos, nor are these ratings about my own personal taste in piano tone or touch. Rather, through my contacts with dozens of piano technicians, dealers, and other industry personnel, and from thirty years of involvement with the piano industry, I have made a good-faith effort to find a consensus of informed opinion to the extent it may exist. Of course, a perfect consensus rarely exists, so I must sometimes use my own judgment to determine how much weight to give different opinions and to decide where the thread of "truth" lies on any given matter. Needless to say, the ratings and commentary are anecdotal and subjective in nature, not scientific, and I cannot guarantee they accurately represent the typical or average opinion about any brand. One thing I *can* guarantee is that the ratings will be controversial. While most knowledgeable people in the industry are likely to agree with the rating system's structure in the broadest sense, they will disagree endlessly about the details. I, myself, change my mind about the details quite frequently, so you should consider this only an approximation intended to start you on your own path of discovery, not something set in stone.

Please use common sense when comparing one brand with another. Compare verticals to verticals and grands to grands, and compare only similar sizes with one another.

Pianos can be divided into two types, largely according to the intention of the manufacturer. One type is built to a high standard, or even to the highest standard possible, and the price charged is whatever it takes to build such a piano and bring it to market. I call this type of piano "Performance-Grade." The other type is built to be sold at a particular price, and adjustments (compromises) to materials, workmanship, and method and location of production are made to meet that price. I call this type "Consumer-Grade." Both types of piano are necessary, of course, as not everyone needs or can afford the best possible piano.

Each type can be further subdivided into two groups, creating a four-group structure. Groups 1 and 3 represent the highest quality within the two types of piano. Groups 2 and 4 represent a slightly lower quality within each type, but at a lower cost, and are often a better value as a result. So if you are buying for quality, you will generally look at Groups 1 and 3. If you looking for the best value for the money, you will generally look at Groups 2 and 4. The four groups are further described and shown below. (In *The Piano Book*, there is a fifth group, consisting of pianos that are not good enough even to be recommended. That group, thank goodness, is currently empty.) This is not a perfect scheme for describing the piano market, and there are some brands that do not neatly fit the above description, but it is close enough that you are not likely to be seriously misled.

For this *Supplement*, I have subdivided each of the four groups into several subgroups, each containing one or more brands that can be recommended about equally. **Within each subgroup, the brands are listed in alphabetical order and no other inference should be made from this order.** It's important to understand that just because two brands are listed together does not mean they are similar in their characteristics. For example, one brand could have an excellent musical design but questionable quality control. Another could have a so-so musical design but terrific quality control. On balance, though different, they might be recommended about equally. Of course, depending on whether musical design or quality control is more important to you, you might place the brands in a different order, another reason why a generic list such as this must be considered only a rough calculation.

Don't get too hung up on small differences. The distinction between one group and the next (especially between Groups 1 and 2) can be subtle, and the difference between adjacent subgroups can be miniscule, even questionable. Furthermore, the preparation of the piano by the dealer can be far more important to the quality of the product you receive than many of the distinctions shown on the chart. When it comes to dealer prep, it really is possible (to some extent, anyway) to turn "a sow's ear into a silk purse." Look for a dealer known for providing thorough and competent make-ready and you won't have to worry so much about what group your piano is in!

Prices shown below are the approximate lowest and highest typical selling prices of new pianos in the least expensive style and finish.

Group 1: Highest quality performance pianos

These pianos are for those who want the best and can afford it. They utilize the very best materials, and the manufacturing process emphasizes much hand labor and refinement of details. Advanced designs are painstakingly executed, putting quality considerations far ahead of cost and production output. They are suitable for the most advanced and demanding professional and artistic uses. Most of the pianos in this group are made in the U.S. and Western Europe. *Comparison with automobiles: think Rolls-Royce, Bentley, Mercedes-Benz.*

    Verticals: $14,000 to $34,000
    Grands 5' to 7': $40,000 to $90,000

Group 1A: Blüthner
                      Bösendorfer
                      Fazioli
                      Steingraeber & Söhne
                      Steinway & Sons (Hamburg)

Group 1B: Bechstein, C. (Concert series)
                      Förster, August
                      Grotrian
                      Sauter

Group 1C: Kawai, Shigeru
                      Steinway & Sons (New York)

<u>Commentary on Group 1</u>: It was easier to arrive at a consensus on Group 1A than on any other subgroup in this rating system. So celebrated are the pianos in this subgroup that dealers eagerly nominated their competitors for the list. These pianos have everything, and the attention to detail can only be called fanatical. Some of the names in this group are well known and expected, but one that is not is Steingraeber & Söhne. I was aware of this brand, but was surprised at how many others with even passing acquaintance with it named it without hesitation. Note that Steinway & Sons (Hamburg) is not routinely available in North America; I include it for informational purposes only.

The pianos in Group 1B are also fabulous, and very "fussy," but there was little doubt that they were second to the pianos in Group 1A, either because their workmanship is not quite as fussy as the first group, or because their musical designs are considered slightly less desirable, or both. However, preference throughout Group 1 is highly dependent on musical taste, and the brands in Group 1B definitely have their devoted following. Sauter pianos, new to Group 1, are beautifully crafted and sound terrific, but the company tends to maintain a low profile in the U.S. and the tone is not as distinctively European as the others, so it's easy to overlook.

As for Group 1C, Shigeru Kawai, another newcomer to Group 1, is the first piano from Japan to make the grade. It is beginning to gain acceptance in universities and other venues as one of the great instruments of the day. I'm still not sure where in Group 1 it belongs, so I've put it in 1C as a start.

Steinway & Sons (New York), at its best, has one of the finest sounds of any piano in Group 1—and, relative to the others in this group, the worst workmanship. It's a testament to the amazing piano designs of this venerable brand, and the integrity of its sound-body construction, that instruments with so little finesse in workmanship can potentially sound and play so well. They vary, but if you bother the salespeople until they get their technicians to prep them, you can find some really nice ones.

A brand I did not feel familiar enough with to place accurately, but which would probably fall in Group 1, is Feurich.

Group 2: High-performance pianos

These instruments are built to a standard favoring high-performance design features, materials, and workmanship. They are suitable for home, institutional, and some professional and artistic uses. Greater hand labor is put into refining touch and tone during manufacture, although perhaps not quite as much as some in Group 1. Cost considerations, virtually absent for Group 1 instruments, may affect decisions regarding materials and production methods to a limited extent. For a variety of reasons, these pianos have not received as much critical acclaim as those in Group 1. Although the difference in quality between the two groups is small—and for many buyers will be undetectable—the price difference is substantial, making these pianos a great value for those who can settle for "almost the best." Most pianos in this group are made in the U.S. and in Eastern and Western Europe. *Comparison with automobiles: think BMW, Saab, Volvo, Audi, Lexus.*

    Verticals: $6,000 to $20,000
    Grands 5' to 7': $18,000 to $50,000

Group 2A: Estonia
                     Mason & Hamlin
                     Schimmel (Konzert series)

Group 2B: Bechstein (Academy series)
Haessler
Schimmel (Classic series)
Schulze Pollmann
Seiler
Steinberg, Wilh.
Walter, Charles R.
Yamaha ("S" series)

Group 2C: Baldwin (grands)
Bohemia
Irmler
Kemble
Petrof
Vogel

<u>Commentary on Group 2:</u> Group 2A contains three brands that are close runners-up for Group 1. Estonia, formerly at the bottom of Group 2, has become so much more advanced over the last five years that it may belong in Group 1. However, this fact has not yet been appreciated or confirmed by much of the piano community, so I am testing the waters by putting it in Group 2A.

I have always thought of Schimmel as being perfectly engineered, but not a luxury instrument and just a little lacking in soul. Apparently Mr. Schimmel decided he wanted to leave a better legacy than that, so before he retired, he pulled out all the stops and used the considerable engineering skills of his company to create a more modern and mature series of instruments. The innovative design decisions he made, combined with the perfect execution for which the brand is known, have elevated the stature of the company's instruments to a new level.

The rating of Mason & Hamlin has been reduced slightly to Group 2A. It is still a great instrument, but I believe the company's current manufacturing approach is more consistent with Group 2 than Group 1.

I found it difficult to further subdivide Group 2, and sensed little agreement among my contacts about how it should be done. I believe the instruments in Group 2B have just a little more finesse (I use that word a lot) than those in Group 2C. Each of the brands in Group 2B is quite different, but I couldn't figure out a way to reliably subdivide them further. Don't be fooled by the fact that Group 2C pianos are at the bottom of Group 2. They are still wonderful instruments, and some of the best values in the piano world.

Baldwin grands are a special case. I have placed them here out of respect for their great designs and specifications and their former reputation. But they are currently not living up to that reputation consistently and must be examined carefully before purchase.

Group 3: Better quality consumer-grade pianos

These instruments give roughly equal weight to economy and performance. The dominant pianos in this group are by Japanese-based companies manufacturing in Japan, the U.S., and Indonesia. They are mass produced but with attention to detail, and are consistent, predictably uniform instruments with few defects, suitable for both home and institutional use. For decades they have been legendary for their high quality-control standards and commitment to excellent warranty service. Also in this group are the higher-level pianos made by Korean-based companies in Korea or Indonesia, with more variation in quality, but enhanced by some advanced design features. *Comparison with automobiles: think Honda, Toyota, Subaru (Group 3A); upper-level Kia, Hyundai (Groups 3B and 3C).*

Verticals: $3,500 to $12,000
Grands 5' to 7': $9,000 to $34,000

Group 3A: Boston (Kawai with Steinway)
Kawai (verticals and RX series grands)
Perzina (verticals)
Pramberger, J.P. (Samick)
Weber, Albert (Young Chang)
Yamaha (verticals and C series grands)
Young Chang (Platinum Edition)

Group 3B: Baldwin (verticals)
Essex (Young Chang/Korea with Steinway)
Kawai (GM and GE series grands)
Knabe, Wm. (Samick)
Weber (Sovereign series) (Young Chang)
Yamaha (GB and GC grands)
Young Chang (Professional Artist series)

Group 3C: Kohler & Campbell (Millennium series) (Samick)
Pramberger, J. (Samick)

<u>Commentary on Group 3:</u> Group 3A consists of most pianos made by the Japanese-based companies Yamaha and Kawai and the highest-level Korean-made pianos of Young Chang and Samick. The latter are built to advanced designs, and when expertly prepared by a technician, can play as well as some pianos in higher

categories. However, their quality is more variable and most dealers do only enough make-ready to make them acceptable. Also in this category are Perzina verticals, the only pianos made in China thus far to make it out of Group 4. They have excellent tone and action, and have been out in the field without problems long enough for me to feel comfortable recommending them.

Group 3B consists of the smaller Kawai and Yamaha grand models with simpler case construction and features, mid-level Korean-made models from Young Chang, and mid- to upper-level pianos from Samick (Wm. Knabe) made in either Korea or Indonesia. I've also put U.S.-made Baldwin verticals in this category though, to be honest, Baldwin has been keeping a low profile of late, and feedback about the verticals is sparse.

Group 3C are mid-level Samick pianos made in Korea or Indonesia (Kohler & Campbell Millennium) and upper-level pianos entirely from Indonesia (J. Pramberger). The same comments made about Korean pianos in Group 3A also apply to the Korean and Indonesia pianos in Groups 3B and 3C.

Group 4: Medium quality consumer-grade pianos

Most of these instruments are somewhat more oriented toward economy than performance. In general, quality control is not as perfect as many in Group 3, so the pianos may need a little more attention by the dealer both before and after the sale. For some upper-level Chinese brands, the quality control and features might normally make the piano a candidate for a higher-level group, but their track record is short, so as a precaution, I am leaving them in this group for the time being. These pianos are suitable at least for average home and lighter institutional use, and sometimes more. Students with smaller models of some of these brands may wish to upgrade to a larger or better instrument after a number of years. Pianos in this group are made in China, or in Indonesia by Korean-based companies. *Comparison with automobiles: think Kia, Hyundai (and Chinese-made cars).*

Verticals:	$2,500 to $7,000
Grands 5' to 7':	$6,000 to $19,000

Group 4A: Brodmann
Ebel, Carl (Perzina)
Heintzman
May Berlin
Perzina (grands)
Steinberg, Gerh. (Perzina)

Group 4B: Everett (grands) (Dongbei)
Hallet, Davis (grands) (Dongbei)
Nordiska (grands) (Dongbei)
Story & Clark (grands) (Dongbei)
Weinbach (grands) (Dongbei/Petrof)

Group 4C: Bergmann (Young Chang)
Essex (Pearl River or Young Chang/China with Steinway)
Hailun
Kohler & Campbell (except Millennium series) (Samick)
Miller, Henry F. (Pearl River)
Palatino (AXL)
Pearl River
Remington (Samick)
Ritmüller (Pearl River)
Samick
Steigerman (Premium series) (Hailun)
Weber (Legend series) (Young Chang)

Group 4D: Cable, Hobart M. (Sejung)
Cristofori (Sejung)
Everett (verticals) (Dongbei)
Falcone (Sejung)
Gulbransen (Sejung)
Hallet, Davis (verticals) (Dongbei)
Hamilton (Sejung/Baldwin)
Hardman, Peck (Beijing)
Meister, Otto (Beijing)
Nordiska (verticals) (Dongbei)
Steck, Geo. (Sejung)
Steigerman (Beijing)
Story & Clark (verticals) (Dongbei)
Suzuki (Artfield)
Vivace (Sejung)
Wurlitzer (Sejung/Baldwin)
Wyman (Beijing)

<u>Commentary on Group 4</u>: Many of the Group 4 piano brands are new or rapidly improving. I have tried as best I can to estimate their relative quality positions, preferring to err slightly on the low side rather than overstate their quality. I expect the future will bring many changes to this list.

Group 4A consists of the best of the Chinese pianos. Some of these actually have the performance characteristics of higher-grade instruments and, like Perzina verticals in Group 3A, may eventually migrate upward on this chart as their track record and reputation warrant. The pianos in this subgroup are distinguished from those in lower subgroups by superiority in a combination of design, materials, and execution. Most use a large amount of parts and material imported from Europe or North America. They also excel in the oversight given them by the sponsoring company. Schimmel, for example, reportedly rejects a substantial percentage of the May Berlin pianos it receives as not meeting the company's rigid standards, and returns them to their origin. It then prepares the remainder of the pianos to even higher standards before sending them on to dealers. My contacts generally gave cautious praise to these brands, recognizing that they provide tremendous value for the money, but were not yet ready to abandon better-known, established, more expensive brands from other parts of the world in favor of them.

Group 4B consists of the grand pianos from Dongbei, distributed in the U.S. under a variety of names by several distributors. These pianos don't have the finesse of the ones in Group 4A, but are clearly distinguished from most other Chinese grands by the excellence of their design. When properly prepared by the dealer, they perform exceptionally well. Note that the Nordiska brand differs from the others, though there is some dispute among the distributors as to the degree of the difference and how consistently it is applied. The Story & Clark brand is prepared in the U.S. by its distributor prior to being shipped to dealers. Weinbach is a deluxe piano from Dongbei with a Petrof keyboard and action. Though it has been grouped with the other Dongbei grands, it's possible it belongs in Group 4A.

Group 4C consists of the large, middle ground of Chinese pianos—those from the Young Chang, Pearl River, Hailun, and AXL factories—and the lower-level pianos from the Samick factory in Indonesia. These pianos are not likely to win awards for anything in particular, but with proper dealer make-ready and some follow-up home service, they should be fine for casual home use and sometimes more.

Group 4D pianos are a little less advanced in design or execution than those in higher categories. The smaller sizes of grands and verticals in particular are for those buyers for whom low price or furniture are the most important considerations. With thorough dealer prep, good after-sale service, and realistic expectations, these brands can be successfully purchased by buyers with simpler needs.

BRAND LISTINGS

ALTENBURG, OTTO

Wyman Piano Company
P.O. Box 218802
Nashville, Tennessee 37221

941-661-0220
george.benson@wymanpiano.com
www.altenburgpiano.com

Pianos made by: Beijing Hsinghai Piano Group, Ltd., Beijing, China

This is the house brand of Altenburg Piano House, a New Jersey piano retailer in business for over 150 years, at one time as a manufacturer. This brand is sold via the internet and through other dealers in addition to the company's own stores. For many years Otto Altenburg pianos have been made by Samick in Korea or Indonesia, though sometimes to musical and cabinet designs different from Samick's own. More recently, Altenburg has engaged the Beijing Hsinghai Piano Group in China to make a new line of pianos, some of which are special to Altenburg with individually-hitched strings. The Beijing models are the ones shown in the Pricing Guide section of this *Supplement*. Grand models up to 5' 3" use a laminated soundboard, larger models use solid spruce.

The F.E. Altenburg line of pianos by Niendorf has been discontinued.

Warranty: Twelve years, parts and labor, transferable to future owners within the warranty period.

ASTIN-WEIGHT

Astin-Weight Piano Makers
P.O. Box 65281
Salt Lake City, Utah 84165

801-487-0641
gr8pianos@networld.com
www.astin-weight.com

Astin-Weight pianos have been made in Salt Lake City since 1959. Due to storm damage at the factory, the company is currently engaged in limited production from several temporary locations.

Astin-Weight vertical pianos, 50" in height, are unusual from a technical standpoint because they have no backposts, instead relying on a massive full-perimeter plate; and because the soundboard takes up the entire back of the piano, behind the pinblock, resulting in a much larger volume of sound than a conventional piano (see *The Piano Book* for an illustration of this feature). Many of the cabinet finishes are simple, hand-rubbed oil finishes. The 41" console has been discontinued.

The Astin-Weight 5' 9" grand is produced in very limited quantities. It has an unusual symmetrical shape and is hinged on the treble side instead of the bass. The company says this shape allows for much longer strings and soundboard area.

Warranty: Twenty-five years, parts and labor

BALDWIN
including D.H. Baldwin, Hamilton, Howard, Chickering, Wurlitzer, ConcertMaster

Baldwin Piano Company
309 Plus Park Blvd.
Nashville, Tennessee 37217

615-871-4500
800-876-2976
800-444-2766 (24/7 consumer hotline)
www.baldwinpiano.com

Baldwin Piano & Organ Co. was established in Cincinnati in 1862 as a retail enterprise and began manufacturing its own line of pianos in 1890. Throughout most of the twentieth century, the company was considered one of the most successful and financially stable piano makers in the United States. Beginning in the 1980s, however, the quality declined, especially as a result of the relocation of action manufacturing to Mexico. A combination of foreign competition and management problems led to bankruptcy in 2000. The company was purchased out of bankruptcy in 2001 by Gibson Guitar Corporation. Baldwin manufactures in Trumann, Arkansas and in several factories in China, where it also maintains a major presence in the Chinese domestic piano market.

All pianos with the Baldwin brand name are made in Trumann, Arkansas. The verticals come in four sizes: 43½", 45", 48", and 52". The 43½" console comes in two basic models, the series 660 "Classic" console and the series 2000 "Acrosonic." They both use the same back and action, but the Acrosonic has fancier cabinet features and hardware. The 45" studio, long known as the "Hamilton," also comes in two levels of cabinetry. Model 243 is the institutional school studio version (one of the most popular school pianos in history) and the series 5000 models are the fancy furniture styles. They are otherwise identical. Model 248, a 48" upright introduced in 1997, and the model 6000 "Concert Upright," both with some interesting technical features, round out the vertical piano line. A Custom Vertical program includes the limited edition Gibson studio, each one signed by guitarist Les Paul; the Elvis Presley Signature model, authorized by the Presley estate; and a B.B. King model (also available as a grand).

All Baldwin verticals share certain technical features, including a 19-ply maple pinblock, a solid spruce soundboard, and a full-size, direct blow action (even the consoles). The action, now made in China, has been redesigned with a Schwander-type hammer-butt return spring and other changes, and is now known as the Stealth™ action (to signify that it is quieter than the previous action). It can be recognized by its visually striking black and deep blue colors. In addition, vertical pianos with the new action have model numbers ending in "E."

Baldwin also makes a line of vertical pianos under the name "D.H. Baldwin." Those in the trade may recall this as a name Baldwin used on a line of pianos made in Korea. The new D.H. Baldwin line, however, is made in Arkansas and is based on the regular Baldwin 43½" vertical scale. The company says these new models are essentially like their higher-priced cousins musically, but with scaled-down cabinetry. Also made in Arkansas are pianos with a variety of minor brand names Baldwin owns and uses at dealer request, such as Ivers & Pond, Cable, J&C Fischer, and others. These are essentially the same as the D.H. Baldwin pianos.

Baldwin grands include the model M1 (5' 2"), R1 (5' 8"), L1 (6' 3"), SF-10E (7'), and SD-10 (9'). Model 225E is the model M1 in French Provincial styling; model 226E is the model R1 in French Provincial styling; and model 227E is the model R1 with round, fluted, tapered legs. Baldwin has introduced a Custom Grand Finishes program, allowing customers to design their own grand piano in several levels of customization: wood-finish accents on regular grand; colors; exotic wood veneers; and "anything goes." Some of the Custom Grand Finishes are also available in regular inventory.

Baldwin grands use a strong, one-piece rim construction made entirely of maple, soundboards of tapered solid spruce, and pinblocks of forty-one highly densified laminations of maple. They also use the patented Accu-just™ hitch pin system (illustrated in *The Piano Book*), in which the downbearing pressure of each string on the bridge can be individually adjusted. This mainly allows for more efficient and uniform construction of grand bridges, but may also occasionally be useful in servicing the piano. The 7' and 9' models use special treble termination pieces to provide more precise termination of each treble string. They also use a Renner action instead of the regular Baldwin action used in the other models. However, all Baldwin grands have Renner hammers. Each piano comes with an adjustable artist bench. Baldwin maintains a long roster of well-known concert artists, musicians, and composers who endorse and use its concert grand.

A "Howard" line of grands is made in Arkansas, complementing the D.H. Baldwin verticals with a lower-cost line of U.S.-made grands. Currently, the Howard line consists of two models, 5' 2" and 5' 8". They are based on regular Baldwin scales, but made with lower-cost materials and components.

Baldwin has also introduced several lower-cost lines of piano made in China. The first of these is the "Hamilton." This is not to be confused with the famous Hamilton model studio piano that says "Baldwin" on the fallboard; rather, this new line says "Hamilton" on the fallboard. Currently, they are made by Sejung to Baldwin's specifications; however, in the future they may be made in one of Baldwin's own factories in China. The verticals are available in both continental and American furniture styles. A 73-note spinet is part of this line. The company says that except for the number of notes, this short-keyboard instrument is a true acoustic piano with all the features of a full-size piano. Both verticals and grands feature a solid spruce soundboard.

In the 1980s, Baldwin acquired the Wurlitzer and Chickering names, and for many years sold a Wurlitzer line of pianos made in Korea. Like the Hamiltons, Wurtlizer pianos are now made in China by Sejung. However, whereas the Hamilton pianos are made with Sejung-designed scales and plates, the Wurlitzer pianos are made with Baldwin-designed sand-cast plates based on old Chickering scale designs. The pianos, all grands, come in six sizes from 4' 7" to 9'.

After Baldwin filed for bankruptcy and until some time after being purchased by Gibson, piano production at Baldwin's Arkansas factories came to a near standstill for a time and a great deal of piano-making talent and know-how was lost to layoffs—at least temporarily. Over the past few years, Baldwin has been very gradually resuming production. As can be expected, quality has been uneven while the factory has been gaining experience. Baldwin grands in particular, though still with great designs and specifications, do not always live up to their former reputation for quality. For protection and peace of mind, I would advise hiring an independent technician to inspect a Baldwin piano before purchasing it.

Warranty: Baldwin and D.H. Baldwin verticals—25 years on parts, 10 years on labor. Baldwin grands—lifetime on parts, 10 years on labor. Howard, Hamilton, and Wurlitzer pianos—10 years on parts and labor.

A note to current Baldwin owners: When Gibson acquired Baldwin out of bankruptcy, it acquired only its assets, not its liabilities. Therefore, the company is not required to honor warranty claims for pianos purchased prior to the acquisition date. Pianos purchased by the consumer from an authorized dealer on or after November 9, 2001 are eligible for warranty coverage, even if the dealer purchased the piano before that date. Warranty coverage for pianos purchased by the consumer before November 9, 2001 will only be considered on a case-by-case basis.

ConcertMaster

Please read "Electronic Player Piano Systems and Hybrid Acoustic/Digital Pianos" on pages 160–161 of *The Piano Book*.

ConcertMaster is an electronic player piano system available only on new Baldwin, Chickering, and Wurlitzer grand and vertical pianos. (ConcertMaster CD is a simplified version that can be installed on any brand of piano, new or old, by a Baldwin dealer.) Sometimes ConcertMaster is installed at the Baldwin factory, sometimes at the local Baldwin dealership. The system comes with a floppy disk drive, a CD drive, and a 1.2-gigabyte hard drive pre-loaded with twenty hours of music. Baldwin says the floppy disk drive can read just about any type of standard MIDI music software on the market, including such software made for other player piano systems. The CD drive can read the QRS CDs containing analog audio accompaniment. The hard drive has a capacity of nearly 10,000 songs, which can be organized into 99 different libraries containing up to 99 songs each. ConcertMaster also reads video discs and can be integrated into whole-house audio and video systems. It comes with a 128-voice General MIDI sound card and two amplified speakers, and can be operated via either a stationary controller or a wireless remote. The operating system is software upgradeable. A new optional feature provides piano accompaniment to a number of popular music CDs available on the general market. When a customer plays one of the CDs, ConcertMaster links the accompaniment, located on the system's hard drive, to the CD and plays them together.

A "Performance Option" adds single or multi-track recording capabilities to ConcertMaster, as well as features found on many digital keyboards, including velocity sensitivity and assignable split point. This option includes a record strip that uses light beams to determine key velocity. There is also an optional stop rail to silence the acoustic piano sound and allow you to listen via headphones to the instrumental sounds from the sound card.

Warranty: ConcertMaster—Two years, parts and labor, to the original purchaser

BECHSTEIN, C.

Bechstein America, LLC
207 West 58th Street
New York, New York 10019

212-581-5550
info@bechstein-america.com
www.bechstein.de

Pianos made by: C. Bechstein Pianoforte Fabrik GmbH, Berlin and Seifhennersdorf, Germany

Bechstein was founded in 1853 by Carl Bechstein, a young German piano maker who, in the exploding world of piano technology of his day, had visions of building an instrument that the tradition-bound piano-making shops of Berlin were not interested in. Through fine workmanship and the endorsement of famous pianists, Bechstein soon became one of the leading piano makers in Europe, producing over five thousand pianos annually by 1900. The two world wars and the Depression virtually destroyed the company, but it was rebuilt successfully, and in 1963 it was acquired by Baldwin. In 1986, Baldwin sold Bechstein to Karl Schulze, a leading West German piano retailer and master piano technician, who undertook a complete technical and financial reorganization of the company. In the early 1990s, Bechstein acquired the names and factories of Euterpe, W. Hoffmann, and Zimmermann. Pianos with these names are currently being sold in Europe, but not in North America. Bechstein pianos are manufactured in Seifhennersdorf, Germany, with final finishing work on the grands done in Berlin. Bechstein also co-owns plants in China and Indonesia, where it makes less expensive pianos for sale in other parts of the world. In 2006, Bechstein purchased a 49 percent interest in the Czech piano maker Bohemia.

Several years ago, Bechstein and Korean piano maker Samick each acquired a small financial interest in the other and agreed to cooperate in technical matters, marketing, and distribution. Pursuant to that agreement, SMC, Samick's North American distributor, also distributed Bechstein pianos. The distribution agreement has terminated, and Bechstein is now distributing through its own North American subsidiary based in New York.

All Bechstein pianos use Abel or Renner hammers, solid European spruce soundboards, and beech or beech and mahogany for grand rims and some structural parts. American maple pinblocks are used in the most expensive grand and vertical pianos, Delignit in the others. Three pedals are standard on all pianos, the grands with sostenuto and the verticals with practice pedal (sostenuto optional). Over the past few years, all Bechstein grands have been redesigned with a capo bar (eliminating the agraffes in the treble), higher tension scale, and front and rear duplex scales for better tonal projection and tonal color. Also, unlike older Bechsteins, which had an open pinblock design, in the redesigned grands the plate covers the pinblock area. For better tuning control, the higher-level pianos are without tuning pin bushings.

Bechstein pianos are available in two levels of quality. The regular verticals and partially redesigned versions of the old grand models are known as the "Academy Series" and say only "Bechstein" on the fallboard. A series of designer verticals that recently received the Chicago Design Award, the Concert 8 vertical, and the fully redesigned grands (models D, C, B, M/P, and L) are called the "Concert Series" and say "C. Bechstein" on the fallboard. (The 51½" Concert 8 vertical, by the way, is one of my all-time favorite vertical pianos.) The company says both lines are made in Germany, though for cost effectiveness some parts and components may originate at the Bohemia Piano Company in the Czech Republic.

The differences between the two lines appear to be primarily in tonal philosophy and cabinetry. C. Bechstein grands were designed with a higher tension scale for better projection and with various components that the company believed would result in the greatest usable palette of tonal color (tapered soundboard, vertically laminated bridges, hornbeam hammer shanks, solid keybed, thicker rim, and hammers with walnut moldings and AAA felt). The grand soundboard is installed after the inner and outer rims are joined. The ribs are tapered after being glued to the soundboard, and the heavy-duty rim posts are dovetailed and embedded into the rim.

The Academy series grands have an untapered soundboard, solid beech bridge with beech cap, maple hammer shanks, expansion-type keybed, and hammers with mahogany moldings and AA felt. The same quality wood and strings are used in both. The rim parts are joined, and the soundboard and ribs installed, in a more efficient, less time-consuming manner than with the C. Bechstein. C. Bechstein keys still use leather key bushings, whereas the Academy series keys use the more conventional cloth bushings. Bone keytops are an option on the C. Bechstein pianos and genuine ebony sharps are used on both series.

Bechstein uses its own action it calls "Silver Line" in the Academy series, and one called "Gold Line," with slightly tighter specifications, in the Concert series. The company says that as part of its global strategy it uses multiple suppliers for nearly all parts and as such, action parts for the Gold Line come from Renner in Germany and for the Silver Line from Ningbo in China. Bechstein says that whatever the origin, all parts are inspected and re-worked as necessary to conform to the company's rigid standards. It's next to impossible, either looking at the actions or playing them, for the average person to tell the two apart. Both appear to be well made, and both are of the Renner design and so have the smooth, responsive touch characteristic of that design. Time will tell if the parts from various sources are as equal as they appear.

The C. Bechstein cabinetry is much sleeker and more sophisticated than the plain Academy series, though both cabinets are finished to the same standards. The C. Bechstein plates receive the royal hand-rubbed finish; the Academy series plates are just spray finished in the conventional manner.

C. Bechstein grands are impeccably made in Europe with the very bright sound generally preferred there, and may need considerable voicing to bring out their potential. The company says that more recently, the sound has been adjusted a bit darker for the American taste. Some customers may still prefer the slightly warmer sound of the Academy series grands, which are also about half the price.

Warranty: Five years, parts and labor, to original purchaser.

[As this *Supplement* goes to press, Bechstein has just announced that it has purchased the remaining interest in the Bohemia Piano Company and integrated it into a new entity called C. Bechstein Europe. Bechstein will also reportedly be distributing a new line of W. Hoffmann pianos through Bechstein dealers.]

BEIJING HSINGHAI

Beijing Hsinghai Piano Group, Ltd., part of the Beijing Hsinghai Musical Instruments Co., has been producing pianos since 1949 and manufactures more than fifty thousand vertical and grand pianos annually, mostly for domestic Chinese consumption. They are available throughout the world under the "Otto Meister" and "Hsinghai" (or "Xinghai") labels, as well as under various other labels as joint ventures with other manufacturers and distributors, including Steigerman, Wyman, and Altenburg. Kawai also has a joint venture with Beijing, though the pianos (formerly under the name "Linden") are distributed only in Canada and Europe.

BERGMANN — See "Young Chang"

BLÜTHNER
including Haessler, Irmler, Breitmann

Blüthner USA LLC
5660 W. Grand River
Lansing, Michigan 48906

517-886-6000
800-954-3200
info@bluthnerpiano.com
www.bluthnerpiano.com

In Canada, contact Blüthner Agency, Canada at 416-236-8870
www.bluethner.ca

Pianos made by: Julius Blüthner Pianofortefabrik GmbH, Leipzig, Germany (and other locations)

Blüthner has been making pianos of the highest quality in Leipzig, in the eastern part of Germany, since 1853 and, though nationalized in 1972, has remained under the management of the Blüthner family to this day. Until 1900, Blüthner was Europe's largest piano factory. During World War II, the factory was bombed, but after the war the East German government allowed the Blüthner family and workers to rebuild it because the Blüthner piano was considered a national treasure (and because the Soviet Union needed quality pianos). With the liberation of Eastern Europe, Blüthner is again privately owned by the Blüthner family.

Blüthner pianos have beech rims (grands), solid spruce soundboards, Delignit pinblocks, Renner actions, Abel hammers, and polyester finishes. Pianos for export have three pedals, including sostenuto on the grands, and celeste (practice) on the verticals. Blüthner builds about 100 verticals a year in four sizes and 500 grands a year in six sizes.

In addition to numerous specialized furniture styles and finishes, Blüthner has two recently-issued special editions. In honor of the company's 150th anniversary, Blüthner introduced a Jubilee model with a commemorative cast-iron plate in the style of the special-edition pianos of a century ago. It is available in several sizes, in any style or finish. A new "Julius Blüthner" edition, in honor of this fifth-generation company's founder, and available in most grand sizes, features a very fancy, elaborately carved music desk in the styling designed by the founder; brass inlays in the lid; and round Victorian legs; among other embellishments.

Blüthner pianos incorporate several unique technical features. With "aliquot stringing," the notes in the highest treble section (about the top two octaves) have four strings each instead of three. The extra string is raised slightly above the others and vibrates only sympathetically. The effect, heard mainly in medium to forte playing, is similar to that of a duplex scale, adding tonal color to the treble and aiding the singing tone. Another feature concerns the angled hammers, which may at first look odd, though the reason may not be readily apparent. It turns out that the angled hammers are actually cut at an angle to match the string line and mounted straight on the shanks instead of being cut straight and mounted at an angle like other brands. The company says that the effect is to more evenly distribute the force of the blow across both the strings and the hammers, and to make a firmer connection with the backchecks, which are also positioned in a straight line. Visually, the effect is an even, rather than a staggered, hammer line.

In what is perhaps a world's "first," Blüthner has designed and built a piano for left-handed pianists. This is a completely "backwards" piano, with the treble keys, hammers, and strings on the left and the bass on the right. When it was introduced, a pianist gave a concert on it after only a couple of hours of practice! It is currently available in the 6' 10" and 9' 2" sizes by special order (price not available).

With voicing, Blüthner pianos have a very full sound that is warm, romantic, and lyrical, generally deeper and darker than some of its German counterparts. Sustain is good, but at a low level of volume, giving the tone a refined, delicate character. The action is a little light, but responsive. The pianos are built of superb materials, and are favorably priced compared to some of their competitors.

In the 1990s, a "Haessler" line of pianos was added to the Blüthner line. (Haessler is a Blüthner family name.) Created to compete better in the American market, Haessler pianos have more conventional technical and cosmetic features than Blüthner pianos and cost about twenty-five percent less. For example, the grands are loop-strung instead of single-strung, there is no aliquot stringing, and the hammers are cut and mounted in the conventional way. Case and plate cosmetics are simpler. The pianos are made in the Blüthner factory in Germany to similar high quality standards.

Blüthner also makes the more modestly priced "Irmler" piano at a factory in Poland. The grands have Renner actions, Abel hammer, and German pinblocks and strings. Final inspection and regulation are performed to rigid Blüthner specifications. The Irmler verticals are equipped with Czech-made Detoa actions, with Renner as an option.

Blüthner makes the low-cost "Breitmann" piano by contract arrangement in a plant in China. Features include Delignit pinblocks, laminated or solid spruce soundboards, German strings, Abel hammers, and Renner action parts in the grands. Scale designs are approved by Blüthner.

Warranty: Blüthner, Haessler, Irmler, Breitmann—Ten years, parts and labor, to original purchaser.

BOHEMIA

German American Trading, Inc.
P.O. Box 17789
Tampa, Florida 33682

813-961-8405
germanamer@msn.com

Pianos made by: Bohemia Piano Company, Hradec Kralove, Czech Republic

The factory that makes Bohemia pianos began production in 1871, after World War II becoming part of the Czech state-owned enterprise that included the better-known Petrof. Privatized in 1993, Bohemia now makes 2,500 verticals and 500 grands per year. Originally it exported to the U.S. under the name Rieger-Kloss, a name now used only in other markets. The name Bohemia is derived from the original term used by the ancient Romans for the part of Europe that is now the Czech Republic.

In 2006, Bechstein purchased a 49 percent interest in Bohemia. Bechstein now provides Bohemia with technical assistance, and the two companies collaborate in the manufacture of certain components. Most of the components for Bohemia pianos are made in the Czech Republic or elsewhere in Europe. Models numbers with "BR" have Renner parts on Bohemia action frames; otherwise they have Czech actions. The pianos have either Abel or Renner hammers. All pianos come with a leather upholstered adjustable artist bench, and the grands have a slow-close fallboard.

Bohemia pianos play very well, with a nice, bright singing treble tone.

Warranty: Ten years, parts and labor, to the original purchaser

[As this *Supplement* goes to press, Bechstein has just announced its acquisition of the remaining interest in the Bohemia Piano Company, which it has integrated into a new entity called C. Bechstein Europe. Sales of Bohemia pianos through the existing Bohemia dealer network will continue as usual.]

BÖSENDORFER

Bösendorfer USA
1771 Post Road East
Suite 239
Westport, Connecticut 06880

203-520-1801
usinfo@bosendorfer.com
www.bosendorfer.com

Pianos made by: L. Bösendorfer Klavierfabrik AG, Vienna, Austria

Bösendorfer was founded in 1828 in Vienna, Austria by Ignaz Bösendorfer. The young piano maker rose to fame when Franz Liszt endorsed his concert grand after being unable to destroy it in playing as he did every other piano set before him. Ignaz died in 1858 and the company was taken over by his son Ludwig. Under Ludwig's direction, the firm greatly prospered and the pianos became even more famous throughout Europe and the world. Ludwig, having no direct descendants, sold the firm to his friend Carl Hutterstrasser in 1909. Carl's sons Wolfgang and Alexander became partners in 1931. Bösendorfer was sold to Kimball International, a U.S. manufacturer of low- and medium-priced pianos, in 1966. In 2002, Kimball, having exited the piano business, sold Bösendorfer to the BAWAG-P.S.K. Group, Austria's third largest banking group. BAWAG recently announced an agreement to be acquired by Cerberus Capital Management, a New York investment firm. Bösendorfer manufactures fewer than five hundred pianos a year, with close to half sold in the U.S.

Bösendorfer makes a 52" upright and seven models of grand piano, from 5' 8" to the 9' 6" Imperial Concert Grand, one of the world's largest pianos. The company also makes a slightly less expensive version of the 6' 7" and 7' grands known as the Conservatory Series (CS). Conservatory Series grands are like the regular grands except that the case and plate receive a satin finish instead of high-polish, and the pianos are loop-strung instead of single-strung. All Bösendorfer pianos for sale in the U.S. have three pedals, the middle pedal being a sostenuto.

One of the most distinctive features of the grands is that a couple of the models have more than eighty-eight keys. The 7' 4" model has 92 keys and the 9' 6" model has 97 keys. The lowest strings vibrate so slowly that it's actually possible to hear the individual "ticks" of the vibration, and it's next to impossible to tune these strings accurately by ear. They are, of course, rarely used, but their presence, and the presence of the extra long bridge and larger soundboard to accommodate them, adds extra power, resonance, and clarity to the lower regular notes of the piano. In order not to confuse pianists, who rely on the normal keyboard configuration for spatial orientation while playing, the keys for these extra notes are usually covered with a black ivorine material.

The rim of the Bösendorfer grand is built quite differently from that of all other grands. Instead of veneers bent around a form, the rim is made in solid sections and jointed together. It is also made of spruce instead of the maple or beech normally used for this purpose. Spruce is better at transmitting sound than reflecting it, and this, along with the scale design, may be why Bösendorfers tend to have a more delicate treble and a bass that features the fundamental tone more than the higher harmonics. Although the stereotype that Bösendorfers are "better for Mozart than Rachmaninoff" may be an exaggeration (as evidenced by the number of performing artists who successfully use the piano in concert for a wide variety of music), the piano's not so "in your face" sound is certainly ideally suited for the classical repertoire in addition to whatever else it can do. In recent years, Bösendorfer has made some refinements to its designs to increase tonal projection. The relatively newer 6' 1", 7' 4", and 9' 2" models have been designed specifically to appeal to pianists looking for a more familiar sound. In all models, however, the distinctive Bösendorfer difference is still readily apparent.

During the past few years, Bösendorfer has introduced a number of interesting instruments in new cabinet styles. These include a Porsche-designed modern piano in aluminum and polished ebony (or special-ordered in any standard automobile finish color); Victorian-styled pianos "Liszt" and "Vienna;" and a model called "Yacht" in wood finish with brass inlay that can be ordered without casters to be bolted to the deck of a ship! "Edge" is a modern piano designed by a group of industrial designers and was the winner of a design competition. "Mozart" commemorates the 250th anniversary of the composer's birth and is limited to twenty-seven individually numbered instruments, one for each Mozart piano concerto. Its case has subtle modifications, including gold leaf trim, round legs and lyre posts, and a carved music desk.

Bösendorfer's SE Reproducer (player piano) system, out of production for a number of years, has been replaced by an all-new design called "CEUS (Create Emotions with Unique Sound)" with updated electronics and solenoids. The visual display is discreetly located on the fallboard and is wireless, so the fallboard can be removed for servicing the piano without the need to disconnect wires. Player controls for recording, playback, and data transfer are by means of a combination of keystrokes on the sharp keys, pedal movements, and fallboard touch sensors. Optical sensors measure key and hammer movement at an extremely high sampling rate for maximum accuracy and sensitivity to musical nuance. Bösendorfer says it intends to build a library of recordings for CEUS, and that the system will also play standard MIDI piano files. CEUS is available in every Bösendorfer grand model and adds about $60,000 (list) to the price of the piano. Retrofitting of CEUS into previously-sold Bösendorfers is available at the factory. A CEUS "Master" keyboard is an optional MIDI controller that contains a complete key and action set from a Bösendorfer model 280 concert grand.

Perhaps the world's most expensive piano inch for inch, Bösendorfer grands make an eloquent case for their prices. They are distinctive in both appearance and sound, and are considered to be among the finest pianos in the world.

Warranty: Ten years, parts and labor, transferable to future owners within the warranty period

BOSTON

Steinway & Sons, Inc.
Steinway Place
Long Island City, New York 11105

718-721-7711
800-842-5397
bostoninfo@steinway.com
www.steinway.com

Pianos made by: Kawai Musical Instrument Mfg. Co., Ltd., Hamamatsu, Japan and Karawan, Indonesia

In 1992, Steinway launched its Boston line of pianos, designed by Steinway & Sons and built by Kawai. Steinway's stated purpose in creating this line was to supply Steinway dealers with a quality, mid-priced piano for those customers "who were not yet ready for a Steinway." In choosing to have a piano of its own design made in Japan, Steinway sought to take advantage of the efficient high-technology manufacturing methods of the Japanese while utilizing its own design skills to make a more musical piano than is usually available from that part of the world. Sold only through select Steinway dealers, Boston pianos are currently available in three sizes of vertical piano and five sizes of grand. All are made in Japan, except the model 118S, which is made in Kawai's Indonesian factory.

Boston pianos are used by a number of prestigious music schools and festivals, including Aspen, Tanglewood, Brevard, and Bowdoin.

The most obvious grand piano design feature, visually (and one of the biggest differences from the Kawai), is the Boston's wide tail. Steinway says this allows the bridges to be positioned closer to the more lively central part of the soundboard, smoothing out the break between bass and treble. This, plus a thinner tapered soundboard and other scaling differences, may give the Boston grands a longer sustain though less initial power. The verticals are said to have a greater overstringing angle for the same purpose. Over the last few years, the Boston verticals have been redesigned for greater tuning stability and musical refinement. There are plans to redesign the grands using the same structural analysis software employed in the design of the new Boston uprights and Steinway's Essex line of pianos (see "Essex").

A number of features in the Boston piano are similar to those in the Steinway, including vertically laminated bridges for better tonal transmission, duplex scaling for additional tonal color, rosette-shaped hammer flanges to preserve hammer spacing, and radial rim bracing for greater structural stability. The Boston grand action is said to incorporate some of the latest refinements of the Steinway action. Cabinet detailing on the Boston grands is similar to that on the Steinway. Boston hammers are made differently from both Kawai and Steinway hammers, and voicers in the Kawai factory receive special instructions on voicing them. All Boston grand models come with a sostenuto pedal; the verticals have a practice pedal.

Boston grands also have certain things in common with Kawai RX series grands: the composition of their rims, pinblocks, and bridges; tuning pins, hardware, and grand leg and lyre assemblies; duplex scaling, radial rim bracing, and a sostenuto pedal; and the level of quality control in their manufacture. The same workers build the two brands in the same factories. One important way they differ is that Kawai uses carbon-fiber reinforced ABS Styran plastic for most of its action parts, whereas Boston uses only traditional wooden parts. At retail, Boston pianos tend to be about twenty percent more expensive than comparably-sized Kawais.

Steinway guarantees full trade-in value for a Boston piano at any time a purchaser wishes to upgrade to a Steinway grand.

Piano technicians are favorably inclined toward Boston pianos. Some find Boston pianos to have a little better sustain and more tonal color than Kawai pianos, though otherwise similar in quality. When comparing the two brands, I would advise making a decision based primarily on one's own musical perceptions of tone and touch, as well as the trade-up guarantee, if applicable.

Warranty: Ten years, parts and labor, to the original purchaser

BREITMANN — See "Blüthner"

BRODMANN

Piano Marketing Group, LLC
752 East 21st Street
Ferdinand, Indiana 47532

812-630-0978
gary.trafton@brodmann-pianos.com
www.brodmann-pianos.com

Company Headquarters: Joseph Brodmann Piano Group, Viktorgasse 14, 1040 Vienna, Austria. Phone: +43-1-890-3203; christian.hoeferl@brodmann-pianos.com

Joseph Brodmann was a well-known piano maker in Vienna in the late eighteenth and early nineteenth centuries. Ignatz Bösendorfer apprenticed in Brodmann's workshop and eventually took it over, producing the first Bösendorfer pianos there. Today's Brodmann is a new company, headquartered in Vienna, started by two former Bösendorfer executives, pursuing a direction they say was planned as a possible second line for Bösendorfer a number of years ago, but never acted upon.

There are three lines of Brodmann pianos. One is made in Yichang, Hubei Province, China by a manufacturer affiliated with Parsons Music, a major music retailer in Hong Kong and China. The pianos are designed in Europe and use European components in critical areas, such as Strunz soundboards, Abel hammers, Röslau strings, and Langer-designed actions (Renner in the 7' 6" grand, a Chinese action in the verticals). Brodmann has its own employees in the factory for quality control purposes.

The other two lines, all verticals, are known as "European Premium Pianos." One is made in a small factory in Vienna and specializes in making pianos with stunning wood veneers, such as Bubinga, Pyramid Mahogany, Pommele, and Brazilian Rosewood. All the pianos have a traditional Viennese curved leg. The other line, made in Germany by the maker of Wilh. Steinberg pianos, features vertical pianos with a straight-leg design in Ebony, Mahogany, and Walnut. Both European lines have the same high-quality components as those listed above, but with a Renner action.

Warranty: Ten years, parts and labor

CABLE, HOBART M. — See "Sejung"

CABLE-NELSON — See "Yamaha"

CHASE, A.B.

Musical Properties, Inc.
823 South Sixth Street, Suite 100
Las Vegas, Nevada 89101

773-342-4212

Pianos made by: Dongbei Piano Company, Ltd., Yingkou, Liaoning Province, China

A.B. Chase is an old American piano name formerly owned by Aeolian Pianos, which went out of business in 1985. Since 2001, the brand has been used by a different distributor on pianos from the Dongbei Piano Company in China (see "Dongbei").

CHICKERING — See "Baldwin"

CONCERTMASTER — See "Baldwin"

CONOVER CABLE — See "Samick"

CRISTOFORI
including Vivace

Jordan Kitt's Music
9520 Baltimore Avenue
College Park, Maryland 20740

Schmitt Music
Butler's Square, Suite 850B
100 North 6th Street
Minneapolis, Minnesota 55403

800-466-9510 x1267
(Chris Syllaba)

800-920-9540 x2372
(Wayne Reinhardt)

info@cristoforipianos.com
www.cristoforipianos.com

Pianos made by: Sejung Corporation, Qingdao, Shandong Province, China

Originally issued under the name "Opus II," the Cristofori piano is a joint venture between Jordan Kitt's Music and Schmitt Music, which own and operate a combined twenty-five piano dealerships throughout the country. At present, Cristofori pianos are sold only in their stores. (Cristofori was, of course, the inventor of the piano.)

Cristofori pianos are made by Sejung in China (see "Sejung"). They are differentiated from Sejung's regular pianos by upgraded feature specifications such as: the use of Mapes' highest quality strings; action parts made from German hornbeam instead of maple; reinforced, T-fastened, double-felted hammers from Japanese felt; and premium solid Siberian spruce soundboards for the grands and taller verticals (veneered spruce soundboard for the smallest verticals). Some vertical models have cabinets that are custom-designed for Cristofori. Grands are pre-marked for more accurate PianoDisc installation should it be desired later by the customer or dealer. Each piano is individually inspected in the Sejung factory by an American piano technician before being boxed and shipped.

"Vivace" is a lower-cost 4' 8" grand similar to Sejung's Hobart M. Cable brand, except with a veneered spruce soundboard. The piano says "Vivace" at Jordan Kitt's stores and "Cristofori" at Schmitt Music stores.

Warranty: Jordan Kitt's Music—Twelve-year full (transferable) warranty on parts and labor. Schmitt Music—Ten-year limited (non-transferable) warranty on parts and labor.

DISKLAVIER
including MIDIPiano. See also Yamaha

Yamaha Corporation of America
P.O. Box 6600
Buena Park, California 90622

714-522-9011
800-854-1569
infostation@yamaha.com
www.yamaha.com

Pianos made by: Yamaha Corporation, Hamamatsu, Japan and other locations

Please read "Electronic Player Piano Systems and Hybrid Acoustic/Digital Pianos" on pages 160–161 of *The Piano Book*.

Disklaviers are regular Yamaha pianos that have been outfitted with an electronic player piano mechanism. These mechanisms are installed only in new Yamahas and only at the factory. They cannot be retrofitted into older Yamahas or any other brand. (There are other systems on the market that do that.)

As with all such systems, the Disklavier consists of a solenoid rail installed in a slot cut in the piano keybed; a processor unit mounted under the piano; and a control box that plays floppy disks and/or CDs, depending on the model, that is either mounted under the keybed at the front of the piano or sits on or near the piano. There is one solenoid for each note and solenoids for the damper and una corda (soft) pedals. When playing Disklavier's specialized software (or other compatible software), one track contains the MIDI signal that drives the piano solenoids, the other tracks provide an instrumental or vocal accompaniment that plays through a stereo system or through amplified speakers that come with the piano. The accompaniment may be in the form of synthesized or sampled sound, or actual recordings of live musicians. Except for playback-only models, Disklavier grands also include an optical record system beneath the keys that records key stroke information in MIDI format. Pedal movement is recorded, and hammer stroke information is also recorded on the larger grand models. This information can be stored for later playback on the same piano, stored on other media, or sent to other MIDI-compatible devices, including if desired, another Disklavier piano.

Disklavier differs from the popular after-market systems PianoDisc and QRS Pianomation in that Disklavier is not modular. That is, you cannot pick and choose which features you wish to buy. For the most part, whatever Disklavier features come with a particular model of piano is what you get. The features vary a little from one model to another. All grands contain the features of the Mark IV (i.e. fourth generation) Disklavier except the model DGB1, which is playback-only, and the model DGC1B, which is Mark III. All verticals contain the features of the Mark II Disklavier except the 48" model U1 Disklavier upright (DU1A), which is a Mark III and thus includes a CD drive (the Mark II plays only floppy disks). A CD upgrade option is available for the other verticals.

The new features of the Mark IV Disklavier, released in 2004, include the following: An 80-gigabyte hard drive capable of holding all the Disklavier software ever written (and then some); a tablet or pocket remote control to communicate wirelessly with the Disklavier (pocket on the GC1, C1, and C2 models; both tablet and pocket on C3 and above); built-in Ethernet for connecting to your network and downloading MIDI files; the ability to play much softer as a result of a higher-speed CPU, greater MIDI resolution, and improved solenoids; more sensitive recording capabilities due to the use of grayscale (continuous) hammershank and key sensors; karaoke capability; and an improved speaker system. The performance level of the standard Mark IV Disklavier is the same as formerly found in the Mark III PRO series. The Mark IV PRO provides the highest level of performance in the Disklavier line. The PRO series has a much higher internal recording resolution and a greater dynamic range in playback.

In addition to the new features mentioned above, the Mark III and IV Disklaviers have the following features as well, described in greater detail in *The Piano Book*: Floppy and CD drives, flash memory (Mark III only), tone generator with hundreds of synthesized or sampled sounds, digital piano sound chip, built-in speakers, 16-

track recording capabilities, Silent Mode (silencing the acoustic piano and listening through headphones), Quiet Mode (silencing the acoustic piano and directing the sound to speakers), Quick Escape Action (maintains correct action regulation when using Silent Mode or Quiet Mode), headphones, SmartKey (a teaching device), and CueTIME (a smart accompaniment feature). Note: Model DGC1B is a Mark III Disklavier, but with some limits to its functionality. It does not support Silent Mode, Quiet Mode, or Quick Escape Action, and does not come with headphones or a digital piano sound chip (it uses the piano sound in the tone generator).

PianoSmart Audio Synchronization technology is a new feature of all Mark III and Mark IV Disklavier pianos. Yamaha has prepared a piano track in MIDI format on a floppy disk to go along with each of a number of popular audio CDs available on the general market. When the owner plays both the floppy and the CD at the same time, PianoSmart links them together, enabling the Disklavier to accurately play along with the CD. One can also record a piano accompaniment to a favorite audio CD. Pop the CD and a blank floppy into a Mark III or Mark IV Disklavier and record yourself playing along. The two will then be linked together for future playback. PianoSmart Video Synchronization works the same way. Plug a camcorder into the Disklavier while videotaping a piano performance, and the Disklavier will play the performance back perfectly on the piano whenever you play back the video of the performance through the camcorder. PianoSmart is available as a free software upgrade from Yamaha.

Yamaha has just released the 2.0 operating system upgrade for Mark IV Disklavier. Among other things, the upgrade will allow the user to purchase and download music over the internet directly to the instrument using the pocket remote controller screen without the use of a computer. It also enables Disklavier Radio, a group of streaming MIDI music stations encompassing a variety of music formats to choose from and play on the Disklavier, available on a subscription basis. In the future, Disklavier will be upgradeable for free over the internet.

For simple playback, most of the player-piano systems on the market are probably equally recommended. The Disklavier, however, has a slight edge on quality control, and its recording system is much more sophisticated than most of the others, especially on the larger grands. For this reason, it is the system of choice for professional applications such as performance and teaching, and much of Yamaha's marketing efforts are directed at that audience.

Two examples are especially noteworthy. Yamaha sponsors regular piano "e-competitions" in which contestants gather in several cities and play on Yamaha Disklavier concert grands. Their performances are transmitted over the internet to judges located far away who listen to the music reproduced perfectly on other Disklavier pianos, rather than listen to recordings. A similar concept is the technology called "Remote Lesson," recently demonstrated and to debut next year, in which a student can take a lesson on one Disklavier, while a teacher located far away teaches and critiques on a second Disklavier connected via the internet, both communicating with each other in real time via videoconferencing. In 2006, the Disklavier received the Frances Clark Keyboard Pedagogy Award from the Music Teachers National Association. Typically awarded to a music educator who has made significant contributions to the field of keyboard pedagogy, this marks the first time the award has been given to a music product.

Yamaha maintains a large and growing library of music for the Disklavier, including piano solo, piano with recorded "live" accompaniment, piano with digital instrumental accompaniment, and PianoSmart arrangements. The system will also play Standard MIDI files type 0 and 1 and most of its competitors' CDs. (Because competitors frequently change their formats and encryption, the ability to play the format of a particular competitor is not guaranteed.)

Yamaha also makes a line of MIDIPianos. Technically, these are not Disklaviers because they do not have playback capabilities. They are included here because they are closely related products that have some similar features. As with the Disklaviers, there are sensors associated with the keys, hammers, and pedals that record their movement in MIDI format and output the information through a digital piano sound chip to headphones or speakers, or to a computer for editing if desired. With the addition of Yamaha's piano mute rail, the acoustic piano can be silenced and the instrument can be used as a digital piano, though with a real piano action. The sophistication of the key, hammer, and pedal sensing will vary depending on which generation of Disklavier (Mark II, III, or IV) is associated with that particular piano model. MIDIPianos don't have disk drives for recording MIDI data, but an optional add-on unit is available with floppy disk drive and tone generator (to create sounds other than piano).

Warranty: Acoustic Piano—Ten years, parts and labor, to original purchaser. Player-piano/MIDIPiano system—Five years, parts; one year, labor, to original purchaser.

DONGBEI

Pianos made by: Dongbei Piano Company, Ltd., Yingkou, Liaoning Province, China

The Dongbei Piano Company in China makes pianos that are sold in North America by various distributors and under a variety of names, including Nordiska, Everett, Story & Clark, and Hallet, Davis & Co., among others (see listing under each name).

Dongbei is Chinese for "northeast." In 1952, Dongbei was formed by splitting off from a government-owned piano factory in Shanghai and establishing a new government-owned factory in the northeastern part of the country. Dongbei began a process of modernization in 1988 when it purchased the designs and manufacturing equipment for a vertical piano model from the Swedish company Nordiska when that company went out of business. The Swedish-designed vertical model 116 was strikingly more advanced than Dongbei's own "Prince" and "Princess" piano lines. At that time, Dongbei made only vertical pianos. In 1991, Dongbei entered into an agreement with Korean piano maker Daewoo whereby Daewoo would assist Dongbei in improving its vertical piano production.

Modernization continued in 1996 when Dongbei entered into a contract with Daewoo under which Daewoo would help Dongbei develop grand piano designs and production facilities. In 1997 Daewoo dispatched Steve Chung, a piano designer with twenty-five years of experience and manager of piano development for that company, to work with Dongbei. Mr. Chung had previously trained with Young Chang and had been manager of Daewoo's grand piano factory. He had also studied piano design and construction with Ibach in Germany when Ibach was involved in a joint venture with Daewoo (see "Ibach"). In 1997 Daewoo decided to exit the piano business and Dongbei purchased nearly all of Daewoo's grand piano manufacturing equipment, including key and action making equipment, and commenced making pianos using Mr. Chung's designs. The first grand pianos were finished and ready to ship in 1998. Mr. Chung has remained with Dongbei as an independent consultant and continues to develop pianos for the company. Export to the U.S. began in 1994 under the brand name Sagenhaft, at first only with vertical pianos. When export of grand pianos began in 1998, other brand names such as Nordiska, Everett, and Story & Clark began to become available.

Over the past ten years, production for both domestic use and for export has grown enormously. Dongbei has about one million square feet of factory space, employs 2,300 workers, and makes about 21,000 vertical and 7,000 grand pianos per year. More than twenty-five percent of Dongbei's production is for export to the United States. In early 2007, Gibson Musical Instruments, parent of Baldwin Piano Company, announced its intent to acquire Dongbei. Baldwin has greatly expanded its presence in China over the last five years and will likely use the manufacturing capacity of Dongbei toward servicing the Chinese domestic market.

In the opinion of many technicians who have examined a variety of pianos from China, the Dongbei grand piano designs are among the best and most successful musically. Dongbei recently upgraded its designs to utilize a focused beam structure that concentrates the piano's structural support toward the nose flange of the plate, a design used by Steinway and others that is thought to increase the tonal projection of the instrument by making the frame more rigid. This design was first brought out under the Nordiska brand name (see "Nordiska"), but may be available to other Dongbei-made brands. You can tell if the Dongbei-made piano you are looking at uses this improved system by looking up at the beam structure of the piano from underneath. If all the beams are more or less parallel to one another, the piano is of the old design. If several of the beams converge toward the front of the instrument, the piano is of the new design.

EBEL, CARL — See "Perzina, Gebr."

ESSEX

Steinway & Sons, Inc.
Steinway Place
Long Island City, New York 11105

718-721-7711
800-842-5397
bostoninfo@steinway.com
www.steinway.com

Pianos made by: Young Chang Co., Ltd., Inchon, South Korea and Tianjin, China; and Guangzhou Pearl River Piano Group Ltd., Guangzhou, Guangdong Province, China

Essex pianos are designed by Steinway & Sons engineers and are made in factories in China and Korea by both Young Chang and Pearl River. Steinway first introduced its Essex line of pianos in early 2001 with a limited offering of models made by Young Chang, and the brand kept an unusually low profile in the piano market for a number of years. In 2006, a major relaunch of Essex was held that included a new and very complete line comprised of thirty-five grand and thirty-one vertical models and finishes.

Four grand sizes and three vertical scales are made. The 44" model EUP-111 console comes in a variety of furniture styles, and 43" model EUP-108 is a version of the console in continental style. The newly-designed 46" model EUP-116 studio is available in fourteen different and striking cabinets, designed by Steinway & Sons and renowned furniture designer William Faber. Styles include: Classic, Queen Anne, Italian Provincial, French Provincial, Formal French, English Country, English Traditional, Contemporary, and Sheraton Traditional. These models incorporate various leg designs (including cabriole leg, spoon leg, and canopy-styled tapered leg and arm designs) and hand-carved trim (such as Acanthus leaf designs, tulip trim, vertical bead molding), highly molded top lids, picture frame front panels, and stylized, decorative music desks. The newly-designed 48" model EUP-123 upright comes in a traditional style in four finishes along with Empire and French styles.

The Essex grands are available in 5' 1" (EGP-155), 5' 3" (EGP-161), 5' 8" (EGP-173), and 6' (EGP-183) sizes in (depending on model) Classic, Neoclassic, Traditional, Renaissance, and French Provincial styles. They come in a variety of regular and exotic veneers in high polish and satin luster (semi-gloss) finishes.

Like the Boston pianos, the Essex line was designed with a lower tension scale and incorporates many Steinway-designed refinements. Included in these are a wide tail design that allows the bridges to be positioned closer to the more lively central part of the soundboard, smoothing out the break between bass and treble. This, plus a thinner, tapered soundboard and other scaling differences produces a tone with a longer sustain. Other Steinway-designed features include an all-wood action with Steinway geometry, and with rosette-shaped hammer flanges to preserve hammer spacing like those used in Steinway grands; pear-shaped hammers with reinforced shoulders and metal fasteners, vertically laminated bridges with solid maple cap, duplex scale, radial bracing in grands, and staggered backposts in verticals.

At present, Young Chang makes Essex vertical models 108, 111, and 116 in its factory in Tianjin, China, and grand models 161 and 183 in Korea. Guangzhou Pearl River makes vertical model 123 and grand models 155 and 173 in China.

Although I do not have much feedback from technicians about the Essex pianos, I do know that Steinway has put an immense amount of time and effort into the relaunch of this brand. The pianos are new designs by Steinway engineers and not just warmed-over designs of other companies. Steinway has a permanent office in Shanghai, China and full-time employees inspecting pianos in the Asian factories. I expect that the quality of the Essex pianos will be at the upper end of what these factories are capable of producing.

Steinway guarantees full trade-in value for an Essex piano toward the purchase of a Steinway grand within ten years.

Warranty: Ten years, parts and labor, to the original purchaser

ESTONIA

Laul Estonia Piano Factory Ltd.
7 Fillmore Drive
Stony Point, New York 10980

845-947-7763
laulestoniapiano@aol.com
www.estoniapiano.com

Pianos made by: Estonia Klaverivabrik AS, Tallinn, Estonia

Estonia is a small republic in northern Europe on the Baltic Sea, near Scandinavia. For centuries it was under Danish, Swedish, German, and Russian domination, finally gaining its independence in 1918, only to lose it again to the Soviet Union in 1940. It became free again in 1991 with the collapse of the Soviet Union.

Piano making in Estonia goes back over two hundred years under German influence, and from 1850 to 1940 there were nearly twenty piano manufacturers operating in the country. The most famous among them was Ernst Hiis-Ihse, who studied piano making in the Steinway Hamburg and Blüthner factories and established his own company in 1893. His piano designs gained international recognition. In 1950 the Communist-dominated Estonian government consolidated many smaller Estonian piano makers into a factory managed by Hiis, making pianos under the Estonia name for the first time. The instruments became prominent on concert stages throughout the East and, amazingly, more than 7,400 concert grands were made. After Mr. Hiis' death in 1964, however, the quality of the pianos gradually declined, partly due to the fact that high-quality parts and materials were hard to come by during the Communist occupation of the country. After Estonia gained its independence in 1991, the factory struggled to maintain production. In 1994, Estonia pianos were introduced to the U.S. market by Paul Vesterstein, an Estonian-American.

In 1994 the company was privatized under the Estonia name, with the managers and employees as owners. During the following years, Indrek Laul, an Estonian with a doctorate in piano performance from the Juilliard School of Music, and a recording artist, gradually bought shares of the company from the stockholders until he became sole owner in 2001. Dr. Laul lives in the United States and represents the company here. In 2005, the Juilliard School named Dr. Laul one of the school's top one hundred graduates at its 100th anniversary celebration. Estonia makes about 350 pianos a year, all grands, mostly for sale in the United States.

Estonia pianos have rims of laminated birch, sand-cast plates, Renner actions and hammers, laminated red beech pinblocks, and European solid spruce soundboards. They come in 5' 6", 6' 3", and 9' sizes. All have three pedals, including sostenuto.

When I reported on Estonia pianos for the fourth edition of *The Piano Book* (2001), it was a good piano with much potential, but as the company was still rebounding from problems suffered during the Communist era, some caution was advised. Since becoming sole owner in 2001, Dr. Laul has made so many improvements to the piano that it is practically a different instrument. Improvements include: rescaling the bass and upgrading bass string making machinery for producing hand-wound bass strings; improving the method of drilling pinblocks; stronger plates and improved plate finishes; thicker inner and outer rims; improved fitting of soundboard to rim; concert-grand quality soundboard spruce on all models; quarter-sawn maple bridge caps; adjustable front and rear duplex scales; wood for legs and keyslips heat-treated to better resist changing climatic conditions; Renner Blue hammers on all models; better quality metal hardware that resists oxidation; suede-covered music desk tray; improved satin finishes; establishing a quality control department headed by Dr. Laul's father (both his father and mother are professional musicians); higher-grade and artistically matched veneers; and establishing a U.S. service center for warranty repairs. All pianos are now accompanied by a quality control certificate signed by a member of the Laul family, and each piano is played and checked by them.

The Estonia factory has recently introduced a new custom line of pianos, offering exotic veneers such as Rosewood and Pyramid Mahogany, and is willing to finish instruments to fit the desire of each individual customer. The custom line is also featuring a number of different Victorian-style legs and ornamental music desks.

In the short time Estonia pianos have been sold here, they have gathered an unusually loyal and devoted following. Groups of owners of Estonia pianos, completely independent of the company, frequently hold musical get-togethers at different locations around the country. The pianos have a rich, warm, singing tone; are very well constructed and well prepared at the factory; and there is hardly a detail that the company has not examined and impressively perfected. The price has risen over the years, but they are still an unusually good value among higher-end instruments.

Warranty: Ten years, parts and labor, to the original purchaser

EVERETT

Wrightwood Enterprises, Inc.
717 St. Joseph Drive
St. Joseph, Michigan 49085

800-445-0695

Pianos made by: Dongbei Piano Company, Ltd., Yingkou, Liaoning Province, China

The Everett Piano Company originated in Boston in 1883 and moved to South Haven, Michigan in 1926. It was acquired by Yamaha in 1973. Until mid-1986, Yamaha made a line of Everett vertical pianos in this factory alongside its U.S.-made Yamaha pianos. When Yamaha moved its U.S. piano manufacturing to Thomaston, Georgia in 1986, it contracted with Baldwin to continue making Everett pianos. The contract terminated in 1989 and Yamaha dropped the line permanently. See the entry for "Everett" in *The Piano Book* for more information about pianos from that era.

The Everett name has been used by Wrightwood Enterprises, Inc. since 1995. The pianos are made in China by the Dongbei Piano Company (see "Dongbei"). The grands have duplex scaling and a bass scale that is custom-made for the Everett brand, the company says.

Warranty: Ten years, parts and labor, to the original purchaser

FALCONE — See "Sejung"

FANDRICH & SONS

Fandrich & Sons Pianos
7411 Silvana Terrace Road
Stanwood, Washington 98292

360-652-8980
877-737-1422
fandrich@fandrich.com
www.fandrich.com

Pianos made by: various makers—see text

In the late 1980s, Darrell Fandrich, an engineer and piano technician, developed a vertical piano action designed to play like a grand. You can see an illustration of the Fandrich Vertical Action™, an explanation of how it works, and some history of its development in the third and fourth editions of *The Piano Book* and on the Fandrich & Sons web site. Since 1994, Darrell and his wife Heather have been installing Renner-made Fandrich actions in selected new pianos, selling them under the Fandrich & Sons label. They also sell some grands (with regular grand actions) under that name.

Over the years, the Fandrichs have installed their actions in over two hundred instruments, including ones from Pearl River, Wilh. Steinberg, Klima, Bohemia, and Feurich. At present, the action is being installed into 50" and 52" Bohemia uprights and 48" Feurich uprights. The converted pianos are available directly from the Fandrichs. The Fandrichs say they are working with factory personnel to train them in completing the actions at the factory, at which time these pianos may also become available from other Bohemia and Feurich dealers.

The grand pianos for sale under the Fandrich & Sons name are made by Dongbei in China (see "Dongbei"), and are available in two models. The "HGS" series instruments are customized by the Fandrichs with Renner hammershanks, either Abel or Ronsen hammers, and Arledge bass strings, and receive a 40-hour make-ready consisting of regulation, proprietary touchweighting, tuning stabilization, and voicing. The "S" series pianos have the original factory parts, but receive the same extensive make-ready as the HGS series.

All Fandrich & Sons pianos come with a Dampp-Chaser humidity control system and an adjustable artist bench.

Warranty: Twelve years, parts and labor, to the original purchaser

Note: Do not confuse the Fandrich & Sons pianos with the 48" Fandrich upright that was once manufacturerd with a Fandrich Vertical Action™ by Darrell Fandrich's brother Delwin Fandrich. That piano has not been made since 1994.

FAZIOLI

Fazioli Pianoforti srl
Via Ronche 47
33077 Sacile (Pn), Italy

+39-0434-72026
info@fazioli.com
www.fazioli.com

In 1978, musician and engineer Paolo Fazioli of Rome, Italy began designing and building pianos, with the object of making the finest quality instruments possible. Now even the most famous piano makers of Western Europe are recognizing his accomplishment, and artists throughout the world are using the instruments successfully on the concert stage and elsewhere.

As a youth, Fazioli studied music and engineering, receiving advanced degrees in both subjects. He briefly attempted to make a living as a concert pianist, but instead joined his family's furniture company, rising to the position of factory manager in the Rome, Sacile, and Turin factories. But his creative ambitions, combined with his personal search for the perfect piano, finally led him to conclude that he needed to build his own piano. With advice and financial backing from his family, in 1977 Fazioli assembled a group of experts in woodworking, acoustics, and piano technology to study and scientifically analyze every aspect of piano design and construction. The following year, prototypes of his new instruments in hand, he began building pianos commercially in a factory housed at one end of the family's Sacile furniture factory, which is a top supplier of high-end office furniture in Italy.

In 2001, Fazioli built a new expanded, modern piano production facility, and in 2005 opened an adjoining 198-seat concert hall with a stage large enough for a chamber orchestra. Fazioli maintains a regular concert schedule of well-known musicians who perform there. The concert hall is designed so that it can be adjusted acoustically with moveable panels and sound reflectors to optimize the acoustics for performing, recording, or testing, and for different kinds of music, musical ensembles, and size of audience. The hall is used for the research and testing of pianos, and every piano Fazioli makes is tested here. In addition to the research activities in the concert hall, the new factory also contains a research department for ongoing research in musical acoustics in cooperation with a number of educational institutions.

Fazioli builds grands only, about 120 per year, in six sizes from 5' 2" to 10' 2", the largest piano in the world. This model also has the distinction of having four pedals. Three are the usual sustain, sostenuto, and una corda. The fourth is a "soft" pedal that brings the hammers closer to the strings—similar to the function in verticals and some older grands—to soften the sound without altering the tonal quality as the una corda often does. A unique compensating device corrects for the action irregularity that would otherwise occur when the hammers are moved in this manner. The fourth pedal is available as an option on the other models. Fazioli also offers two actions and two pedal lyres as options on all models. Having two actions allows for more voicing possibilities without having to constantly revoice the hammers. A second pedal lyre containing only three pedals can be a welcome alternative for some pianists who might be confused by the presence of a fourth pedal.

All Fazioli pianos have inner and outer rims of maple. Pinblocks are of Delignit, except for the largest two models, which use five-ply maple pinblocks from Bolduc in Canada. The pianos have Renner actions, Kluge keyboards, and either Renner or Abel hammers. The bronze capo d'astro bar is adjustable in the factory for setting the strike point and treble string length, and is also removable for servicing if necessary, and the front and rear duplex scales are tunable. The company says that a critical factor in the sound of its pianos is the scientific selection of its woods, such as the "resonant spruce" obtained from the Val di Fiemme, where Stradivarius reportedly sought woods for his violins. Each piece of wood is said to be carefully tested for certain resonant properties before being used in the pianos.

An incredible level of detail has gone into the design and construction of these pianos. For instance, in one small portion of the soundboard where additional stiffness is required, the grain of the wood runs perpendicular to that of the rest of the soundboard, cleverly disguised so as to be almost unnoticeable. The pianos are impeccably prepared at the factory, including very fine voicing—even perfect tuning of the duplex scales.

Those most familiar with Fazioli pianos describe them as combining both great power and great warmth in a way that causes the music played on them to "make sense" as few other pianos can.

Warranty: Ten years, parts and labor, transferable to future owners within the warranty period.

FEURICH
including Siegfried Hansing

Unique Pianos
159 Park Hill Blvd.
West Melbourne, Florida 32904

888-725-6633
321-725-5690
www.feurich.com
www.atlanticmusiccenter.com

Pianos made by: Julius Feurich Pianofortefabrik GmbH, Gunzenhausen, Germany

This German piano manufacturer was founded in Leipzig in 1851 by Julius Feurich. At its height in the early part of the twentieth century, the company employed 360 people, producing 1,200 upright and 600 grand pianos annually. Like many German manufacturers, however, Feurich lost its factory during the Second World War. Following the war, the fourth generation of the Feurich family rebuilt in Langlau in what became West Germany.

In 1991, Bechstein purchased Feurich and closed the Langlau factory, but in 1993 the name was sold back to the Feurich family. For a time, production was contracted out to other German manufacturers, including Schimmel, while the Feurich family marketed and distributed the pianos. In 1995, Feurich opened a new factory in Gunzenhausen, Germany. Under the direction of Julius Feurich, the fifth generation, the company began building its own pianos once again, and is currently building about fifty to sixty instruments per year in two sizes of grand and three sizes of vertical. All pianos and parts are made in Germany. The 49" model 123 vertical is available with a choice of actions, either the traditional Feurich action made by Renner or the Fandrich Vertical Action™, made by Renner under license from the Fandrichs (see "Fandrich & Sons" for more information).

A new piano, the Siegfried Hansing, made by Feurich is being introduced in 2007 to the United States. It employs the designs of the 5' 8" model 172 Feurich grand and the 49" model 123 Feurich vertical, but in a more contemporary case. These pianos will be available at a lesser cost by using some action parts made by Detoa in the Czech Republic and case parts made by Artfield in China. However, assembly of all models and technical work are completed in Germany. Siegfried Hansen was a celebrated piano designer in the early twentieth century who worked for Feurich.

Feurich has a partnership in China to produce pianos for the mainland Chinese market. These pianos are not available elsewhere.

Warranty: Five years, parts and labor, to the original purchaser

FÖRSTER, AUGUST

German American Trading Co., Inc.
P.O. Box 17789
Tampa, Florida 33682

813-961-8405
germanamer@msn.com
www.august-foerster.de

Pianos made by: August Förster GmbH, Löbau, Germany

The Förster factory was founded by Friedrich August Förster in 1859 in Löbau, Germany, after Förster studied the art of piano building with others. During the years of control by the government of East Germany, the factory was managed by the fourth generation pianomaker, Wolfgang Förster. Since the reunification of Germany and privatization, Wolfgang and his family are once again the owners of the company.

Förster makes about 120 grands a year in four sizes, and 150 verticals a year in two sizes, with a workforce of forty, using a great deal of hand labor. The pianos are very well built structurally and the cabinets elegant. Rims and pinblocks are of beech, soundboards of Siberian spruce, and bridges are of hardrock maple (without graphite). Each string is individually terminated (single-strung). The actions are made by Renner with Renner hammers. A sostenuto pedal is standard on all grand models.

The tone of August Förster grands is quite unique, with a remarkable bass, dark, deep, yet clear. As delivered from the factory, the treble is often quite bright, and for some American tastes might be considered a bit thin. It is a less complex sound emphasizing clarity. This, however, can be modified somewhat with voicing and a good dealer preparation. The instruments are quite versatile, at home with Mozart or Prokofieff, classical or jazz. The 6' 4" model is often said to have an especially good scale. The concert-quality 7' 2" and 9' 1" models are well balanced tonally and, over the years, have been endorsed by many famous artists. The Renner actions are very responsive and arrive in exacting regulation.

Most of the comments regarding the quality of materials and workmanship of the grands also apply to the verticals. The cabinet of the vertical is of exceptional width, with extra-thick side panels of solid-core stock. Counter bridges are used on the outside of the soundboard to increase its mass. The verticals have a full set of agraffes and all the hardware and handmade wood parts are of elegant quality. The actions are built by Renner. The verticals possess the same warm, rich, deep bass tone as the grands.

Warranty: Ten years, parts and labor, to the original purchaser

GROTRIAN

Grotrian Piano Company
P.O. Box 5833
D-38049 Braunschweig, Germany

+49-531-210100
+49-531-2101040 (fax)
contact@grotrian.de
www.grotrian.de

Friedrich Grotrian was born in Schöningen, Germany in 1803, and as a young man lived in Moscow, where he ran a music business and was associated with piano manufacturing. Later in his life, he teamed up with Heinrich Steinweg and Heinrich's son Theodore to build pianos in Germany. Heinrich emigrated to the United States about 1850, soon to establish the firm of Steinway & Sons. Theodore followed in 1865, selling his share in the partnership to Friedrich's son Wilhelm, Friedrich having died in 1860. Thereafter, the firm became known as Grotrian-Steinweg. (In a legal settlement with Steinway & Sons, Grotrian-Steinweg agreed to use only the name Grotrian on pianos sold in North America.)

Even as early as the 1860s, Grotrian pianos were well known and highly respected throughout Europe. Each successive generation of the Grotrian family maintained the company's high standards and furthered the technical development of the instrument. Today the company is owned by the sixth generation of Grotrians. Housed in an up-to-date factory, and using a combination of modern technology and traditional craftsmanship, Grotrian makes about 500 verticals and 100 grands a year.

Grotrian grands have beech rims, solid spruce soundboards, laminated beech pinblocks, Renner actions, and are single-strung. Grotrian prides itself on what it calls its "homogeneous soundboard," in which each piece of wood is specially chosen for its contribution to the tone of the soundboard. The cast-iron plate is attached with screws along the outer edges of the rim, instead of on top of the rim, which the company says allows the soundboard to vibrate more freely. The vertical pianos have a unique star-shaped wooden back structure and a full-perimeter plate.

Grotrian makes five sizes of grand and six sizes of vertical piano. The 43½" "Friedrich Grotrian" vertical is a lower-cost piano with a beech back frame but no back posts, and a simpler cabinet. New in 2006 is a 6' 10" grand model called "Charis."

Grotrian has introduced the Duo Grand Piano, two grand pianos placed side by side with keyboards at opposite ends, as in a duo piano concert, with removable rim parts, connected soundboards, and a common lid (price on request).

The treble of Grotrian pianos has extraordinary sustaining characteristics. It also has a pronounced sound of attack, subtle and delicate. The tenor is darker than many other brands. The bass can be powerful, but without stridency. Overall, Grotrian pianos have a unique, expressive sound and are a pleasure to play.

Warranty: Five years, parts and labor, transferable to future owners

GULBRANSEN

QRS Music Technologies, Inc.
2011 Seward Avenue
Naples, Florida 34109

800-247-6557
www.gulbransen.com

Pianos made by: Sejung Corporation, Qingdao, Shandong Province, China

Founded in 1904, Gulbransen was a well-regarded piano and organ manufacturer of the early twentieth century, and at one time was the world's largest maker of player pianos. In more modern times, the company was known for its electronic organs and MIDI products. In 2004, QRS Music Technologies, maker of the Pianomation player piano systems and distributor of Story & Clark pianos, purchased Gulbransen's MIDI products and company name.

Currently, the Gulbransen line consists of two sizes of grand, both with and without player systems, and two sizes of vertical, made by Sejung (see "Sejung"). The pianos are tuned, inspected, and adjusted at the Story & Clark facility in Pennsylvania prior to being shipped to the dealer.

Warranty: Eight years, parts and labor, to the original purchaser

HAESSLER — See "Blüthner"

HAILUN

Hailun Distribution, LLC
5400 Lawrenceville Hwy., N.W.
Suite E-2
Lilburn, Georgia 30047

770-381-3871
678-898-9931
Aspire@HailunUSA.com
www.hailunusa.com

Pianos made by: Ningbo Hailun Musical Instrument Co., Ningbo, Zhejiang Province, China

Ningbo Hailun began making piano parts in 1986 under the Ningbo Piano Parts Factory name. Ningbo is a city near Shanghai which, the company says, is the birthplace of the maker of the first pianos built in China. In the mid-1990s, the company began assembling entire pianos. Most of the production is for export to Asia and Europe. This is the first foray into the U.S. market, where a dealer network is currently being established.

The Ningbo Hailun factory has over 400,000 square feet of production capacity and 800 employees. A 200,000 square foot production expansion project is underway to accommodate distribution in the U.S. market. Since 2001, the company has invested heavily in computer-controlled manufacturing equipment and has hired an impressive group of experts from Japan, Austria, and the United States to help it reach the highest quality standards.

At present, the company offers three sizes of vertical piano and three sizes of grand to U.S. customers, but several more grand and vertical models, including a group of "designer" models, are expected during 2007. The distributor says the models offered in the U.S. are aimed at the mid-level market. Initial reports about these pianos, based on inspection at trade shows and discussions with people in the industry, suggest that the quality is better than average for a Chinese-made piano.

HALLET, DAVIS & CO.

North American Music, Inc.
11 Kay Fries Drive
Stony Point, New York 10980

800-782-2694
www.namusic.com

Pianos made by: Dongbei Piano Company, Ltd., Yingkou, Liaoning Province, China

This famous old American piano brand name dates back to at least 1843 and changed hands many times over the years. It eventually became part of the Aeolian group of piano brands, and instruments bearing the name were manufactured at Aeolian's Memphis plant before that company went out of business in 1985. For a time, Hallet & Davis pianos were made by Samick in Korea. At the present time, most Hallet, Davis & Co. pianos are made in China by the Dongbei Piano Company (see "Dongbei"). In general, they are similar to pianos built by Dongbei under other names for several other distributors. However, the distributor says that pianos in the "Imperial Collection" (model numbers ending in "I") use higher-quality imported veneers provided to Dongbei by the distributor.

HAMILTON — See "Baldwin"

HANSING, SIEGFRIED — See "Feurich"

HARDMAN, PECK & CO.

Hardman Pianos
11 Kay Fries Drive
Stony Point, New York 10980

800-782-2694
info@hardmanpiano.com
www.hardmanpiano.com

Hardman, Peck & Co. was an old American piano company whose roots can be traced back to 1842. In the early twentieth century it was absorbed into the Aeolian Corporation, which went out of business in 1985. Until recently, most Hardman, Peck pianos were made in China by the Dongbei Piano Co. (see "Dongbei"), and were similar to those built by Dongbei under other names for several other distributors. Beginning this year, Hardman, Peck's distributor is using the Beijing Hsinghai Piano Group (see "Beijing Hsinghai") to manufacture most of the pianos. However, for a time, there may be some pianos from each of the two factories available on the showroom floor. Prices were not available at press time.

HAZELTON BROS. — See "Samick"

HEINTZMAN & CO.
including Gerhard Heintzman

Heintzman Distributor Ltd.
210-2106 Main Street
Vancouver, British Columbia
Canada V5T 3C5

604-801-5393
info@hzmpiano.com
www.hzmpiano.com

Pianos made by: Heintzman Piano Company, Ltd., Beijing, China

Heintzman & Co. Ltd. was founded by Theodore August Heintzman in Toronto in 1866. By 1900, Heintzman was one of Toronto's larger manufacturing concerns, building 3,000 pianos per year and selling them throughout Canada and abroad through a network of company stores and other distributors. The pianos received high praise and won prizes at exhibitions. Even today, technicians frequently encounter old Heintzman pianos built in the early part of the twentieth century and consider them to be of high quality. In the latter decades of the century, Heintzman, like other North American brands, struggled to compete with cheaper foreign imports. The factory finally closed its doors in 1986 and relocated to China. (Some pianos continued to be sold in Canada under the Heintzman and Gerhard Heintzman names for a few years thereafter).

The new company, known as Heintzman Piano Company, Ltd., is Canadian owned and managed and has a private, independent factory dedicated to producing Heintzman brand pianos. Heintzman makes pianos to the original Canadian Heintzman designs and scales utilizing some of the equipment from Canada. Manufacturing is supervised by James Moffat, who was plant manager of the Canadian Heintzman factory for forty years. The company even utilizes some components from Canada, such as Bolduc soundboards, in grands and larger verticals. The factory makes about 5,000 pianos per year.

The smallest vertical made under the Heintzman name is 43½" tall, but pianos for export to North America typically start at 47½" and contain a mixture of Chinese and imported parts such as pinblocks and treble strings from Germany and Mapes bass strings from the U.S. Verticals 48½" and above use Renner Blue hammers, and the largest two sizes have Canadian Bolduc solid Eastern white spruce soundboards. All verticals have a middle pedal that operates a bass sustain mechanism, as well as a "Silent Switch" that operates a mute bar for silent practice.

The grands, 5' 6", 6' 8", and 9' in size, also use German pinblocks and strings, Mapes bass strings, Renner Blue hammers, and Canadian Bolduc soundboards. The 9' concert grand comes with a full Renner action and Kluge keys from Germany. A Renner action is a higher-priced option on the other models. All grands come with a sostenuto pedal. A 6' 2" model patterned on the old Heintzman model D is being introduced in 2007.

Heintzman Piano Company also makes the "Gerhard Heintzman" brand, intended to compete with less expensive Chinese-made pianos. Most of the pianos in this line are smaller than in the Heintzman line. This brand uses less expensive materials and components than the Heintzman, including Japanese hammers and a laminated spruce soundboard.

Warranty: Heintzman and Gerhard Heintzman—Ten years, parts and labor, from the factory, transferable to future owners within the warranty period.

HOFFMANN, W. — See "Bechstein, C."

HOWARD — See "Baldwin"

HSINGHAI — See "Beijing Hsinghai"

IBACH

Resource West, Inc.
2295 East Sahara Avenue
Las Vegas, Nevada 89104

702-457-7919
800-777-6874
info@ibachpiano.com
www.ibachpiano.com

Pianos made by: Rud. Ibach Sohn, Schwelm, Germany

Established by Johannes Adolf Ibach in 1794, Ibach has the distinction of being the oldest existing manufacturer of fine pianos in the world. (For perspective, in 1794, Haydn was writing his last works while Beethoven was writing his Opus 1 piano trios.) Ibach is still owned and managed by the original family, Messers. Christian and Rolf Ibach, the sixth generation.

Ibach has been notable in the development of both piano construction and the piano industry in general. Although not as well known in North America as some other European manufacturers, Ibach has quietly built a solid reputation in Europe over the last two centuries through fine craftsmanship and by supplying pianos to a long list of famous composers and artists, such as Wagner, R. Strauss, Liszt, Bartok, Schoenberg, and others.

Economic conditions in Germany during the last couple of decades have hit all the small piano makers very hard. In order to survive, in 1991 Ibach sold a thirty-three percent interest in the company to Daewoo, the Korean former manufacturer of Sojin pianos. The plan was that Ibach was to sell Korean-made Ibach pianos worldwide in addition to a small number of German-made Ibachs. This joint venture did not survive very long and the Korean manufacturing operation was eventually abandoned by Daewoo.

German-made Ibach pianos are being distributed in the United States by Resource West, a Las Vegas retailer. Resource West says it will be distributing these fine pianos through interior design professionals and some smaller piano dealers. No investment is needed by the dealer. In lieu of stocking the pianos and receiving a regular retail markup, the dealer instead refers interested customers to the Resource West/Ibach showroom in Las Vegas and receives a substantial commission when a sale is made. The price list in this *Supplement* is the suggested retail price at the Las Vegas showroom.

IRMLER — See "Blüthner"

KAWAI
including Shigeru Kawai

Kawai America Corporation
2055 East University Drive
P.O. Box 9045
Compton, California 90224

310-631-1771
800-421-2177
310-223-0900 (Shigeru Kawai)
acoustic@kawaius.com
www.kawaius.com
www.shigerukawai.com

Pianos made by: Kawai Musical Instrument Mfg. Co., Ltd., Hamamatsu, Japan and Karawan, Indonesia

Kawai was founded in 1927 by Koichi Kawai, an inventor and former Yamaha employee who was the first person in Japan to design and build a piano action. While Kawai is second in size to Yamaha among Japanese piano manufacturers, it has a well-deserved reputation all its own for quality and innovation. Nearly all Kawai grands and taller uprights are made in Japan; most consoles and studios are made in Indonesia. The company closed its North Carolina factory in 2005.

One of Kawai's most important innovations is the use of ABS Styran plastic in the manufacture of action parts. Nearly forty years of use and scientific testing have shown this material to be superior to wood for this purpose. ABS does not swell and shrink with humidity changes, so actions made with it are likely to maintain proper regulation better than wood actions. The parts are stronger and without glue joints, so breakage is rare. Kawai calls this advance the "Millennium" action and it is present in every Kawai piano. In the current "Millennium III" version found in some models, the ABS is reinforced with carbon fiber so it can be stronger with less mass. With less mass to "push around" (less inertia), the action can be more responsive to the player's intentions, including faster repetition. Certain contact surfaces on the action parts are also micro-engineered for ideal shape and texture, resulting in a more consistent touch. Although it took a number of years to overcome the idea that plastic parts must be inferior, there is essentially no dispute anymore among piano technicians on this subject.

Kawai's vertical piano offerings change frequently and are sometimes confusing. At present there are three basic series of Kawai vertical pianos. The console series begins with the 44½" model 506, a basic entry-level console in an institutional-style cabinet (legs with toe blocks). Model K-15 is a 44" version of this in a continental-style cabinet (no legs), and model 508 is a 44½" version in a simple furniture-style cabinet (free-standing legs). Model 607 is the same piano in a fancier furniture-style cabinet. All have the same internal workings. The action in this series is slightly smaller than a full-size action, so it will be slightly less responsive. However, it is more than sufficient for beginner or casual use.

The studio series used to consist primarily of the 46" school models UST-7 and UST-8. The UST-7 was a workhorse, with a very strong back, and would stay in tune well even when moved. The UST-8 was a less-expensive piano with a thinner back and simpler cabinet, developed to be more competitive in school bidding situations. It didn't have the same tuning stability as the UST-7, especially when moved, but was otherwise adequate. Kawai has just replaced both of these models with the 46" model UST-9. This model has the stronger back of the UST-7, but the simpler cabinet of the UST-8. It also contains the Millennium III action; an angled, leather-lined music desk to better hold music; and a stylish, reinforced bench. Because it is made in Indonesia, the price is only a little higher than the UST-8. It is probably one of the better "deals" in the Kawai vertical piano line. Rounding out the studio series is the 46½" model 907, which is essentially the model UST-9 in a fancy, furniture-style cabinet and with a standard ABS action.

Kawai's upright series is known as the "K" series. It consists of the K-2 (45"), K-3 (48"), K-5 (49"), K-6 (52"), and K-8 (52"). All have the Millennium III action, a soft-close fallboard; a wide, leather-lined music desk; a somewhat stylish cabinet; and come with an adjustable bench. The larger models also feature agraffes, duplex scaling, Kawai's NEOTEX synthetic ivory keytops, and various kinds of tone escape mechanisms. The K-8 has a true sostenuto pedal.

Kawai has invented a variable-touch action for vertical pianos in which the player can vary the touchweight by sliding a lever. The lever operates a set of sliding weights behind the fallboard. The touchweight varies depending on the point at which the keys contact the sliding weights. The touchweight can be adjusted from about 48 to 70 grams (normal for Kawai is 56 grams). The "Vari-Touch" feature is currently available only on the 46" UST-8 upright (model VT-118).

Kawai has three series of grand pianos: RX, GE, and GM. The RX series is the most expensive and has the best features. It is designed for the best performance, whereas the GE and GM series are designed more for efficiency in manufacturing, with fewer performance features. The RX pianos have a radial beam structure, focused and connected to the plate using a cast-iron bracket at the tenor break. This system makes for a more rigid structure, which translates into better tone projection. The soundboard of the RX models is tapered for better tonal response, and the rim is thicker and stronger than in the GE and GM models. The RX series pianos also use the new Millennium III action, have duplex scaling, lighter hammers (less inertia), and NEOTEX synthetic ivory keytops (though some of these features are being introduced into the GE and GM pianos as well). The RX grands get more precise key weighting, plus more tuning, regulating, and voicing at the factory. The cabinetry is nicer-looking and of better quality than that of the GE and GM series pianos. The difference between the GE and GM pianos is primarily that the GM grands have simpler cabinetry and internal design (no agraffes, for example) than the GE. The 5' model GM-10K is Kawai's first grand made in Indonesia; the others are made in Japan.

Kawai's quality control is excellent. Major problems are rare and after-sale service other than normal maintenance is usually limited to fixing the occasional minor buzz or squeak. Kawai's warranty service is also excellent and the warranty is transferable to future owners within the warranty period (a benefit that is not common these days). The tone of most Kawai pianos, in my opinion, is not ideal for classical music, but when expertly voiced, it is not far off, and in any case is quite versatile musically. In part because the touch is so good, Kawai grands are often sought by classical pianists as a less-expensive alternative to a Steinway or other high-end piano. Kawai dealers tend to be a little more aggressive about discounting than their competition (Yamaha). There is also a thriving market for used Kawais. (If you are considering buying a used Kawai, please read "Should I Buy A Used 'Gray Market' Yamaha or Kawai Piano?" on pages 176–177 of *The Piano Book*.)

Kawai has invented an Acoustic Piano Recording System (PR-1) that allows one to create a CD of a piano performance right from the piano. It contains two specially-designed microphones that attach easily to the piano, and a CD read/write player with built-in reverb and EQ that connects to any sound system. The system retails for $1,595.

The Shigeru Kawai line of grands represents Kawai's ultimate effort in producing world-class pianos. Named after Kawai's former chairman (and son of company founder Koichi Kawai), the limited edition Shigeru Kawai grands are made at the separate facility where Kawai's EX concert grands are made.

Although based on the Kawai RX designs, the Shigeru Kawai models are "hand-made" in the extreme. Very high-grade soundboard spruce is air dried for multiple years and then planed by hand by a worker who knocks on the wood and listens for the optimum tonal response. Ribs are also hand planed for correct stiffness. String bearing is set in the traditional manner by planing the bridges by hand instead of having pre-cut bridges pinned by machine. Bass strings are wound by hand instead of machine wound. Plate castings are buried in sand for a year to make sure all internal tensions are gone before using them. Cold-pressed hammers have felt fibers that are sorted bass to treble by the length and texture of the wool fibers for better voicing. Hammer shanks are thinned along the bottom so that their stiffness is matched to the hammer mass. These procedures represent a level of detail relatively few manufacturers indulge in.

Each buyer of a Shigeru Kawai piano receives a visit within the first year by a Kawai master technician from Japan, who performs concert-level voicing and regulation of the piano. According to those who have watched them work, these Japanese master technicians are amazingly skilled. Although not many U.S. technicians are familiar with Shigeru Kawai pianos, those who are tend to rank them among the world's finest instruments. In addition, Shigeru Kawai pianos have been chosen by top prize winners at a number of prestigious piano competitions.

Warranty: Kawai and Shigeru Kawai—Ten years, parts and labor, transferable to future owners within the warranty period.

KEMBLE

Kemble & Company Ltd.
Mount Avenue
Bletchley, Milton Keynes MK1 1JE
United Kingdom

+44-1908-371771
+44-1908-270448 (fax)
brian.kemble@gmx.yamaha.com
www.kemble-pianos.co.uk

The Kemble family has been manufacturing pianos since 1911. In 1985, Kemble started making pianos for Yamaha for the European market, and in 1988 Yamaha bought a majority interest in the company and expanded and modernized the factory. Kemble is England's only, and Western Europe's largest, piano manufacturer.

Kemble makes verticals from 43" to 52" and a 5' 8" grand. The quality of the materials used in the Kemble is comparable to that in the Yamaha pianos Kemble makes. The soundboard of the Kemble is of German spruce which, the company says, gives it more of a "European" tone. The cabinets tend to be much fancier than Yamaha's, with some very interesting and beautiful designer models and finishes. For example, the 48" Shaker-inspired designer upright called "Vermont" was designed by the famous British designers Conran and Partners. The Empire and Prestige models have beautiful inlaid panels of mahogany curl and burr yew, respectively. There is also a 45" model called "Classic-T," available in black and chrome or in a delicious chocolate color called "Mocha Oak;" a 49" "Conservatoire" upright with "softline" design (rounded edges and profile) and brass inlay; and a limited-edition (250) "Mozart" model celebrating the 250th anniversary of the composer's birth. A new 52" model K131SN with sostenuto pedal is being introduced in 2007.

The 5' 8" model KC173 grand is essentially like the Yamaha model C2 grand, with design differences such as plate color and music desk shape. It is also voiced to Kemble's specs, sounding to me more "European," i.e. a bass with less-pronounced high overtones.

Warranty: Ten years, parts and labor, to the original purchaser

KIMBALL

Kimball Pianos
Brighton Music, Inc.
2647 North Western Avenue
Chicago, Illinois 60647

800-445-0695
www.kimballpiano.net

Kimball, a name with a long history in the piano world (see *The Piano Book* for details), is now being produced by Brighton Music, Inc., which acquired the rights to the Kimball name in 2005. Kimball International, the previous owner of the Kimball brand, which produced Kimball pianos from 1959 to 1996, was primarily a furniture maker that mass-produced a very average piano.

In contrast, Kimball is now controlled by an American piano technician who has returned Kimball to its historical roots in Chicago and says he is placing the company's focus on the musical instrument and on technical details of American piano design and construction. The result of this new focus is a new line of Kimball grands that include the 5' 1" model K1 and the 6' 2" model K3. A 5' 9" model K2 will be introduced in late 2007.

Parts and components for the new Kimball grands are being sourced from many parts of the world, primarily China and Europe. In the U.S., Kimball is doing final assembly and detailing of the instruments. Components include a rim made of maple and oak; bridges planed and notched by hand in the traditional manner; a wet-sand cast plate; Langer keys, action, and hammers; and a solid spruce soundboard.

Warranty: Twelve years, parts and labor, to the original purchaser

KNABE, WM. — See "Samick"

KOHLER & CAMPBELL — See "Samick"

MASON & HAMLIN

Mason & Hamlin Piano Company
4111 North Freeway Blvd.
Sacramento, California 95834

800-566-3472
916-567-9999
www.masonhamlin.com

Pianos made by: Mason & Hamlin Piano Co., Haverhill, Massachusetts and Sacramento, California

Mason & Hamlin was founded in 1854 by Henry Mason and Emmons Hamlin. Mason was a musician and businessman and Hamlin was an inventor working with reed organs. Within a few years, Mason & Hamlin was one of the largest reed organ manufacturers in the country. The company began making pianos in 1881 in Boston, and soon became, along with Chickering, among the most prestigious of the Boston piano makers. By 1910, Mason & Hamlin was considered Steinway's chief competitor. Over the next eighty-five years, Mason & Hamlin changed hands many times. (You can read the somewhat lengthy and interesting history in *The Piano Book*.) In 1996, the Burgett brothers, owners of PianoDisc, purchased Mason & Hamlin out of bankruptcy and set about re-establishing manufacturing at the factory in Haverhill, Massachusetts. At present, the company manufactures about three hundred pianos per year at this factory.

Since acquiring the company, the Burgetts have brought back most of the piano models from the company's Boston era (1881-1932) that originally made the company famous. Some have been refinements of original designs, others have been completely new. First came the 5' 8" model A and 7' model BB, both of which had been manufactured by the previous owner and so needed less work to resurrect. Then, in fairly rapid succession, came the 6' 4" model AA, the 9' 4" model CC concert grand, and the 5' 4" model B. The development of the model AA was an especially interesting project because in the process the engineering staff standardized certain features, refined manufacturing processes, and modernized jigs and machinery, improvements that afterward were applied to the company's other models. The 50" model 50 vertical piano has also been re-introduced and redesigned, with longer keys for a more grand-like touch, and improved pedal leverage. Internal parts for the verticals are made in Haverhill, then installed into an imported cabinet in the company's Sacramento factory, where it also installs PianoDisc systems.

All Mason & Hamlin grands have certain features in common, including a wide-tail design, a full-perimeter plate, an extremely thick and heavy maple rim, solid spruce soundboard; five-ply, quartersawn maple pinblock; and the patented "tension resonator" crown retention system. The tension resonator (illustrated in *The Piano Book*), invented by Richard Gertz in 1900, consists of a series of turnbuckles that connect various parts of the inner rim. In theory this web of turnbuckles, nicknamed "the spider," locks the rim in place so that it cannot expand with stress and age, thereby preserving the soundboard crown (curvature). (The soundboard is glued to the inner rim and would collapse if the rim expanded.) There is no modern-day experimental evidence to confirm or deny this theory, but many technicians believe in its validity nevertheless because unlike most older pianos, the soundboards of old Mason & Hamlins almost always have plenty of crown.

In the early part of the twentieth century, Wessell, Nickel & Gross was a major supplier of actions to American piano manufacturers, including Mason & Hamlin. Over the years, the name fell into disuse. In 2004, Mason & Hamlin revived the name by registering the trademark, which now refers to the design and specifications of Mason & Hamlin actions.

The grands are available in ebony and several standard and exotic wood finishes, in both satin and high polish. Satin finishes are lacquer, the high polish finishes are polyester. Most sizes are also available in a stylized case design called "Monticello," which has fluted, conical legs, similar to Hepplewhite, with matching lyre and bench.

The tone of Mason & Hamlin pianos is typically American—lush, singing, and powerful, not unlike the Steinway in basic character, but with an even more powerful bass and a clearer treble. The designers have done a good job of making a recognizable Mason & Hamlin sound that is consistent throughout the model line. The 5' 8" model A has a particularly powerful bass for a piano of its size. The treble, notably weak in prior versions, has been beefed up, but the bass is still the showpiece of the piano. The new 5' 4" model B also has a large-sounding bass for its size. The "growling" power of the Mason & Hamlin bass is most apparent in the 7' model BB. 6' 4" model AA is a little better balanced between bass and treble, one reason why it is a personal favorite.

The basic musical design of Mason & Hamlin pianos is very good, as is most of the workmanship. As with other American-made pianos, musical and cabinet detailing, such as factory voicing and regulation and plate and cabinet cosmetics, are reasonable but lag somewhat behind the company's European competitors in finesse. Some of this can be finished off by thorough and competent dealer make-ready. Dealers report that like its competitor Steinway, the Mason & Hamlin piano requires a substantial amount of preparation by the dealer.

In recent years, many companies have turned to Asia for parts and materials, both to save money and to increase the security of supply. Among makers of high-end pianos, Mason & Hamlin has been pioneering in this regard and more aggressive than most, now importing cast-iron plates, hardware, and many of its action parts from China. The company also maintains traditional sources of supply, such as Renner, for some of the action parts. As the company explains:

> "... we are pleased to say that we source our materials, brass, iron, steel, hard wood, felt, leather etc. and components from the four corners of the earth in an effort to maintain steady production and to control quality and price levels. Likewise as the artisans who built Mason & Hamlin pianos in the early Boston days, immigrants and direct descendents of immigrants, we are proud to report that the artisans who build our instruments today continue to represent a diverse mix of cultures and races from many parts of the world."

Though this approach has raised eyebrows in some circles, and there is obviously some risk, the company says it has kept a close eye on quality. In fact, for some items, it's possible that the quality available from China is better than from other sources. Most of my contacts felt that the quality of the piano had not diminished during this time and may, in fact, have improved. A smaller number of contacts said they felt the quality had diminished somewhat but that the piano was still very good. What *has* been affected, however, is the price of the piano. The list price has not been affected much; however, substantial discounts from list are routinely available from Mason & Hamlin dealers, making the piano quite a good value among high-end instruments.

Warranty: Twelve years, parts and labor, transferable to future owners within the warranty period; except lifetime, non-transferable warranty on case and action parts.

MAY BERLIN — See "Schimmel"

MEISTER, OTTO

The Piano Group, Inc.
P.O. Box 14128
Bradenton, Florida 34280

941-794-5157
thepianogroup@yahoo.com
www.ottomeisterpianos.com

Otto Meister pianos are made by the Beijing Hsinghai Piano Group, Ltd. in Beijing, China. See "Beijing Hsinghai."

MILLER, HENRY F.

Henry F. Miller
236 West Portal Avenue #568
San Francisco, California 94127

800-511-0083
info@henryfmiller.com

Henry F. Miller is the name of an old American piano maker dating back to 1863. The name eventually became owned by Aeolian Pianos, which went out of business in 1985. The name is now owned by the Sherman Clay chain of piano stores and used on a mid-priced line of pianos carried by these and other major piano retailers around the country. Current Henry F. Miller pianos are made by Pearl River in China. Some models are similar to pianos sold under the Pearl River name. The 4' 10" and 5' 3" grands feature solid spruce soundboards.

MOOG PIANO BAR

Moog Music Inc.
2004-E Riverside Drive
Asheville, North Carolina 28804

828-251-0090
info@moogmusic.com
www.moogmusic.com

Moog Music Inc., founded by electronic music pioneer Robert Moog, has introduced an amazingly simple and elegant way of turning any acoustic piano into a MIDI controller without modifying the piano in any way. The system consists of three parts: A *scanner bar* sits on the cheek blocks, spanning the keyboard immediately in front of the fallboard and slightly above the keys. Optical sensors in the scanner bar measure the movement of the keys and translate it into note and velocity information. A *pedal sensor* rests beneath the pedals and detects their motion. A *control module* sits on the piano, receiving the data from the scanner bar and pedal sensor, turning it into MIDI information that can trigger over 300 built-in sounds. The control module can hold up to 100 setups, twenty of which can be stored on a portable "library card," twenty that are factory-supplied, and sixty that are user-determined. The control module also contains a headphone jack, audio outputs, and MIDI in and out ports. The Moog Piano Bar is completely portable and comes with a carrying case. It sells for about $1,595 from piano dealers, selected piano technicians, and musical instrument dealers.

NORDISKA

Geneva International Corporation
29 East Hintz Road
Wheeling, Illinois 60090

800-533-2388
847-520-9970
pianos@geneva-intl.com
www.geneva-intl.com

Pianos made by: Dongbei Piano Company, Ltd., Yingkou, Liaoning Province, China

Nordiska was a hundred year old Swedish piano manufacturer that sold its designs, equipment, and technology to the Chinese company Dongbei when it went out of business in 1988. See "Dongbei" for more information.

Dongbei pianos are sold in the United States under a number of different brand names, among them Nordiska. The importer says the Nordiska brand differs from the others in several ways: The Nordiska brand has Abel hammers (except the 43" model). The grands use a higher grade of felt, cloth, and buckskin throughout the action, keys, and key frame, resulting in an action that is quieter and more durable than that of its competitors. The Nordiska pianos utilize the best-quality soundboard wood and are worked on by the most experienced technicians. Finally, only the Nordiska pianos use the Petrof leg attachment system. The importer says that other exclusive upgrades are planned for the future.

Nordiska grands now utilize the focused beam structure described under "Dongbei," plus a maple rim, heavier plate, and better plate cosmetics. The 7' and 9' models also feature Renner actions assembled by Renner, Kluge keys and key frame, and a Bolduc (Canadian) white spruce soundboard. Imported American veneers are being used on all grands. The 7' grand has an especially good sound and touch, perhaps the best yet on a Chinese-made piano.

Warranty: Ten years, parts and labor, to the original purchaser

OPUS II — See "Cristofori"

PALATINO

The Music Link
P.O. Box 162
Brisbane, California 94005

888-552-5465

piano@palatinousa.com
www.palatinausa.com

Pianos made by: AXL Musical Instrument Co., Ltd. Corp., Shanghai, China

Although this company is new to the piano world, it is not new to music. For some time, AXL has been manufacturing a full range of musical instruments under its own name and under OEM agreements with other companies. The company says that its factory is very automated, employing CNC routers from Japan and Germany, and that it sources materials for the pianos from around the world.

At present the company makes three sizes of vertical piano and three sizes of grand. Specifications include solid spruce soundboard in both verticals and grands, hard rock maple pinblock and bridges, and adjustable artist bench and slow-close fallboard on all models.

Based on personal observation and dealer reports, Palatino pianos appear to have good quality control and are prepared well at the factory before being shipped to dealers.

Warranty: Ten years, parts and labor, transferable to future owners within the warranty period.

PEARL RIVER
including Ritmüller

Pearl River Piano Group America, Ltd.
2260 South Haven Avenue, Suite F
Ontario, California 91761

909-673-9155
800-435-5086
sales@pearlriverusa.com
www.pearlriverusa.com

Pianos made by: Guangzhou Pearl River Piano Group Ltd., Guangzhou, Guangdong Province, China

Originally established in 1954 through the consolidation of several piano making facilities, the Guangzhou Pearl River piano factory is now China's largest piano manufacturer and one of the largest in the world, with production of over 100,000 pianos annually by move than 4,000 workers. The company says the average length of service of its workers is seventeen years. Pianos are made under the Pearl River and Ritmüller names, and under a few other names under OEM contract with distributors, such as Henry F. Miller (with Sherman Clay) and Essex (with Steinway) (see separate listings under those names).

Pearl River verticals begin with 42½" console model 108 in continental style (no legs) and in a style with curved leg and toe block, and with 43½" model 110 in a variety of American furniture styles. It continues with a series of studio models, including 45" model 115 in a traditional institutional style (legs with toe blocks), a school-friendly institutional style, and a furniture style; and 47" model 118 in institutional style. Finally, there are upright models 120 (48"), 125 (49"), and 130 (51½") in institutional style. The 49" model is a joint venture with Yamaha. The 51½" model has a decorative upper panel.

Pearl River grands come in ten sizes, from 4' 7" to 9'. In addition to a number of models with decorative legs and music desk, there are two unusual pianos: a 6' 1" model 186 in "European" style with angled case sides and a cast-iron plate in silver; and a 6' 6" model 198 "Butterfly" style with U-shaped body, clear acrylic lid that hinges in the middle, and other modern design features.

Pearl River's Ritmüller line uses the same strung back (structural and acoustical components) as the Pearl River line, but has upgraded cabinets and finishes. It also has more furniture options in the larger sizes of vertical. The 7' and 9' grand models in both lines come with Renner actions; all other models use Chinese actions. Most Pearl River and Ritmüller pianos have a veneer-laminated soundboard, but now that the company has invested in climate control in its tropically-situated factory, it is in the process of switching over to solid spruce soundboards in some of its models.

Warranty: Ten years, parts and labor, to the original purchaser

PERZINA, GEBR.
including Carl Ebel and Gerh. Steinberg

Piano Empire, Inc.
13370 East Firestone Blvd., Suite A
Santa Fe Springs, California 90670

800-576-3463
562-926-1906
info@pianoempire.com
www.perzinapianos.com

Pianos made by: Yantai-Perzina Piano Manufacturing Co., Ltd., Yantai, Shandong Province, China

The Gebr. Perzina (Brothers Perzina) piano company was established in the German town of Schwerin in 1871, and was a prominent piano maker until World War I, after which its fortunes declined. In more recent times, the factory was moved to the nearby city of Lenzen and the company became known as Pianofabrik Lenzen GmbH. In the early 1990s, the company was purchased by Music Brokers International B.V. in the Netherlands. Eventually it was decided that making pianos in Germany was not economically viable, so manufacturing was moved to Yantai, China, where a range of verticals and grands were made for a number of years by the Yantai Longfeng Piano Co. under the Perzina name. In 2003, Music Brokers International established its own factory in Yantai, called Yantai-Perzina, where it now builds the Perzina, Carl Ebel, and Gerh. Steinberg pianos. (Note: Do not confuse Gerh. Steinberg with Wilh. Steinberg, a German piano brand.)

The Carl Ebel and Gerh. Steinberg pianos are based on the same scale design, but the Perzina scale design is different. Further technical differences revolve primarily around the choice of action, hammers, and soundboard design, among other things. In particular, the Perzina brand is distinguished by use of a solid, tapered, Austrian white spruce soundboard in both verticals and grands, whereas the Carl Ebel and Gerh. Steinberg soundboards are of veneer-laminated Austrian white spruce. In addition, the Perzina verticals have several interesting features rarely found in other pianos, including a "floating" soundboard that is unattached to the back at certain points for freer vibration, and a reverse, or concave, soundboard crown. (There may be something to this, as the Perzina verticals are the best sounding verticals from China, the bass being particularly notable.) The Perzina grands are available with either Detoa ("G" models) or Renner ("E" models) action. The company says that the Perzina pianos also receive a higher level of attention to detail at the end of the manufacturing process than do the other two brands. In 2007 Perzina plans to bring out new "GX" and "EX" versions of its grands with Renner "AA" hammers, exclusive to Perzina; new scale designs; and other upgrades and modifications.

The company's European headquarters says it ships many European materials to Yantai, including Roslau strings, Delignit pinblocks, Abel hammers, English felts, European veneers, and Austrian white spruce soundboards. New machinery is from Germany, Japan and Italy. According to the company, all the piano designs are the original German scales. The Renner actions used in some of the Perzina grands are ordered complete from Germany, not assembled from parts.

Warranty: Ten years, parts and labor, to the original purchaser

PETROF
See also Weinbach

Geneva International Corporation
29 East Hintz Road
Wheeling, Illinois 60090

800-533-2388
847-520-9970
pianos@geneva-intl.com
www.geneva-intl.com
www.petrof.com

Pianos made by: Petrof, spol. s.r.o., Hradec Králové, Czech Republic

The Petrof piano factory was founded in 1864 by Antonin Petrof in Hradec Králové, an industrial town located 100 kilometers east of Prague in the Czech Republic. Three generations of the Petrof family owned and managed the business, during which time the company kept pace with technical developments and earned prizes for its pianos at international exhibitions. The Czech Republic has long been known for its vibrant musical instrument industry, which also includes makers of brass, woodwind, and stringed instruments.

In 1947, all businesses in the Czech Republic were nationalized by the state and the Petrof family was forced out of the business. In 1965, Petrof, along with other piano manufacturers, was forced to join Musicexport, the state-controlled import-export company for musical instruments. Since the fall of the Soviet Union and the liberation of Eastern Europe, the various factories that were part of Musicexport have been spun off as private businesses, including Petrof, which is once again owned and controlled by the Petrof family. Currently Petrof manufactures 4,500 vertical pianos and 900 grands annually.

Petrof makes seven sizes of grand and four sizes of vertical. The majority of components are produced in Petrof or other Czech factories, including hardware, plates, and cabinetry. Soundboards are of solid Bohemian spruce, grand rims are largely of beech, and plates are of the wet sand-cast type. The grands and largest verticals use seven-ply beech pinblocks, the other verticals use Delignit pinblocks. All grands produced for the United States now use Abel hammers. Keys are individually weighted. The grands all have a sostenuto pedal, the verticals a practice pedal (except 53" model P135, which has a sostenuto).

For many years Petrof used a combination of Czech Detoa actions and German Renner actions or action parts, depending on the model. The company has recently designed new grand and vertical actions, called "Petrof Original," which are being manufactured in a separate section of the Detoa factory under the supervision of Petrof engineers. All Petrof grand pianos and the larger verticals produced for the U.S. now use these actions. Most of the smaller verticals use a standard Detoa action. The action for the smallest vertical has been converted from a console to a full-size action. Several parts, both grand and vertical, have been re-designed to achieve greater rigidity and less weight.

Petrof has also invented and patented a version of its new grand action that uses tiny opposing magnets on the wippens and wippen rail. These magnets allow for the removal of the usual lead counterweights in the keys and, according to the company, significantly alter the dynamic properties of the action. "The hammer receives an inertial boost from the magnets as the key begins to move from the rest position. When the key is fully depressed, the effect of the magnets is minimal, allowing gravity to work in giving the hammer another inertial boost on the way down. The effect is faster repetition, less fatigue, and less physical work needed to reach higher dynamic levels." The new action also furthers the European Union's stated environmental goal of phasing out the use of lead in pianos. The action is adjusted in the factory for a standard touchweight. If necessary, it can be adjusted up or down five grams by a technician (not the customer) in an hour or so. Otherwise, the action can (and should) be serviced in exactly the same way as a standard action. The "Sterling Original" action, as it is known, is an option on 5' 3", 5' 8", and 6' 4" Petrof grands.

Petrof's research and development department, one of the largest in the piano industry, has been busy of late. In addition to the innovations mentioned above, Petrof recently introduced the 6' 10½" "Pasat B" grand, which contains a myriad of novel and interesting technical features. The inner rim is built up by hand of alternating layers of solid pieces of red beech and spruce instead of laminations bent around a mold. The company says this is the way several piano makers formed their grand rims in the nineteenth century before modern technology made the bent-lamination rim possible, and that this method results in a more stable, stress-free rim. The bridges are of solid maple, but the treble bridge is capped with solid ebony wood to increase sound projection of the higher frequencies. The piano is single-strung with front and rear tuned duplexes (duplex scale) thoughout the treble. The solid spruce soundboard is asymmetrically crowned, and each soundboard is custom-tapered based on tests of its vibrating characteristics. The piano utilizes a focused beam structure to increase rigidity of the structure for better tonal projection. A densified beam of red beech further stiffens the treble area to enhance projection of the treble tone. The result is a very impressive sounding and playing instrument.

Petrofs are known for their warm, rich, singing tone, full of color. The pianos are solidly built and workmanship is good, but can vary a little as they come from the factory. After careful preparation, though, the pianos can sound and feel quite beautiful and hold their own against some of the better-known European pianos. Due to lower labor costs, however, the prices are significantly lower than many other European instruments and sometimes even less expensive than pianos from Japan. As a result, they are a very good value.

Note: For years, Weinbach pianos were made by the Petrof company and were virtually identical to Petrof brand pianos. The Weinbach name is now being used differently. See under "Weinbach" for more information.

Warranty: Ten years, parts and labor, to the original purchaser. The first five years are from Petrof, the second five from Geneva International, the importer.

PIANODISC

PianoDisc
4111 North Freeway Blvd.
Sacramento, California 95834

800-566-3472
916-567-9999
www.pianodisc.com

Please read "Electronic Player Piano Systems and Hybrid Acoustic/Digital Pianos" on pages 160–161 of *The Piano Book*.

PianoDisc is an electronic player piano system that can be installed into virtually any piano, grand or vertical, new or used. Most manufacturers endorse PianoDisc and install it at dealer request at one of their manufacturing or distribution points. It can also be installed at a dealer location by a technician who has been specially trained by PianoDisc.

As with all such systems, PianoDisc consists of a solenoid rail installed in a slot cut in the piano keybed, a processor unit mounted under the piano, and a control box that plays floppy disks and/or CDs, depending on the model, that is either mounted under the keybed at the front of the piano or sits on or near the piano. There is one solenoid for each note and solenoids for the damper and una corda (soft) pedals. When playing PianoDisc's specialized software, one channel contains the MIDI signal that drives the piano solenoids, the other is an instrumental or vocal accompaniment that plays through a stereo system or through optional amplified speakers.

PianoDisc offers several different systems and options. The basic system is the model 228CFX. It has both a floppy drive and a CD drive as standard equipment. The company says that the control box is the smallest such box with both floppy and CD drives on the market. It can be mounted on the piano or can be located up to 100 feet away and operated with the included infrared wireless remote control.

The 228CFX has several options available that allow one to customize the system to one's needs. SymphonyPro is a sound module with a 128-voice General MIDI sound set to provide sampled-sound orchestration as an accompaniment to the piano. TFT ("Touch Film Technology") MIDI Record allows one to record one's playing or turn the piano into a MIDI controller. A sensor strip installed beneath the keys turns each key stroke into a MIDI signal containing information on note, speed, and duration. The information can be put into memory for later playback or output to speakers or headphones. A Performance Package with sensor strip, mute rail, and headphones turns the piano into a MIDI controller.

The MX (Music Expansion) option is flash memory in which to store music and play it back without having to change a disc. MX Basic has 32 MB of flash memory and comes with 25 hours of pre-selected music; MX Platinum has 64 MB of memory and comes with 35 hours of music. One can also add music from floppy disks, TFT MIDI Record, and standard MIDI files (but not PianoDisc CDs).

PianoDisc's entry-level system is called PianoCD. It is an easy to use system that plays only CDs—both PianoDisc CDs and regular audio CDs—and has fewer features than the 228CFX.

The flagship of the PianoDisc line is the Opus7 system, released in 2004. In addition to the PianoDisc playback system and SymphonyPro sound module, Opus7 features a wireless, internet-ready Web Tablet with touchscreen and full color, high resolution grahics as the system's "Conductor." It has the ability to download music and system upgrades directly from PianoDisc's website, and surf the web and receive email (broadband connection required), among other features. The Opus7 system is invisible, mounted completely out of sight under the piano, but with an access panel that allows the user to connect the included floppy and CD drives for copying music to the system's "MX3" music storage hard drive.

The MX3 hard drive comes with forty hours of pre-loaded music. Its MX3 media format will accept standard MIDI files type 0 and 1 available from a wide variety of standard MIDI file publishers, PianoDisc CDs, and standard audio CDs. (The company says that while playback of non-PianoDisc media is supported, it is not guaranteed.) Music saved to the MX3 hard drive from diverse sources can be organized into separate "libraries" and played back from a single source for convenience without having to change CDs. Music can also be purchased online from PianoDisc's new "eMusic" store and downloaded directly to the hard drive. A "Schedule" feature allows one to program a start time and end time for selected music to play.

Opus7 comes in two versions, Opulence and Luxury. Opulence is the full system. Luxury is designed to integrate with home automation systems, and so does not come with the web tablet, router, or floppy and CD drives, as it is assumed that the home automation system will already include these or similar interfaces. Owners of 228CFX or the older PDS128 PianoDisc systems can upgrade to Opus7 at a modest discount to the full system price. Opus7 is distributed through an exclusive network of authorized dealers.

PianoSync is a MIDI-controlled piano performance that synchronizes with a commercially available audio CD of a major recording artist. When a PianoSync performance is purchased from PianoDisc's growing collection, Opus7 will recognize the matching audio CD and accompany the original recording on the piano whenever the CD is played. Both can be copied to MX3 for more convenient playback.

Using PianoCast and broadband internet, Opus7 can connect to PianoDisc's internet radio station. The station will feature special events, interviews, and performances, combining a traditional audio broadcast with a piano performance that will play the Opus7.

Another PianoDisc product is QuietTime model GT-2, a silent system that can be installed in virtually any new or used piano. Once installed, one can mute the acoustic piano and listen to one's playing with sampled sound through headphones. The GT-2 has a control unit with two sampled sounds—piano and church organ. It also includes a metronome with adjustable beat, rhythm, and volume. A MIDI key sensor strip is installed under the keys, and a padded mute rail prevents the hammers from hitting the strings while still allowing the motion and feel of the piano action. The mute rail is activated by moving a small lever under the keyboard, which also turns on the sampled sound. The GT-2 comes with a control unit, power supply, MIDI cable, MIDI strip, pedal switches, headphones, and a mute rail. *Note*: If you purchase the PianoDisc playback system with the SymphonyPro sound module, the TFT MIDI Record system, and the PianoMute rail, you have already purchased virtually all the components of the QuietTime system. The separate listing for QuietTime in the price list is for those who wish to purchase it without the PianoDisc playback.

PianoDisc maintains a large and growing library of floppy disks and CDs for use on its systems, including solo piano with famous artists, piano with orchestrated accompaniment (some "live"), and piano and vocal. PianoDisc says its system will also play any standard MIDI file (type 0 format), much of the PianoSoft (Yamaha Disklavier) library, and disks of independent producers. PianoDisc is currently offering $1,000 in free music software with each PianoDisc system purchased.

PIANOFORCE

Pianoforce LLC
1251 East Fowler Avenue
Tampa, Florida 33612

813-631-8888
sales@pianoforce.com
www.pianoforce.com

Please read "Electronic Player Piano Systems and Hybrid Acoustic/Digital Pianos" on pages 160–161 of *The Piano Book*.

Pianoforce is a new entrant into the player piano market under its own name, but the company that makes the Pianoforce product—Ncode Ltd. of Bratislava, Slovakia—has been developing and manufacturing front-end controllers for the player piano systems of other companies, such as Baldwin and QRS, since 1995. In 2005, Pianoforce was first offered as a complete system in the pianos of selected piano makers. In 2006, it was introduced as a retrofit kit that can be installed into any piano, new or old. The kit is designed and built by Ncode in Europe. It is ordered through a piano dealer and is typically installed in a new piano either at a distribution point or at the dealer location.

Like other such systems, Pianoforce consists of a solenoid rail installed into a slot cut in the keybed of the piano, with one solenoid for each note and one for the damper pedal, and a CD drive/controller mounted under the keybed at the front of the piano. Traditionally, one CD channel contains the MIDI information that drives the piano solenoids, while the other channel contains instrumental or vocal accompaniment that plays through a stereo system or optional amplified speakers. In addition, the new Pianoforce CD format uses both channels for full stereo audio, with embedded MIDI information for the player mechanism. An infrared remote control device is included.

The company says that its system differs from that of its competitors in that the main rail component also contains all the controlling electronics, eliminating the need for a lot of complicated wiring and making for a neater and simpler installation. Also, a technician can plug a laptop computer into a USB port on the rail and, using software supplied by the company, can customize the system to the piano and to the customer's preferences through the software control of many playing parameters, such as solenoid force, note release, and pedal release. These customized parameters can then be archived on the laptop. The system automatically calibrates itself with the help of a small sensor mounted on the soundboard. The combination of automatic calibration with manual setup ensures the best playback performance for each individual piano after installation.

In 2007, Pianoforce introduced its latest controller, called "Performance." Expanding on its experience supplying control components for other companies in the past, the new controller contains some of the newest and most advanced features in the player piano arena, such as the ability to read the software of other systems, including Yamaha Disklavier, QRS (except SyncAlong), and Web Only software, plus standard MIDI files; onboard connections to the internet via an ethernet or wireless hookup through which the user can download music from Pianoforce, or even have system problems diagnosed and fixed from Europe; and three USB ports for greater versatility, such as plugging in flash memory. There is a digital optical stereo output and a dedicated sub-woofer output line.

The system comes with 256 MB of internal memory, pre-loaded with approximately 25 hours of piano music, and is expandable to 8 GB. The units are also shipped with approximately 400 "Star Tracks" piano recordings. A "Star Track" is a piano file in MIDI format synchronized to an original audio CD. When the audio CD is inserted, the corresponding Star Track is activated and plays a 30-second sampler piano accompaniment on the piano. The customer can then order a key via email or phone to unlock the entire song or album from Pianoforce.

The company says that a record strip, a General MIDI sound card, and other optional accessories are coming in the near future. In addition to the system's ability to play other makers' software, Pianoforce is also building its own library of CDs. To start the customer's collection, five Pianoforce CDs are supplied with the system.

The MSRP for the installed system, including pedal solenoid, two amplified speakers, and remote control, is $5,695. As with other such systems, discounts may be available, especially as an incentive to purchase a piano.

Warranty: Five years parts, one year labor, to the original purchaser

PLEYEL

Pleyel & Co.
Manufacture Française de Pianos
Z.I. de Croupillac
30 319 Alès Cédex, France

+33-4-66 56 25 13
+33-4-66 86 92 21 fax
info@pleyel.net
www.pleyel.fr

Two U.S. dealers who are serving as informal U.S. contacts for Pleyel are:

Jim Callahan	Brian Gatchell
Piedmont Piano Co.	Unique Pianos
510-547-8188	888-725-6633

Ignace Pleyel, an accomplished musician and composer, patron of music, and publisher, began manufacturing pianos in 1807 with the aim of adapting instruments to the new requirements of the composers and musicians of his day. By the time of his death in 1831, Pleyel pianos were known and exported throughout the world. His son, Camille, an accomplished pianist, continued the family business and brought it to new heights of success. As part of his work, Camille established the legendary music salons that served as a focus for the Parisian music scene of his time and where many famous musicians and composers were heard for the first time. It was at one of these concerts, in 1832, that Frederic Chopin made his Paris debut, and he played his final concert there in 1848. In addition to Chopin, who is closely associated with Pleyel pianos, other notable users included Claude Debussy, Cesar Frank, Edward Grieg, and Maurice Ravel. In 1927, the company established the Salle Pleyel, an important Paris concert venue.

Pleyel was also responsible for some of the technical innovations of his day. The company first introduced iron bracing into a piano in 1826, was the first to bring the upright piano to France, and is credited with inventing the sostenuto in 1860.

Over the years, Pleyel acquired the piano names of former French piano makers Rameau, Gaveau, and Erard. From 1971, these names were made under contract by Schimmel in Germany, returning to France in 1994. In 2000, a private investor associated with the Salle Pleyel acquired the trademarks under the name Manufacture Française de Pianos and moved the factory to the south of France, where for several years it produced high-quality instruments using a combination of high-tech machinery and hand craftsmanship. As this edition of the *Supplement* goes to press, the company is in the process of moving to a new location in the outskirts of Paris, not far from its original factory and the Salle Pleyel. The company says it plans to reduce the size of production and concentrate only on building a small number of instruments to the highest standards. The company principally makes pianos only under the Pleyel name at this time. Pleyel is France's only piano manufacturer.

At present, Pleyel has available in inventory vertical pianos in 47", 49", and 51½" sizes and grands 5' 7", 6' 3", and 9' 2½" in length. All models feature Renner action and hammers, Kluge keyboard on the grands, beech multi-laminated pinblock, and solid European spruce soundboard. The verticals have a one-piece multi-laminated back. Sostenuto is optional on the 51½" upright. The concert grand has white keytops made of mammoth bone, comparable in feel to ivory.

The company also specializes in creating instruments with art cases, marquetry, and unusual designs. Some interesting recent models include a 47" vertical model P118 in luxury leather, a new line of contemporary verticals, and a 6' 3" model P190 grand in bird's-eye poplar.

Pleyel pianos appear to be of very high quality. Those I've played have generally had a bright, singing treble; a light touch; and an unusually deep, dark sounding bass. The larger uprights are particularly nice sounding instruments.

Warranty: Ten years, parts and labor, to the original purchaser

PRAMBERGER — See "Samick;" also see "Young Chang"

QRS / PIANOMATION

QRS Music Technologies, Inc.
2011 Seward Avenue
Naples, Florida 34109

800-247-6557
www.qrsmusic.com

Please read "Electronic Player Piano Systems and Hybrid Acoustic/Digital Pianos" on pages 160–161 of *The Piano Book*.

Pianomation is an electronic player piano system that can be installed into virtually any piano, grand or vertical, new or used. Most manufacturers endorse Pianomation and install it at dealer request at one of their manufacturing or distribution points. It can also be installed at a dealer location by a technician who has been specially trained by QRS.

As with all such systems, Pianomation consists of a solenoid rail installed in a slot cut in the piano keybed, a processor unit mounted under the piano, and a control box that usually plays CDs, either mounted under the keybed at the front of the piano or that sits on or near the piano. There is one solenoid for each note and a solenoid for the damper pedal. (The solenoid for the damper pedal is now standard. If this solenoid is for any reason disabled, software-based commands called "Magic Pedal" will simulate it.) When playing Pianomation software, one channel contains the MIDI signal that drives the piano solenoids, the other is an instrumental or vocal accompaniment that plays through a stereo system or through optional amplified speakers.

QRS offers several different Pianomation systems and options. The simplest and least expensive controller is the model 2000C. The control box is hidden under the piano. It has no built-in disk drives, but instead uses the owner's stereo components to play QRS CDs and DVDs. The background music comes from the user's stereo system, while a wireless transmitter sends the piano data to the Pianomation system, even through walls.

The model 2000CD+ is like the 2000C, above, but has a CD drive with a slim profile of just two inches. It is most often installed with an optional speaker. Its "plug and play" simplicity has made it a popular entry-level system.

The Petine, introduced in 2005, is just over one and a half inches tall, and includes both a DVD ROM drive and a compact flash reader. The drive will play both audio CDs and data CDs (CD ROMs), the latter potentially containing thousands of MIDI files on a single CD. This controller will also play Standard MIDI files type 1 and 0. The unit features a 3-digit LED display and can be controlled by either a data wheel or infra-red remote control. The Petine has a headphone output, microphone input for karaoke, and a 1.44 megabyte internal memory storage capacity. The operating system is flash upgradeable.

The Ancho controller has all the functionality of the Petine, but with the more user-friendly, 20-character alpha-numeric display plus dedicated transport controls, unique among Pianomation controllers. It comes standard with a sound card (optional on the Petine).

Both systems are most often installed with an optional speaker. Both the Ancho and Petine have mixed and unmixed audio outputs so that the background music track and the piano track can be mixed for piping around the house, but the piano track can be omitted from the speakers located in the room containing the piano. Individual sources of audio sound can be finely adjusted so they will sound properly balanced at any volume level. On board but not yet implemented on both controllers are dual USB ports and an S-video output.

The MIDI information on Pianomation CDs is in analog format, which is compressed by QRS' patented AMI (Analog MIDI interface) technology, then uncompressed and translated back into digital format as it is sent to the piano for playback. Being able to translate the MIDI signal into analog form also allows it to be recorded on the audio track of a standard DVD so that video entertainment, such as lyrics or images of a pianist's hands, can be shown in synch with the piano playback. The analog signal can also be transmitted to the piano by radio waves using the optional wireless transmitter and receiver, which could be handy for use in commercial establishments or when one doesn't want to run wires from the CD player to the piano.

SyncAlong is a MIDI-controlled piano performance that synchronizes with a commercially available audio CD of a major recording artist. SyncAlong CDs play on the Ancho and Petine as well as the discontinued Chili and Serenade Pro controllers. QRS has prepared a piano track in MIDI format, stored on a CompactFlash card, to go along with each of a number of popular audio CDs available on the general market. When the owner plays the CD, SyncAlong links it with the stored piano track, enabling Pianomation to accurately play along with the CD. A Transcription series, similar to SyncAlong but without the background music, is also available. In this series, a solo performance audio CD is transcribed and offered as a Pianomation CD so the customer can hear the performance on his or her own piano.

Qsync™, just released, is a DVD interface designed to implement QRS' patent-pending DVD SyncAlong technology. With the addition of Qsync, a Pianomation player piano will play along with any of a number of popular concert DVDs available to the general market. The owner plays the DVD on his or her own DVD player, which is hooked up to the Pianomation system. Qsync links it with the stored piano track, enabling Pianomation to accurately play along with the DVD.

The QRS record option used to be offered in both "LiteSwitch" and "OptiScan" versions. These have been discontinued and replaced with QRS' own optical recording strip called PNOscan™. Placed under the keys, PNOscan translates each key stroke into MIDI information on note, speed, and duration without affecting the piano's touch. This MIDI information can be output to Pianomation for storage and later playback, or stored as a standard MIDI file on CompactFlash for computer editing if desired. Coupled with Ancho or Petine (with optional sound card), the pianist can play General MIDI sounds. SilentPNO™, formerly called "Practice Session," consists of the PNOscan record strip, a piano sound module, and a stop rail for muting the acoustic piano. By muting the piano and turning on the sound card, the pianist can play in privacy with headphones.

Playola is a portable Pianomation system that sits atop the keys and plays them with little rubber fingers, either alone or with accompaniment. It comes configured with one of the controllers described earlier (2000C, 2000CD+, Ancho, Petine), and does not require professional installation by a technician.

Pianomation systems and controllers, excluding the Ancho, can be ordered or installed through any dealer doing business with QRS. The Ancho can be purchased through Story & Clark dealers only.

QRS has developed an extensive library of CDs, with over 3,000 selections in every imaginable genre, for use with its systems. The library is made up almost entirely of live performance recordings rather than synthesized music, including solo piano, piano with orchestral accompaniment, and piano with background music and vocals. CDs can be purchased one at a time or obtained through NetPiano™, a service through which customers can download any of the thousands of songs from the QRS library to their Pianomation-equipped piano through their personal computer. A wireless transmitter plugged into the computer's audio jack transmits the music to the piano. The service is subscription based, and allows the customer to have access to songs anytime, day or night, without having to build their own CD library. Subscriptions are available only through QRS dealers or through the QRS web site.

QRS also has available the Qtouch Tablet™, an optional tablet remote control, from which the user can control Pianomation, access NetPiano, or surf the web via the user's computer from anywhere in the home (requires an 80211 wireless).

Apart from its player piano systems, QRS is constantly inventing new gadgets and gizmos for pianos that can be installed independently of Pianomation. Recent inventions include a mute rail for quieting the sound of a grand piano (these have existed for verticals before, but not for grands); a Grand Fallboard Closer that allows a grand fallboard to close gently and avoid hurting the player's fingers (available on many new pianos for some time, but not previously as an add-on accessory); the PNObar™, a bar attachment designed to fit any Story & Clark grand piano, creating a natural setting for socializing (it comes with four bar stools); and GloKeys™, a customized keyboard option where the black keys have been replaced by clear keys that are illuminated using state-of-the-art Superflux RGB LED (red, green, blue light emitting diode) technology to produce a wide array of dazzling colors and effects.

REMINGTON — See "Samick"

RITMÜLLER — See "Pearl River"

SAMICK
including Kohler & Campbell, Conover Cable, Remington, J.P. Pramberger, J. Pramberger, Wm. Knabe, Hazelton Bros (disc.). See separate listing for Sohmer & Co.

SMC (formerly Samick Music Corp.)
575 Airport Road
Gallatin, Tennessee 37066

800-592-9393
615-206-0077
info@smcmusic.com
www.smcmusic.com

Pianos made by: Samick Musical Instrument Mfg. Co. Ltd., Incheon, South Korea and Bogor, West Java, Indonesia

Samick was founded by Hyo Ick Lee in 1958 as a Baldwin distributor in South Korea. Facing an immense challenge in an impoverished and war-torn country, in the early 1960s Lee began to build and sell a very limited quantity of vertical pianos using largely imported parts. As the economy improved, Lee expanded his operation, and in 1964 began exporting to other parts of the world, eventually becoming one of the world's largest piano manufacturers, making most of the parts in-house. Over the next several decades, Samick expanded into manufacturing guitars and other instruments and opened factories in China and Indonesia, where it shifted much of its production as Korean wages rose. The Asian economic crisis of the late 1990s forced Samick into bankruptcy, but it emerged from bankruptcy in 2002 and is now on a sound financial footing.

In 2002, Samick and C. Bechstein, a major European piano maker, each acquired a financial interest in the other and agreed to cooperate on technical issues and marketing. Samick has used that collaboration to upgrade its manufacturing capabilities. The two companies also own a joint-venture factory in Shanghai, China. For a few years, Samick distributed Bechstein pianos in North America, but that distribution agreement has ended (see "Bechstein, C.").

In 2004, Samick acquired a controlling interest in its competitor Young Chang and briefly took over distribution of Young Chang and Bergmann pianos in the United States. However, court rulings in Korea and the United States ended this arrangement a year later. Young Chang is once again an independent company and distributes those brands itself (see "Young Chang").

The company says that "Samick" means "Three Benefits" in Korean, symbolizing the wish that the activities of the company benefit not only the company itself, but also the customers and the Korean economy.

Samick Music Corporation, the North American marketing arm of the Korean company, is now known as SMC, and distributes Samick, Kohler & Campbell, Conover Cable, Pramberger, Remington, Wm. Knabe, and Sohmer & Co. pianos in North America. (See separate listing for Sohmer.) Samick no longer makes pianos under the Bernhard Steiner and Hazelton Bros. names. SMC is in the process of building a new manufacturing, warehousing, and office facility in Tennessee. It says it intends eventually to assemble its upper-level instruments there instead of in Korea. Some parts and assemblies will continue to be made elsewhere, especially in Indonesia, and Samick will continue to make pianos in Korea for the Korean domestic market.

Until just a few years ago, Samick primarily made pianos under the Samick and Kohler & Campbell brand names. (Kohler & Campbell was an American company that was established in 1896 and closed its doors in 1985; see *The Piano Book* for more information.) In the 1980s, Klaus Fenner, a German piano designer, was hired to revise the Samick scale designs and make them more "European." Most of the present Samick and Kohler & Campbell pianos are based on these designs. The Conover Cable name (another old American name) was introduced for markets that needed an additional line. It is identical to the Samick piano, however, and is gradually being phased out.

Although in most respects the Samick and Kohler & Campbell pianos are similar in quality, so as not to compete with one another the grands are available in different sizes and have some different features. The two lines are primarily differentiated by the fact that Kohler & Campbell grands (except the 4' 7" model) have solid spruce soundboards and individually-hitched stringing (also known as single-stringing), whereas the Samick grands have veneer-laminated soundboards and conventional loop stringing. A veneer-laminated soundboard (which Samick calls a "surface tension soundboard") is essentially a solid spruce soundboard surrounded by two thin veneers. Samick pioneered the use of this soundboard and it is now used by others as well. Tonally, it behaves much more like a solid spruce soundboard than the old kind of laminated soundboard that was essentially plywood. Like the old kind, however, it won't crack or lose its crown. The solid spruce soundboard may have a slight advantage tonally, but the laminated one will last longer, so take your pick.

Likewise, single stringing is more elegant to those who know pianos, but otherwise offers little or no advantage over loop stringing. The two brands' vertical pianos are more alike: They have the same difference in soundboard as the grands, but are all loop-strung and come more or less in the same sizes.

One big way in which Samick and Kohler & Campbell pianos differ is that Kohler & Campbell has an upper-level group of models called the "Millennium" series with higher-quality features. The grands have a maple rim, premium Canadian Bolduc tapered solid spruce soundboard, Renner action and hammers, and satin wood finishes available in lacquer semi-gloss. The verticals have Renner parts on a Samick-made "Pratt-Reed" hornbeam action rail, Bolduc solid spruce soundboard, Renner hammers, lacquer semi-gloss wood finishes, and a sostenuto pedal on the 52" model. All Samick pianos and regular series Kohler & Campbell pianos are made in Indonesia for the U.S. market. Smaller Millennium series verticals and grands are made in Indonesia, larger ones in Korea. However, all Millennium series pianos are shipped to the U.S. for inspection and tone and action regulation before being shipped to dealers. *Note*: The Samick line also has an upper-level series, called the "World Piano." In the North American market, however, this has become the "Wm. Knabe" line of pianos. See below for more information.

[In the Kohler & Campbell price list, KC models are Indonesian-made, regular series verticals; KM are Indonesian-made Millennium series verticals; KMV are Korean-made Millennium series verticals; KCG are Indonesian-made regular series grands; KCM are Indonesian-made Millennium series grands; KFM are Korean-made Millennium series grands.]

Another brand name Samick makes and sells is Pramberger, a name that was used by Young Chang for its premium-level pianos under license from the late piano engineer Joseph Pramberger, who at one time was head of manufacturing at Steinway & Sons. When Mr. Pramberger died in 2003, his estate terminated its relationship with Young Chang and signed up with Samick. However, since Young Chang still holds the rights to its piano designs, Samick has designed new pianos to go with the name.

The "J.P. Pramberger" piano is a higher-end instrument made in Korea, then shipped to the U.S. for inspection, voicing, and regulation. Several American technicians who had known and worked with Joe Pramberger went to Korea at Samick's request to design this piano. Benefiting by work previously done by Bechstein engineers at the Samick factory, they began with a modified Bechstein scale, then added several features found on current or older Steinways, such as an all-maple rim, an asymmetrically tapered white spruce soundboard, vertically laminated maple and mahogany bridges with maple cap, duplex scaling, and Renner action and hammers. One of the technicians told me the group feels that its design is an advancement of Mr. Pramberger's work that he would have approved of.

The "J. Pramberger" is a more modestly-priced instrument from Indonesia. Its design is based on the former Young Chang version of the Pramberger piano. It uses Samick's Pratt-Reed Premium action, Renner hammers, and a Bolduc solid spruce soundboard.

[Note: Samick's Pratt-Reed Premium action should not be confused with the Pratt-*Read* action used in many American-made pianos in the mid to late twentieth century and eventually acquired by Baldwin. Samick says its Pratt-Reed action is made in Korea and designed after the German Renner action.]

Remington is a new line of low-cost, no-frills piano made in Indonesia, similar to the Samick piano, with a veneer-laminated soundboard and simple cabinetry.

Wm. Knabe is an old, distinguished American piano brand dating back to 1854 and eventually becoming part of the Aeolian family of brands. Following Aeolian's demise in 1985, the Knabe name became part of Mason & Hamlin, which was purchased out of bankruptcy in 1996 by the owners of PianoDisc. For a time, a line of Knabe pianos was made for PianoDisc by Young Chang in Korea and China. That line has been discontinued, and Samick has acquired the Wm. Knabe name. (Note: "Knabe" is pronounced using the hard "K" sound followed by "nobby.")

Samick is now using the Wm. Knabe name on the pianos formerly sold as the "World Piano" premium line of Samick pianos. The 5' 8" and 6' 4" grand models have been redesigned, however, the new models based on the original nineteenth and early twentieth Knabe scale designs and cabinet styles in use when the company was based in Baltimore. Features include sand-cast plates, lacquer semi-gloss wood finishes, Renner actions and hammers, and maple and oak rims. As with the other upper-level Samick lines, the pianos are serviced in the company's U.S. facility before being shipped to dealers.

Quality control in Samick's Korean and Indonesian factories has steadily improved, especially in the last few years, and the Indonesian product is said to be almost as good as the Korean, but consistency can still be a problem in both factories. Many large-scale issues have been addressed and engineers are now working on smaller refinements. Climate control in the tropically-situated Indonesian factory and action geometry issues are among the areas that have recently seen improvement. Samick's upper-level pianos—Kohler & Campbell Millennium series, J.P. Pramberger, and Wm. Knabe—have met with a very positive response from technicians as to their musical design, exceeding comparably priced pianos from Japan in that regard, but workmanship is still not as consistent as in the Japanese pianos. Many of Samick's Indonesian pianos are priced similarly to low-cost pianos from China, and some technicians find the Samicks to be more consistent than those. Although many of the Samick-made pianos are inspected and prepared in the U.S. prior to being shipped to dealers, the quality of the preparation can vary, so preparation by the dealer is very important. With good dealer prep, I recommend Samick-made pianos for average use. In difficult climates humidity control is recommended.

[Samick-made pianos have an odd serial numbering system consisting of a series of letters and numbers. The system appears to vary from one factory to another. Please contact SMC for information on the date of manufacture of a Samick-made piano.]

Warranty: Samick, Kohler & Campbell, Conover Cable, J.P. Pramberger, J. Pramberger, Wm. Knabe, Remington—Twelve years, parts and labor, to the original purchaser; lifetime on "surface tension soundboard" where applicable.

SAUTER

Sauter USA
P.O. Box 1130
Richland, Washington 99354

509-946-8078 (U.S.)
877-946-8078 (toll-free)
+49-7424-94820 (factory)
info@sauteramerica.com (U.S.)
info@sauter-pianos.de (factory)
www.sauter-pianos.de

Pianos made by: Carl Sauter Pianofortemanufaktur GmbH&Co.KG, Max-Planck-Strasse 20, 78549 Spaichingen, Germany

The Sauter piano firm was founded in 1819 by Johann Grimm, stepfather to Carl Sauter I, and has been owned and managed by members of the Sauter family for six generations, currently by Ulrich Sauter. The factory currently produces about 800 vertical pianos and 120 grand pianos a year in its factory in the extreme south of Germany at the foot of the Alps. Structural and acoustical parts are made of high-quality woods, including solid Bavarian spruce soundboards and beech pinblocks. Actions are made by Renner and Sauter makes its own keys. The keybed is reinforced with steel to prevent warping and all pianos are fully tropicalized for humid climates. The larger verticals use an action, designed and patented by Sauter, that contains an auxiliary jack spring to aid in faster repetition. Sauter calls this the "R2 Double Escapement" action. (Although the term "double escapement" does not apply here as it has historically been used, the mechanism has some of the same effect.)

Sauter pianos are especially known for the variety of finishes and styles in which they are available, many with intricate detail and inlay work. It is common to find such rare woods as Yew, Burl Walnut, Pyramid Mahogany, and genuine Ebony in the cabinets of Sauter pianos, as well as special engravings, which can be customized to any customer's desires. Sauter has a line of vertical pianos designated the "M line" which feature exclusive cabinet detailing and built-in features such as a hygrometer to measure relative humidity. "Amadeus" is a special-edition 6' 1" grand in celebration of the 250th anniversary of Mozart's birth. The styling of this model is reminiscent of that in Mozart's time. The natural keytops are of polished bone, the sharps of rosewood with ebony caps. Only thirty-six are to be made, one for each year of Mozart's life.

The company also has introduced versions of its 48" upright and 6' 11" and 7' 6" grands with cabinets designed by the famous European designer Peter Maly. Some recent Peter Maly designs include the 48" upright "Vitrea," after the Latin word for "glass," with a veneer of greenish glass covering the front of the cabinet; and "Ambiente," a 7' 6" grand that is curved asymmetrically on both the bass and treble sides. In the recent past, Sauter has won several prestigious design awards for its Peter Maly–designed pianos.

A couple of extremely unusual models bear mentioning. The 7' 3" model 220 contains colored lines painted on the soundboard and white inlays on the tops of the dampers as guides for musicians performing music for "prepared piano," ultra-modern music requiring the insertion of foreign objects between the strings or the plucking or striking of strings directly by the performer. The 1/16 tone microtonal piano is an upright with 97 keys that has a total pitch range from the lowest to the highest note of only one octave, with the pitch difference from key to key being only 1/16 of a tone (1/8 of a semitone). You can read more about these strange instruments in *The Piano Book*.

Sauter pianos are high quality instruments with a lush, full, singing tone, closer to an "American" sound than most other European pianos.

Warranty: Ten years, parts and labor, to the original purchaser.

SCHIMMEL
including Vogel and May Berlin

Schimmel Piano Corporation
577B Hackman Road
Lititz, Pennsylvania 17543

800-426-3205
schimmel@ptd.net
www.schimmel-piano.de

Pianos made by: Wilhelm Schimmel Pianofortefabrik GmbH, Braunschweig, Germany (Schimmel pianos); Schimmel Holzwerkstätten Leipzig GmbH (all cabinets), Leipzig, Germany; PianoEurope, Kalisz, Poland (Vogel pianos); various factories in China (May Berlin).

Wilhelm Schimmel began making pianos in Leipzig in 1885, and his company enjoyed steady growth through the late nineteenth and early twentieth centuries. The two world wars and the Depression disrupted production several times, but the company has gradually rebuilt itself over the past sixty years with a strong reputation for quality. Today, Schimmel is managed by Viola Schimmel, great granddaughter of the founder, and her husband Hannes Schimmel-Vogel. Schimmel makes about 3,000 verticals and 800 grands per year and is one of Europe's most important piano makers. Yamaha owns a 24.9 percent non-voting interest in the Braunschweig company.

Among European piano manufacturers, Schimmel has been a pioneer in the use of computer-aided design and manufacturing. The company has used its CAPE software (Computer Assisted Piano Engineering) to research, design, and implement virtually every aspect of making a piano, from keyboard layout and action geometry to soundboard acoustics and scale design. Because of the extreme precision with which its pianos are designed and built, less hand work is necessary to create a quality product than with many other makers. Schimmel also believes that precision is aided by controlling as much of the production process as possible. To that end, it is the only German piano manufacturer making its own keyboards. For the same reason, Schimmel established its current Leipzig factory to produce piano cabinets, which it also supplies to other German piano makers.

Over the last few years, Schimmel has reorganized its model lineup into two categories: "Konzert" (models beginning with "K") and "Classic" (models beginning with "C"). The Konzert series consists of some of the newer and larger vertical models and the six most recently-designed and advanced grand models. The company says that the purpose of the Konzert series was to expand the Schimmel line upward to a higher level of quality than it had previously attained. The Classic series consists of the rest of the verticals and the 6' grand model 182. This grand model was recently reintroduced from Schimmel's regular line. It is still a good model, but doesn't have some of the newest refinements. Other grand models will follow in the Classic series. Certain Schimmel Classic models are getting their finish and some action work done at the Schimmel factory in Kalisz, Poland before returning to Braunschweig for further preparation and voicing.

The Konzert series uprights—48" model K122, 49" model K125, and 52" model K132—are based on a more traditional philosophy of construction than the Classic series. In the Classic series, the plate is the main structural support and the pinblock is located in a pocket in the plate. The backposts are used primarily to support the soundboard. In the Konzert series, traditional back posts assume a greater role for support, and the pinblock and soundboard are attached to the posts. The company says that the joining of wooden structural and acoustical parts enhances the tone. These models also incorporate duplex scaling and other advanced design features. Schimmel's philosophy for these uprights was to design them to be as much like the grands as possible. The treble scales, in fact, are exactly the same as in the Konzert series grands.

The Konzert series grands consist of two model groups. In the first, Schimmel has created a "trilogy" of redesigned grands by marrying the front end (keyboard) of its 7' grand to two new models: 5' 7" and 6' 3". The company says the new models all have the same treble scale, keyboard, and action as the 7' grand, and so all three have a similar sound and touch. The case sides are angled slightly to obtain a larger soundboard, a technique now applied to all the grand models. The pianos also have duplex scaling for greater tonal color. The second group, also a "trilogy," consists of the 7' 5", 8' 4", and 9' 2" semi-concert and concert grand models, of which the first and last are new. In this group, all three models have the same keyboard and action as the concert grand. These models also have tunable front and rear duplex scales, reinforced keys for optimal energy transmission, and mineral keytops to mimic the feel of ivory, among other advanced features.

The 6' 3" model K189 and 7' model K213 are currently available in a "Nikolaus W. Schimmel" (NWS) model. Built to commemorate the retirement of the elder Mr. Schimmel, this model has many small technical and cosmetic refinements, uses top-quality soundboard material, and receives greater final preparation at the factory to create a really superior instrument.

Schimmel grand pianos have historically had a tone that was very bright and clear, but a bit thin and lacking in color in the treble. The grands have been redesigned, in part, to add additional color to the tone. The result is definitely more interesting than before. Sustain is also very good. The pianos are being delivered to U.S. dealers voiced less bright than previously, as this is what the American ear tends to prefer. As for the verticals, the smaller ones tend to have a very big bass for their size, with a tone that emphasizes the fundamental, giving the bass a warmer character. The 51" model C130, which features a grand-shaped soundboard, has a very big sound, and listening to it, one might think one was in the presence of a grand.

In 2002, Schimmel acquired the PianoEurope factory in Kalisz, Poland, a piano restoration and manufacturing facility. Schimmel is using this factory to manufacture its Vogel brand, a less expensive line named after the company's president. Schimmel says that although the skill level of the employees is high, lower wages and other lower costs result in a piano approximately thirty percent less costly than the Schimmel. Vogel pianos feature full Renner actions, with other parts mainly made by Schimmel in Braunschweig or by the Kalisz factory. The pianos are designed by Schimmel, but don't have all the refinements and advanced features of the latest Schimmel models. Nevertheless, the pianos have received praise from many quarters for their high-quality workmanship and sound. The company also uses the Kalisz factory to perform some work on selected Schimmel pianos (as mentioned earlier).

Schimmel now imports an entry-level series of pianos from China under the name "May Berlin," a name long owned by Schimmel but not used recently. The pianos are made by several selected suppliers. The company says it sends soundboard wood and hammer felt to the factory in China for use in its pianos. When completed, the pianos are first shipped to the Schimmel factory in Germany for inspection and final preparation before being sent on to dealers around the world.

Warranty: Schimmel, Vogel, May Berlin—Ten years, parts and labor, to the original purchaser

SCHULZE POLLMANN

North American Music Inc.
11 Kay Fries Drive
Stony Point, New York 10980

800-782-2694
www.schulzepollmann.com
www.namusic.com

Pianos made by: Schulze Pollmann s.r.l., Fermingnano, Italy

Schulze Pollmann was formed in 1928 by the merger of two German piano builders who had moved to Italy, where the company still resides today. Since 1973 the firm has been owned by Generalmusic, best known for its digital pianos and organs and other musical electronics. Schulze Pollmann utilizes both sophisticated technology and hand work in its manufacturing. The pianos contain Delignit pinblocks, solid European spruce soundboards, and Renner actions and hammers. Interesting features include a one-piece solid lock (laminated) back and agraffes on the larger verticals, and finger-jointed construction on all soundboards to discourage future cracking. Many of the cabinets have beautiful designs and inlays. A new entry-level 45" vertical has a traditional back, Czech Detoa action, Renner hammers, and a lesser-quality solid spruce soundboard.

The two larger uprights are well built and have a sound that is warm and colorful with a good amount of sustain. The treble is not nearly as brittle sounding as in some of the other European uprights. The smallest vertical is quite different and clearly made to lower quality standards, though with nicely finished furniture. Schulze Pollmann grands are likewise very nicely crafted and arrive at the dealer in good condition. However, they need solid preparation by the dealer to sound their best.

Italian auto manufacturer Ferrari Motor Car has selected Schulze Pollmann as a partner in the launch of its new Ferrari 612 Scaglietti series of automobiles. For the occasion, Schulze Pollmann has crafted a limited edition grand piano whose case sports the Ferrari racing red while the cast-iron plate is in the Ferrari gray carbon, the same as the engine of the Scaglietti. The car and the piano are being exhibited together in cities around the world.

Warranty: Ten years, parts and labor, transferable to future owners within the warranty period.

SEILER

Piano Marketing Group, LLC
752 East 21st Street
Ferdinand, Indiana 47532

888-621-1137
america@seiler-pianos.com
www.seiler-pianos.com

Pianos made by: Ed. Seiler Pianofortefabrik, Kitzingen, Germany

Eduard Seiler, the company's founder, began making pianos in Liegnitz, Silesia, Germany in 1849. The company grew to over 435 employees, producing up to 3,000 pianos per year in 1923. Seiler was the largest piano manufacturer in Eastern Europe at that time. In 1945 and after World War II, the plant was occupied by Poland and the Seiler family left their native homeland with millions of other refugees. In 1951 Steffan Seiler re-established the company in Copenhagen under the fourth generation of family ownership, and in 1962 moved it to Kitzingen, Germany, where it resides today. The company produces approximately 2,000 pianos annually.

Seiler makes high quality pianos using a combination of traditional methods and modern technology. The scale designs are of relatively high tension, producing a brilliant, balanced tone that is quite consistent from one Seiler to the next. The grands have wide tails for greater soundboard area and string length. Although brilliant, the tone also sings well due to, the company says, a unique soundboard feature called a Membrator—a tapered groove running around the perimeter of the board—that gives the soundboard flexibility without losing necessary stiffness. The pianos feature Bavarian spruce soundboards, multi-laminated beech pinblocks, quarter-sawn beech bridges, Renner actions, and slow-close fallboards. A few years ago, the grands were redesigned with a duplex scale for greater treble tonal color, and with longer keys and a lighter touch. Muiscally, these redesigns were very successful. They retained the typical Seiler clarity, but with longer sustain and a marvelously even-feeling touch. Both the verticals and the 6' 1" grands are available in dozens of models with beautiful wood inlays and brass ornamentation.

Seiler's 48" and 52" uprights are now available with the optional "Super Magnet Repetition" (SMR) action, a patented feature that uses magnets to increase repetition speed. Tiny magnets are attached to certain action parts of each note. During playing, the magnets repel each other, forcing the parts to return to their rest position faster, ready for a new key stroke.

Seiler has introduced its "Value Added Warranty." The warranty states that at the end of ten years from date of purchase, a purchaser who has maintained his or her Seiler piano as required under the terms of the warranty may trade it in toward a new Seiler and receive a credit of the full original purchase price paid.

Warranty: Ten years, parts and labor, to original purchaser

SEJUNG
including Falcone, Hobart M. Cable, Geo. Steck, Vivace (disc.)

America Sejung Corporation
5300 East Ontario Mills Parkway
Suite 100
Ontario, California 91764

909-484-7498
866-473-5864
sales@sejungusa.com
www.sejungusa.com

Pianos made by: Sejung Corporation, Qingdao, Shandong Province, China

Sejung is a Korean-based textile, construction, and information technology business that was established in 1974, but the musical instrument portion of the business began only in 2001. In that year, the company's chairman received a proposal from an old friend with extensive experience in piano and guitar manufacturing to enter those businesses in a big way by manufacturing in China. Within a year, the company had partnered with a Chinese manufacturer (necessary for doing business in China); built a 700,000 square foot factory in Qingdao, a port city on the Eastern coast with a temperate climate; hired dozens of manufacturing managers who had once worked for Young Chang and Samick, and staffed the factory with some 2,000 workers, whom the company also feeds and houses in dormitories (necessary to attract good labor and reduce turnover). Although wages are incredibly low in China, the company says it has invested millions in automated production equipment in areas where precision counts, rather than just relying on cheap labor. The company produces just about every piano component in its own factories.

For marketing the pianos in the U.S., Sejung has licensed the Falcone and Geo. Steck names from PianoDisc/Mason & Hamlin and the Hobart M. Cable name from Story & Clark (see "Mason & Hamlin" and "Story & Clark" in *The Piano Book*). The names Vivace and Sejung were used briefly but have been discontinued (the Vivace name is now used as part of the Cristofori line of pianos – see "Cristofori"). The Geo.Steck and Hobart M. Cable lines are similar technically, with some style differences; the Falcone line is a little higher quality. Most of the Falcone models have a slow-close fallboard, cast pedals and maple trapwork on the verticals, and slightly nicer cabinets. In addition, a new Falcone Georgian (FG) series includes such features as Abel hammers on grands 5' 4" and larger, upgraded soundboard material, bubinga veneer on the inside of the grand rim, real ebony sharps, and gold-colored hardware.

The first pianos from Sejung were shown in the U.S. in early 2003, less than one year after production began. I and other technicians examined a number of instruments at a trade show. Although still a little rough, they were definitely satisfactory, and remarkably good for having been only an idea in someone's head less than two years earlier! Since that time, the quality has improved, but so have the products of its competitors. The smaller sizes of grand and vertical in particular are most appropriate for those buyers whose primary considerations are price or furniture.

For model and price information, see under "Sejung" in the Model and Pricing Guide section of this *Supplement*.

Warranty: Twelve years on parts and ten years on labor, to the original purchaser.

SHERMAN CLAY

Correction to *The Piano Book*: I have been told that for much of the 1970s and 1980s, pianos sold under the Sherman Clay label were made by Kimball or Aeolian. In the mid to late 1980s, some Sherman Clay pianos were made by Daewoo (Sojin).

SOHMER (& CO.)

Founded by German immigrant Hugo Sohmer in 1872, Sohmer & Co. was owned and managed by the Sohmer family in New York City for 110 years. Having no descendants to take over the business, the founder's grandsons sold the company in 1982. As the company changed hands several times over the following decade, limited production of Sohmer pianos took place in Connecticut and Pennsylvania, finally ceasing in 1994 (see the Sohmer entry in *The Piano Book* for a more detailed recent history).

Pianos are again being made under this venerable name, once considered among the finest of American-built instruments. However, there appears to be a dispute over the ownership of the Sohmer trademark, with pianos bearing this name being manufactured and distributed by two different companies.

SMC, North American distributor of Samick pianos, says it holds a license from the Burgett brothers, owners of PianoDisc, to use the Sohmer name. The Burgetts acquired the Sohmer trademark registrations when they purchased the assets of Mason & Hamlin out of bankruptcy in 1996. A distributor doing business under the name Persis International, Inc., who applied for the Sohmer trademark in 2001, claims that the registrations acquired by the Burgetts are expired and have been legally abandoned, not having been used since the 1994 closing of the Sohmer factory in Pennsylvania. The U.S. Patent and Trademark Office confirms that the government considers all past registrations of the Sohmer trademark to be expired or canceled and that the Burgetts' new application was refused. Further action on Persis' application has been temporarily suspended pending the Burgetts' appeal. At press time, the application process was still ongoing and it may be some time before the issue is settled for good. In the meantime, piano shoppers may find two "Sohmer" pianos in the marketplace. (Note: Persis' pianos are labeled "Sohmer" and SMC's are labeled "Sohmer & Co.") Both companies submitted product information, including model and price data, for this *Supplement*.

Persis International, Inc.
3540 North Southport #116
Chicago, Illinois 60657

773-342-4212

Sohmer pianos from this distributor are manufactured by Royale, a Korean firm that is descended from the now-defunct joint venture between Ibach and Daewoo (see "Ibach"). Models include a 50" vertical and 5' 3", 5' 10", and 7' 2" grands. The pianos have high quality components, such as Renner actions, Abel hammers, Delignit pinblocks, and Ciresa soundboards.

Warranty: Ten years, parts and labor, to the original purchaser

SMC
575 Airport Road
Gallatin, Tennessee 37066

615-206-0077
800-592-9393
www.smcmusic.com

The Sohmer & Co. model 34, a 42" vertical, features full-length backposts, a sand-cast plate, solid spruce soundboard, exposed 16-ply pinblock, and a slow-close fallboard—virtually identical (except for the slow-close fallboard) to the original, highly regarded Sohmer & Co. console. A new Sohmer & Co. studio piano has a design based on the Bechstein 116 centimeter scale. At present, the consoles are made in Indonesia, the studio pianos in Korea.

Sohmer & Co. grands are similar to the pianos Samick made for Baldwin under the Chickering label. They have maple outer rims, sand-cast plates, German solid spruce soundboards, Renner hammers, spruce beams, solid brass hardware, agraffes, lacquer semi-gloss wood finishes, and other higher quality features, and are available in a variety of furniture styles. Sohmer & Co. grands are made in Korea, except the 5' model, which is from Indonesia. All Sohmer & Co. pianos are inspected, voiced, and regulated in the U.S. before being shipped to dealers.

Warranty: Twelve years, parts and labor, to original purchaser

STECK, GEO. — See "Sejung"

STEIGERMAN

Steigerman Music Corporation
4902 — 217B Street
Langley, British Columbia
Canada V3A 9K1

888-651-8119
pianos@steigerman.com
www.steigerman.com

Pianos made by: Beijing Hsinghai Piano Group, Ltd., Beijing, China; and Ningbo Hailun Musical Instrument Co., Ningbo, Zhejiang Province, China

Steigerman is a name, owned by a Canadian distributor, that has appeared over the years on pianos from a number of Asian manufacturers.

At present, Steigerman's regular line of pianos is made by the Beijing Hsinghai Piano Group in Beijing, China, where, the company says, it has two full-time inspectors overseeing quality control (see "Beijing Hsinghai"). The Beijing models have a three-ply laminated soundboard, except for the 6' grand, which has a solid spruce board.

Steigerman now has a new premium line of pianos made by Ningbo Hailun in Ningbo, China (see "Hailun"). Features of both grands and verticals include: a tapered, solid spruce soundboard, sand-cast plate, agraffes, Renner hammers, and optional Renner action. Additionally, the verticals have a maple back and an easy-to-remove practice rail; grands have a maple rim and front and rear duplex scale.

Warranty: Ten years, parts and labor, to the original purchaser

STEINBERG, GERH. — See "Perzina, Gebr."

STEINBERG, WILH.

Piano Marketing Group, LLC
752 East 21st Street
Ferdinand, Indiana 47532

812-630-0978
gtrafton@pianomarketinggroup.com
www.Wilh-Steinberg.com

Pianos made by: Thüringer Pianoforte GmbH, Eisenberg, Germany

This company, formerly known as Wilhelm Steinberg Pianofortefabrik, was formed from the merger of several East German piano companies following the unification of Germany. These companies collectively trace their origin back to 1877. Steinberg also makes cabinets for other German piano makers, and makes several European piano brands under OEM agreement. The company also specializes in custom cabinets and finishes. Piano production is about 900 verticals and 50 grands per year.

Steinberg makes three models of vertical piano (46", 48½", and 51") and two sizes of grand (5' 8" and 6' 4"). These high quality pianos have beech rims with spruce bracing (grands), solid Bavarian spruce soundboards, maple bridges with maple cap, Renner actions and hammers, and Kluge keys.

Warranty: Five years, parts and labor, to the original purchaser

STEINGRAEBER & SÖHNE

Unique Pianos
165 Park Hill Blvd.
West Melbourne, Florida 32904

888-725-6633
321-725-5690
www.steingraeber.de
www.steingraeberpianos.com

Pianos made by: Steingraeber & Söhne, Bayreuth, Germany

Bayreuth is famous the world over for its annual summer Wagner festival. But tucked away in the old part of town is a second center of Bayreuth musical excellence and one of the piano world's best-kept secrets: Steingraeber & Söhne. Founded in Bayreuth in 1852, and in its present factory since 1872, Steingraeber is one of the smaller piano manufacturers in the world, producing fewer than 250 pianos per year for the top end of the market. It is owned and operated by sixth-generation family member Udo Steingraeber, who still makes pianos using the traditional methods of his forebearers.

Steingraeber makes three sizes of vertical piano—48", 51", and 54"—and three sizes of grand—5' 7", 6' 9", and 8' 11". The 5' 7" grand model has an unusually wide tail, allowing for a larger soundboard area and longer bass strings than is customary for an instrument of its size. One interesting option on the vertical pianos is "twist and change" panels. These are two-sided top and bottom panels, one side finished in polished ebony and the other in a two-toned combination of a wood veneer and ebony. The panels can be reversed as desired by the piano owner to match room décor or just for a change of scenery. Steingraeber also specializes in so-called ecological or biological finishes, available as an option on most models. This involves the use of only organic materials in the piano, such as natural paints and glues in the case, and white keytops made from cattle bone.

Steingraeber is known for its many innovative technical improvements to the piano. One new one is a cylindrical knuckle (grand piano action part) that revolves. It acts like a normal knuckle until the hammer reaches the let-off position. After that point, in soft playing, the knuckle revolves, reducing friction and making pianissimo playing easier, smoother, and more accurate. Another innovation is a new action for upright pianos. The "SFM" action, as it is called, contains no jack spring, instead using magnets to return the jack more quickly under the hammer butt for faster repetition. It is available in all three models of vertical piano.

The 6' 9" model 205, known as the "Chamber Concert Grand," was designed to embody the same tone quality of the Steingraeber Liszt grand piano of circa 1873. The 8' 11" model E-272 concert grand was introduced in 2002 for Steingraeber's 150th anniversary. Unique features include: a drilled capo bar for more sustain in the treble, unusually-shaped rim bracing, smaller soundboard resonating area in treble to better match string length. In 2007, Steingraeber will introduce a new 7' 7" concert grand to provide an additional, smaller, concert-size instrument. Its design will feature many of the innovations of the E-272.

Steingraeber pianos have a unique sound, with an extensive tonal palette derived from a mixture of clarity and warmth.

In addition to its regular line of pianos, Steingraeber makes a piano that can be used by physically handicapped players who don't have the use of their legs for pedaling. A switch in a backrest cushion operates the sustain pedal and a switch under the keybed operates the soft pedal. This mechanism can be installed in pianos of other makers if certain technical requirements are met.

The Steingraeber engineering department has designed and manufactured prototypes of new piano models for a number of other European piano manufacturers. These designs are not the same as Steingraeber's own current models.

Warranty: Ten years, parts and labor, to original purchaser

STEINWAY & SONS

Steinway & Sons, Inc.
Steinway Place
Long Island City, New York 11105

718-721-2600
800-366-1853
www.steinway.com

Heinrich Englehard Steinweg, a cabinetmaker and piano maker from Seesen, Germany, emigrated with his family to the United States in 1850 and established Steinway & Sons in 1853. Within a relatively short time, the Steinways were granted patents that revolutionized the piano, and which were eventually adopted or imitated by other makers. Many of these patents concerned the quest for a stronger frame, a richer, more powerful sound, and a more sensitive action. By the 1880s, the Steinway piano was in most ways the modern piano we have today, and in the next generation the standards set by the founder were strictly adhered to. (The early history of Steinway & Sons is fascinating, and is intimately connected to the history of New York City and the piano industry in general. You can read a summary of it in *The Piano Book*, and there are several excellent books devoted to the subject as well.)

Jumping ahead to the 1960s, the fourth generation of Steinways found themselves without any heirs willing or able to take over the business, and with a lack of capital with which to finance much needed equipment modernization, so in 1972 the Steinways sold their company to CBS. CBS exited the musical instrument business in 1985, selling Steinway to an investment group. In 1995, the company was sold again, this time to a major manufacturer of brass and woodwind instruments. The combined company, now known as Steinway Musical Instruments, Inc., is listed on the New York Stock Exchange under the symbol LVB. Day-to-day management of the company has remained unchanged since at least 1985. Steinway also owns a branch factory in Hamburg, Germany, which serves the world market outside of the Americas; and two major suppliers, the Herman Kluge company, Europe's largest maker of piano keys, and the O.S. Kelly company, the only remaining piano plate foundry in the U.S.

Steinway makes two types of vertical piano in three sizes: a 45" model 4510 studio, a 46½" model 1098 studio, and a 52" model K-52 upright. Models 4510 and 1098 are technically identical—only the cabinet is different—the former being in a period style for home use, the latter in an institutional cabinet for school use or less furniture-conscious home use. In all three models, the middle pedal operates a sostenuto mechanism. All Steinway verticals use a solid spruce soundboard, have no particle board, and in many other ways are similar in design, materials, and quality of workmanship to Steinway grands. Actions are made by Renner. Model K-52 in ebony, and model 1098 in ebony, mahogany, and walnut come with an adjustable artist bench, the others with a regular bench.

Technicians have always liked the performance of Steinway verticals, but used to complain that the studio models in particular were among the most difficult pianos to tune and would jump out of tune unexpectedly. Over the last few years, Steinway has made small design changes to alleviate this problem. The feedback I'm receiving is that the pianos are now mechanically more normal to tune and are stable, but an excess of false beats (tonal irregularities) still make the pianos difficult to tune at times.

Steinway makes six sizes of grand piano, two of which are new within the last few years. All ebony, mahogany, and walnut grand models come with an adjustable artist bench, the others with a regular bench.

The 5' 1" model S is very good for a small grand, but has the usual limitations of any small piano and so is only recommended where space considerations are paramount. The 5' 7" model M is a full six inches longer, but costs little more than the S. Historically, it has been one of Steinways more popular models and is found in living rooms across the country. Its medium size makes the tone in certain areas slightly less than perfect, but it's an excellent home instrument.

The 5' 10½" model L has been replaced with the model O of the same size. Model O was first produced in 1902, but discontinued in 1924 in favor of the model L. Changes over time in both engineering and musical taste, as well as a desire to better synchronize the offerings of the New York factory with Hamburg, where the model O was never abandoned, seemed to dictate a return to the O. The main difference between the two models is in the shape of the tail—the L has a squared-off tail and the O has a round tail—but this can also affect the soundboard and bridges and therefore the tone.

Reintroduction of the model O followed by one year the reintroduction of the legendary 6' 2" model A. First offered in 1878 and discontinued in New York in 1945, model A revolutionized piano making by featuring for the first time radial rim bracing and one-piece bent rim construction, now used in all Steinway grands. Over the years, the model A has gone through several makeovers, each of slightly different size and scaling. The version being reintroduced was made in New York from 1896 to 1914 and is the same size as the model A that has been made at the Hamburg factory for more than a century. Models O and A are suitable for the larger living room or for many school and teaching situations.

The 6' 10½" model B is the favorite of many piano technicians. It is the best choice for the serious pianist, recording or teaching studio, or small recital hall. Small design changes and other refinements to this model in recent years have brought a steady stream of accolades. The 8' 11¾" model D, the concert grand, is the flagship of the Steinway line and the piano of choice for the overwhelming majority of concert pianists. It's too large for most places other than the concert stage.

Steinway uses excellent materials and construction techniques in the manufacture of its grands. The rims, both inner and outer, are made in one continuous bend from layers of maple, and the beams are of solid spruce. The keybed is of quartersawn spruce planks freely mortised together, and the keys are of Bavarian spruce. The pinblock consists of seven laminations of maple with successive grain orientations of 45 and 90 degrees. The soundboard is of solid Sitka spruce, the bridges are vertically laminated of maple with a solid maple cap, and all models have duplex scaling.

It is well known that Steinway's principal competition comes from used and rebuilt Steinways, many of which come in exotic veneers or have elaborately carved or customized "art cases." The company has responded by expanding its product line to include modern-day versions of these collector's items. The Crown Jewel Collection consists of the regular models in natural wood (non-ebonized) veneers, many of them exotic. They are finished in a semi-gloss finish Steinway calls Satin Lustre. Limited Edition models, issued at irregular intervals, are reproductions of turn-of-the-century designs, available only in models O and B. The newest Limited Edition model is one honoring Henry Z. Steinway, the oldest living member of the Steinway family, now 91. This model has Victorian-style legs and lyre, an intricately carved music desk, and period cabinet detailing, and is available in Ebony with chrome-plated hardware or East Indian Rosewood. Each instrument is personally signed by Henry Steinway.

During the early 1900s, ownership of art case Steinways became a symbol of wealth and culture. Steinway has resumed this tradition by regularly commissioning noted furniture designers to create new ones. Most are created around a theme. For example, in 1999 Frank Pollaro designed an art case called "Rhapsody" to commemorate the 100th anniversary of the birth of George Gershwin. The piano featured a blue-dyed maple veneer adorned with more than 400 hand-cut mother-of-pearl stars and a gilded silver plate. Each year sees new art case pianos from Steinway and they are truly stunning. Steinway's Legendary Collection consists of occasional one-of-a-kind reproductions of historical art case pianos.

As another way of capitalizing on the popularity of older Steinways, the company also operates the world's largest Steinway piano rebuilding facility at the factory for the restoration of older Steinways. *The Piano Book* contains a great deal of additional information on the purchase of an older or restored Steinway.

The underlying excellence of the Steinway musical designs and the integrity of the construction process are the hallmarks of the Steinway piano. Steinway pianos at their best have the quintessential American piano sound: a powerful bass, a resonant mid-range, a singing treble with plenty of tonal color. Although other brands have some of these characteristics, it is perhaps the particular combination of harmonics that comprise the Steinway's tonal coloration that distinguishes it from other brands more than anything else and gives it its richness, depth, and power. The construction process creates a very durable and rigid framework, which also contributes to the power of its sound. As with other American-made pianos, musical and cabinet detailing, such as factory voicing and regulation and plate and cabinet cosmetics, are reasonable but lag somewhat behind the company's European competitors in finesse. Some of this can be finished off by thorough and competent dealer make-ready.

Steinway pianos require more preparation by the dealer than most pianos in their class, but over the last several years the factory preparation has greatly improved, so the work required by the dealer is no longer excessive. Still, some dealers are more conscientious than others, and I occasionally hear of piano buyers who "can't find a good Steinway." How much of this is due to inherent weaknesses in some pianos, how much to lack of dealer preparation, and how much to customer bias or groundless complaining is hard to tell. I suspect it is a little of each. Piano technicians who work on these pianos do sometimes remark that some seem to have more potential than others. Many dealers do just enough regulating and voicing to be acceptable to the average customer, but reserve the highest level of work for those situations where a fussy customer for one of the larger models is trying to decide between a few particular instruments. Most customers for a Steinway will probably find one they like on the sales floor. However, if you are a discriminating buyer who has had trouble finding a Steinway that suits your preferences, I recommend letting the salesperson know as precisely as you can what you are looking for. Give the salesperson some time to have a few instruments prepared for you before making a decision. It may also help to tactfully let the salesperson know that you are aware there are other options available to you in the market for high-end pianos. By the way, customers seeking to purchase a model B or D Steinway who have not found the piano they are looking for at their local dealer can make arrangements with that dealer to visit the Steinway factory in New York, where a selection of the larger models is kept on hand for this purpose.

As mentioned earlier, Steinway owns a branch factory in Hamburg, Germany, established in 1880. The "fit and finish" (detailing) of the pianos at this factory is reputed to be better than at the one in New York, although pianists sometimes prefer the sound of the New York Steinway. Traditionally, the Hamburg factory has operated somewhat autonomously, but more recently, the company has been synchronizing the two plants through technical exchanges, model changes, jointly-built models, and by shipping materials from New York to Hamburg. It's possible to special-order a Hamburg Steinway through an American Steinway dealer, or an enterprising American customer could travel to Europe, buy one there, and have it shipped back home.

Warranty: Five years, parts and labor, to the original purchaser

STORY & CLARK

Story & Clark Piano Co.
Quaker Drive
Seneca, Pennsylvania 16346

800-247-6557
www.qrsmusic.com

Owned by: QRS Music Technologies, Inc., Naples, Florida

Pianos made by: Dongbei Piano Company, Ltd., Yingkou, Liaoning Province, China and by Heintzman Piano Company, Ltd., Beijing, China

Hampton Story began making pianos in 1857 and was joined by Melville Clark in 1884. The business settled in Grand Rapids, Michigan in 1901, where it remained, under various owners, until about 1986. Around 1990, a new owner moved the company to its present location in Seneca, Pennsylvania. Over the years, pianos were manufactured under a number of different names, including in recent years, Story & Clark, Hobart M. Cable, Hampton, and Classic. In 1993, QRS Piano Rolls, Inc., now QRS Music Technologies, Inc., purchased Story & Clark. (Ironically, QRS itself was founded in 1901 by Melville Clark of the Story & Clark Piano Co. of old.) QRS, historically the nation's major source of music rolls for traditional player pianos, now manufactures electronic player piano systems that can be retrofitted into any piano (see "QRS/Pianomation").

Story & Clark no longer manufactures pianos in the U.S. Pianos bearing the Story & Clark name are now made in China by the Dongbei Piano Co. (see "Dongbei"), except for the vertical models 120 and 140, which are made in China by Heintzman (see "Heintzman"). (Note: The Heintzman-made models are not made to the same specifications as those sold under the Heintzman brand name.) To maintain quality control, all pianos go to the Seneca, Pennsylvania facility for inspection and adjustment before being shipped to U.S. dealers. The majority of Story & Clark grands are outfitted with the QRS Pianomation system in the factory in China, where the pianos are pre-slotted and modified to accept the player systems without cutting into the keys and key frame.

Warranty: Ten years, parts and labor, to the original purchaser

SUZUKI

Suzuki Corporation
P.O. Box 261030
San Diego, California 92196

800-854-1594
858-566-9710
www.suzukipianos.com

Pianos made by: Artfield Piano Co., Qingpu, Shanghai, China; possibly others

Suzuki Corporation, the world's largest producer of musical instruments for education, has entered the acoustic piano business with a line of vertical and grand pianos made in China. The pianos are sold online at www.suzukipianos.com and through Costco, as well as through regular piano dealers. The company prefers not to be specific as to the source of its pianos, but it appears to me that most are now manufactured by Artfield Piano Co.

Warranty: Ten years, parts and labor, to the original purchaser

VIVACE — See "Cristofori"; also see "Sejung"

VOGEL — See "Schimmel"

VOSE & SONS

Wrightwood Enterprises, Inc.
717 St. Joseph Drive
St. Joseph, Michigan 49085

800-445-0695

Pianos made by: Dongbei Piano Company, Ltd., Yingkou, Liaoning Province, China

Vose & Sons was established in 1851 in Boston by James Whiting Vose. Ownership eventually transferred to the American Piano Company, and later to Aeolian Pianos, which went out of business in 1985. Since 2004, the brand has been used by a different distributor on pianos from the Dongbei Piano Company in China (see "Dongbei").

WALTER, CHARLES R.

Walter Piano Company, Inc.
25416 CR 6
Elkhart, Indiana 46514

574-266-0615
www.walterpiano.com

Charles Walter, an engineer, was head of Piano Design and Developmental Engineering at C.G. Conn in the 1960s, when Conn was doing important research in musical acoustics. In 1969 Walter bought the Janssen piano name from Conn, and continued to make Janssen pianos until 1981. In 1975, he brought out the Charles R. Walter line of consoles and studios, based on his continuing research in piano design. Walter began making grands in 1997.

The Walter Piano Company is fairly unique among U.S. piano manufacturers in that it is a family business, staffed by Charles and his wife, several of their grownup children and various in-laws, in addition to unrelated production employees. The Walters say that each piano is inspected and signed by a member of their family before being shipped. Dealers and technicians report that doing business with the Walters is a pleasure in itself.

The Charles R. Walter line consists of 43" and 45" studio pianos in various decorator and institutional styles, and 5' 9" and 6' 4" grands. The 43" pianos are called "consoles" for marketing purposes because of their styling, but both the 43" and 45" pianos are really studios (as I define the term) by virtue of their full-size actions, and are actually identical pianos in different sized cabinets. Because of the larger action, the "console" will outperform many real consoles on the market.

Although Mr. Walter is not oblivious to marketing concerns, his vertical piano bears the mark of being designed by an engineer who understands pianos and strives for quality. The pianos are built in a traditional manner, with heavy-duty, full-length, spruce backposts; a solid spruce soundboard; and Delignit pinblock. Exceptionally long, thick keys that are individually lead-weighted provide a very even feel across the keyboard. The scale design is well thought out and the bass sounds good most of the way to the bottom. The cabinetry is substantial, contains no particle board, and is beautifully finished. Some of the fancy consoles in particular, such as the Queen

Anne models, are strikingly beautiful. The pianos are well prepared at the factory and so need minimal preparation by the dealer.

The vertical pianos now use Renner actions, but a Chinese-made action is available as a lower-cost option, reducing the price of the piano by about $1,200 (list). The Chinese parts are virtually indistinguishable from the Renner parts, but they make the action feel just slightly lighter due to differing spring tensions.

The Walter 5' 9" and 6' 4" grands were designed by Del Fandrich, one of the nation's most respected piano design engineers. Both models have high-quality features such as a maple rim, Renner action, Kluge keys, Delignit pinblock, tapered solid spruce soundboard, and Abel hammers (Ronsen hammers in the 5' 9" model). The 5' 9" grand also has a number of innovative features: A portion of the inner rim and soundboard at the bass end of the piano are separated from the rest of the rim and allowed to "float." Less restricted in its movement, the soundboard can reproduce the fundamental frequencies of the lower bass notes more like a larger piano can. A special extension of the tenor bridge creates a smoother transition from bass to treble. Eight plate nosebolts increase plate stability, helping to reduce energy loss to the plate and thus increase sustain. Inverted half-agraffes embedded in the capo bar maintain string alignment and reduce unwanted string noise. The Walter grands are competently built and play very well.

Warranty: Twelve years, parts and labor, transferable to future owners within the warranty period.

WEBER — See "Young Chang"

WEINBACH

Geneva International Corporation
29 East Hintz Road
Wheeling, Illinois 60090

800-533-2388
847-520-9970
pianos@geneva-intl.com
www.geneva-intl.com

Pianos made by: Dongbei Piano Company, Ltd., Yingkou, Liaoning Province, China

Formerly made by Petrof and for years virually identical to Petrof pianos, the Weinbach piano line was given a complete makeover in 2006. The pianos are now assembled in the section of the Dongbei Piano Co. in China in which Nordiska pianos are manufactured (see "Nordiska" and "Dongbei").

The Weinbach grand rim structure is the same as for the Nordiska, but the scale designs are modified, and the plate designs are completely new. The pianos are strung with a combination of loop and single stringing (one loop and one single-tied string per unison), with bass strings made in the U.S. by Mapes. Like the Nordiska, the Weinbach grands have maple rims, solid spruce soundboards, Abel hammers, and an advanced leg plate design, among other features. The action is Petrof's new "Petrof Original" action made by Detoa (see "Petrof" for details). Fully-assembled actions, keys, and key frames are shipped from Petrof to Dongbei and added to the Chinese-made strung back and cabinet. At present only grand models exist, but vertical models will follow soon.

Warranty: Ten years, parts and labor, to original purchaser

WEINBERGER

Cathy Harl
Harl Pianos
318 Montgomery Street
Alexandria, Virginia 22314

703-739-2220
800-440-HARL (4275)

Pianos made by: Klavierhaus Weinberger, Enns, Austria

Bruno Weinberger is an Austrian piano technician who markets his own line of pianos. Distribution in the U.S. is very limited. For the most part, the pianos are manufactured by Thüringer Pianoforte GmbH, the maker of Wilh. Steinberg pianos, with Mr. Weinberger providing the musical finishing work. Mr. Weinberger says that the verticals are similar to the Wilh. Steinberg line, but that the grands are built to his own design. The grands have a couple of unique cabinet design features. The closed lid is supported on short posts so that even in the closed position there is a small space for sound to escape. The music desk folds down into the front part of the lid.

WURLITZER — See "Baldwin"

WYMAN

Wyman Piano Company
P.O. Box 218802
Nashville, Tennessee 37221

615-356-9143

info@wymanpiano.com
www.wymanpiano.com

Pianos made by: Beijing Hsinghai Piano Group, Ltd., Beijing, China

Wyman Piano Company is a relatively new venture created by experienced former Baldwin executives. The regular Wyman line consists of seven vertical piano sizes and four grand sizes in a variety of cabinet sizes and finishes. All are manufactured in China by the Beijing Hsinghai Piano Group (see "Beijing Hsinghai"). Wyman says that its executives make frequent trips to Beijing to monitor manufacturing and inspect finished instruments. A premium line of Wyman "Pianoforte" models, made in a small production facility in the Beijing area, features deluxe cabinets and some upgraded technical features.

Wyman now offers a CD player piano system by Pianoforce, a new entrant into the field of player piano systems (see "Pianoforce"). The optional CD systems are installed at the Beijing factory and add about $4,200 to the retail price of the piano.

Warranty: Ten years, parts and labor, transferable to future owners within the warranty period. Lifetime warranty on the soundboard.

XINGHAI — See "Beijing Xinghai"

YAMAHA
including Cable-Nelson. See separate listing for Disklavier.

Yamaha Corporation of America
P.O. Box 6600
Buena Park, California 90622

714-522-9011
800-854-1569
infostation@yamaha.com
www.yamaha.com

Pianos made by: Yamaha Corporation, Hamamatsu, Japan; Thomaston, Georgia; and other locations (see text)

Torakusu Yamaha, a watchmaker, developed Japan's first reed organ, founding Yamaha Reed Organ Manufacturing in 1887. In 1899, Yamaha visited the United States to learn to build pianos. Within a couple of years, he began making grand and vertical pianos under the name Nippon Gakki, Ltd. Beginning in the 1930s, Yamaha expanded its operations, first into other musical instruments, then into other goods and services, such as sporting goods and furniture, and finally internationally.

Export of pianos to the United States began about 1960. In 1973 Yamaha acquired the Everett Piano Co. in South Haven, Michigan and made both Yamaha and Everett pianos there until 1986. In that year, the company moved its piano manufacturing to a plant in Thomaston, Georgia, where it has made Yamaha consoles, studios, and some grands until this year. Citing a depressed piano market and increasing competition from China and Indonesia, Yamaha closed its Thomaston facility just prior to this *Supplement* going to press. The company plans to introduce new models in the near future, from other Yamaha factories, in styles similar to those made in Thomaston.

Yamaha is probably the most international of the piano manufacturers. In addition to its factories in Japan, Yamaha has plants and partnerships with other companies all over the world, including the United States (until recently), Germany (with Schimmel), England (with Kemble), Mexico, China, Indonesia, and Taiwan. Currently, most of the Yamaha pianos sold in the United States are made in Japan or the U.S., but there are a few models made in China and Indonesia, and with the closing of the U.S. factory, more are sure to come.

Yamaha's console line consists of the 44" model M112 in continental style (no legs) and models M425, M450, M475, and M500 in furniture style (free-standing legs) with increasing levels of cabinet sophistication and price. All are the same internally and have a compressed action typical of a console, so the action will not be quite as responsive as with larger models.

The studio line consists of the popular 45" model P22 in institutional style (legs with toe blocks) with school-friendly cabinet; the furniture-style version P600; model T116 in a less-expensive, traditional institutional-style cabinet; and the new, even slightly less-expensive 46" model T118 in institutional style, made in China. All are more or less the same internally, with a full-size action.

The uprights are the very popular 48" model U1, the 48" model T121 in a less-expensive cabinet (otherwise the same), and the 52" model U3. Models U1 and U3 now sport a longer music desk—a very welcome addition. Model U3 joins model U5 (discontinued in this form) in the use of a "floating" soundboard—the soundboard is not completely attached to the back at the top, allowing it to vibrate a little more freely for enhanced tonal performance. A new "Super U" series of uprights (YUS1, YUS3, YUS5) have different hammers and get additional tuning and voicing at the factory, including voicing by machine to create a more consistent, more mellow tone. Model YUS5 uses German Röslau music wire instead of Yamaha wire, also for a more mellow tone. This top-of-the-line 52" upright also has agraffes, duplex scaling, and a sostenuto pedal. (All other Yamaha verticals have a practice/mute pedal.)

Yamaha vertical pianos are very well made for a mass-produced piano. The taller uprights in particular are considered a "dream" to service by technicians and are very much enjoyed by musicians. Sometimes the pianos can sound quite bright, though much less so than in previous years. The model P22 school studio in particular, in my opinion, can sound quite brash and loud. This is great for classroom use, but may need voicing to be suitable for the home. Double-striking of the hammer in the low tenor on a soft or incomplete stroke of the key is a common problem mentioned in regard to Yamaha verticals by those who play with an especially soft touch. This tendency of double-striking in soft playing is a characteristic of the action design, the trade-off being better-than-normal repetition for a vertical piano. It's possible that a technician can lessen this problem if necessary with careful adjustment, but at the risk of sacrificing some speed of repetition.

Yamaha grands come in four levels of sophistication and size. The "Classic Collection" consists of the 4' 11" model GB1 and the 5' 3" model GC1. The GB1 has simplified case construction and cabinetry, no duplex scale, and the middle pedal operates a bass sustain mechanism. It is currently the only Yamaha grand sold in the U.S. that is made in Indonesia. The GC1 has regular case construction and duplex scale, but simplified cabinetry and a bass sustain.

The "Conservatory Classic Collection" consists of the 5' 3" model C1 and 5' 8" model C2; and the "Conservatory Collection" the 6' 1" C3, 6' 7" C5, and 6' 11" C6. Both collections have the advanced construction, scaling, and cabinetry mentioned above, plus a true sostenuto pedal and a soft-close fallboard. Other than the size, these two collections differ primarily in that the former have solid maple bridges with maple cap, where the latter have vertically-laminated bridges with maple or boxwood cap. The vertically laminated design is similar to that found in Steinways and other fine pianos, and is considered to give the bridges greater strength and resistance to cracking and better transmission of vibrational energy. The larger grands also use Yamaha's ivory-alternative Ivorite™ keytops.

Finally, the "Concert Collection" consists of the 7' 6" model C7, the 9' model CFIIIS concert grand, and the two "S" series Yamahas: 6' 3" model S4B and 6' 11" model S6B. The C7 is pretty much like the Conservatory Collection grands, but the others in the Concert Collection are "hand-built" in a separate factory to much higher standards and with some different materials. For example, they use maple and mahogany in the rim, which has recently been made more rigid for greater tonal power; higher-grade soundboard material; a treble "bell" (as in the larger Steinways) to enhance the treble tone; German strings and recent hammer and scaling changes for a more mellow tone; as well as the more advanced features of the other collections. The result is an instrument capable of greater dynamic range, tonal color, and sustain than the regular Yamahas. The CFIIIS concert grand made in this factory is endorsed and used by a number of notable musicians, including Michael Tilson Thomas, Chick Corea, and Elton John, among others.

Other than the special grands just described, Yamaha grands are a little on the percussive side and do not "sing" as well as some more expensive pianos. The tone is very clear and often bright, especially in the smaller grands, although the excessive brightness that once characterized Yamahas seems to be a thing of the past. The clarity and percussiveness are very attractive, but less well-suited, in my opinion, for classical music, which often requires a singing tone and lush harmonic color. On the other hand, Yamaha tends to be the piano of choice for jazz and popular music, which may value the clarity and brightness more than the other qualities mentioned. In recent years, the larger grands in particular (C3 and larger) have come from the factory better voiced and more musically versatile.

Both Yamaha's quality control and its warranty and technical service are legendary in the piano business. They are the standard against which every other company is measured. For general home and school use, piano technicians probably recommend Yamaha pianos more often than any other brand. Their precision, reliability, and performance make them a very good value for a consumer product.

The Yamaha Servicebond program encourages Yamaha dealers to provide customers with follow-up service during the first six months of ownership by reimbursing the dealers for part of the cost of providing the service. Services for which a dealer can be reimbursed include a tuning and a general maintenance check (tightening screws, among other things). The program is voluntary, however, on the part of the dealer. When negotiating the sale, the customer might wish to inquire as to whether the dealer participates in the program, and if so, to make sure the service is actually provided.

Yamaha now makes a piano under the name Cable-Nelson. It is made in Yamaha's factory in Hangzhou, Zhejiang Province, China, southwest of Shanghai, where the company also makes guitars. The Cable-Nelson 45" model CN116 is identical in quality and musical specifications to Yamaha's model T116, except that the Cable-Nelson has a laminated soundboard, whereas all Yamaha pianos sold in the U.S. have a solid spruce soundboard. (This same Cable-Nelson is sold in Canada under the Yamaha name.) The Cable-Nelson model CN216 is a furniture-style version of the 116.

Cable-Nelson is the name of an old American piano maker that traces its roots back to 1903. Yamaha acquired the name when it bought the Everett Piano Company in 1973, and used the name in conjunction with Everett pianos until 1981.

There is a thriving market for used Yamahas. If you are considering buying a used Yamaha, please read "Should I Buy A Used, 'Gray Market' Yamaha or Kawai Piano?" on pages 176–177 of *The Piano Book*.

To help its dealers overcome competition from "gray market" pianos, Yamaha has begun an "Heirloom Assurance" program that provides a five-year warranty on a used Yamaha piano less than twenty-five years old purchased from an authorized Yamaha dealer. See a Yamaha dealer for details.

Yamaha also makes electronic player pianos called Disklaviers, as well as hybrid acoustic/digital pianos called MIDIPianos, that account for a substantial percentage of the company's sales. These products are reviewed separately under "Disklavier."

Warranty: Yamaha and Cable-Nelson—Ten years, parts and labor, to the original purchaser. Cable-Nelson pianos do not come with the Yamaha Servicebond.

YOUNG CHANG
including Bergmann and Weber

Young Chang North America, Inc.
19060 South Dominguez Hills Drive
Rancho Dominguez, California 90220

310-637-2000
800-874-2880
www.youngchang.com

Pianos made by: Young Chang Akki, Ltd., Inchon, South Korea and Tianjin, China

In 1956, three brothers, Young-Sup, Chang-Sup, and Jai-Sup Kim founded Young Chang and began selling Yamaha pianos in Korea under an agreement with that Japanese firm. Korea was recovering from a devastating war, and only the wealthy could afford pianos. But the prospects were bright for economic development, and as a symbol of cultural refinement the piano was much coveted. In 1962, the brothers incorporated as Young Chang Akki Co., Ltd. In 1964, Young Chang began importing partially completed instruments from Yamaha, doing final assembly work itself to reduce high import duties. This led to an agreement with Yamaha under which Yamaha helped Young Chang set up a full-fledged manufacturing operation. In 1975, the two companies parted company when Young Chang decided to expand internationally, thus becoming a potential competitor. Young Chang began exporting to the United States in the late 1970s. In 1995, Young Chang built a factory in Tianjin, China and gradually began to move manufacturing operations there for some of its models as Korean wages rose.

In 2004, Young Chang's Korean rival Samick acquired a controlling interest in the company and began to consolidate the two companies' administrative and distribution functions in North America. A few months later, however, the Korean Fair Trade Commission ruled that the purchase violated Korean anti-monopoly laws and ordered Samick to sell its interest. Naturally, Samick stopped making payments to creditors on Young Chang's behalf, forcing Young Chang into bankruptcy. For a couple of years, while these issues wound their way through the courts, there was a question of which of the two companies was entitled to distribute Young Chang pianos in North America, but the courts finally ruled that Young Chang was a separate entity entitled to distribute its own pianos. In 2006, Hyundai Development Company purchased Young Chang and is in the process of re-establishing Young Chang's presence in North America. Hyundai Development is a Korean civil engineering and construction company that helped create Hyundai Motor Company. Young Chang also owns Kurzweil Music Systems, a manufacturer of digital pianos and other electronic music products.

During the mid-1990s, Young Chang employed the services of Joseph Pramberger, at one time an engineer and manufacturing executive at Steinway & Sons, to evaluate its piano designs and make improvements. The pianos that resulted from this process were known as the "Pramberger Signature Series." The company also produced a completely new line of premium pianos designed by Mr. Pramberger with maple inner rim (grands), upgraded hammers and soundboard material, Renner action parts (grands), and exotic veneers that was called the "Pramberger Platinum Series" and said "Pramberger" on the fallboard instead of "Young Chang." After Mr. Pramberger died in 2003, his estate terminated its relationship with Young Chang and signed up with Samick. Samick now uses the Pramberger name on a completely different piano design (see "Samick"). Young Chang continues to use the original Pramberger designs, but names them differently. The Pramberger Signature Series is now called the Young Chang Professional Artist Series. The Pramberger Platinum Series is now called the Young Chang Platinum Edition. Both of these lines are made in Korea. Pianos made in Young Chang's factory in Tianjin, China bear the name "Bergmann" and are made to lesser specifications at a much lower cost.

Following the demise of the Samsung-owned Weber Piano Company, Young Chang took back the Weber name, which it owns, and brought out a line of Weber pianos patterned after existing Young Chang and Bergmann pianos and the former Pramberger line. The Weber "Legend" series is like the Bergmann line, the "Sovereign" series is like the Young Chang Professional Artist series (formerly Pramberger Signature Series), and the "Albert Weber" series is like the Young Chang Platinum Edition (formerly Pramberger Platinum).

Quality control in Young Chang's Korean factory has improved little by little over the years, always with the promise that it would one day be as good as Yamaha, but never quite making it. Still, most of the problems are ones that can be cured by a good dealer make-ready and a little follow-up service, and the pianos seem to hold up pretty well in the field, even in institutions. The tone of Young Chang pianos used to be bright and sterile, but the work of Joseph Pramberger changed that. He introduced some tonal color and sustain into the pianos he designed. The medium-level pianos are still not exactly what I would call "warm," but with some voicing, they can definitely be made reasonably musical. The Platinum Edition and Albert

Weber pianos have greater musical potential and respond well to expert voicing. Pianos from the factory in China, like other pianos from that country, have been erratic in quality, but generally improving. Hyundai Development says it is in the process of upgrading the factories in both countries with help from engineers at Hyundai Motors.

Young Chang also makes "Essex" pianos under contract with Steinway for sale by Steinway dealers. See "Essex" for more information.

Warranty: Young Chang Platinum Edition—Fifteen years, parts and labor. Young Chang Professional Artist series—Twelve years, parts and labor. Bergmann—Ten years, parts and labor. All warranties are transferable to future owners within the warranty period. Parts are further warranted for the lifetime of the original owner.

MODEL and PRICING GUIDE

This guide contains the "list price" for nearly every brand, model, style, and finish of new piano that has regular distribution in the United States and, for the most part, Canada. Some marginal, local, or "stencil" brands are omitted. Except where indicated, prices are in U.S. dollars and the pianos are assumed to be for sale in the U.S. (Canadians will find the information useful after translation into Canadian dollars, but there may be differences in import duties and sales practices that will affect retail prices.) Prices and specifications are, of course, subject to change. Most manufacturers revise their prices at least once a year; two or three times a year is not uncommon when currency exchange rates are unstable. The prices in this edition were compiled in the spring of 2007.

Note that prices of European pianos vary with the value of the dollar against the Euro. For this *Supplement*, the exchange rate used by most manufacturers was in the range of Euro = $1.30–1.35. All prices are "landed" prices, i.e., including import duties and estimated costs of freight to the U.S. warehouse or port of entry. However, such costs will vary depending on the shipping method employed, the port of entry, and other variables.

Some terms used in this guide require special explanation and disclaimers:

List Price

The list price is usually a starting point for negotiation, not a final sales price. The term "list price," as used in this *Supplement*, is a "standard" or "normalized" list price computed from the published wholesale price according to a formula commonly used in the industry. Some manufacturers use a different formula, however, for their own "manufacturer's suggested retail price" (MSRP), usually one that raises the price above "standard" list by ten to fifty percent so that their dealers can advertise a larger "discount" without losing profit. Because the formula for MSRP varies from one company to another, price-shopping by comparing discounts from the MSRP may result in a faulty price comparison. To provide a level playing field for comparing prices, all prices in this guide are computed according to a uniform "standard" formula, *even though it may differ from the manufacturers' own suggested retail prices.* Where my list prices and those of a manufacturer differ, then, no dishonesty should be inferred; we simply employ different formulas.

For most brands, but not all, the price includes a bench and the standard manufacturer's warranty for that brand. Prices listed here for some European brands do not include a bench, though the dealer will almost always provide a bench and quote a price that includes it. Most dealers will also include moving and one or two tunings in the home, but these are optional and a matter of agreement between you and the dealer.

A note to piano dealers: To more accurately reflect the actual cost of acquiring and displaying product, beginning with this year's *Supplement*, an allowance for dealer freight and make-ready has been factored into the wholesale price before converting to retail. This accounts for what may appear to be a sharp increase in the retail price of lower-cost pianos, which are proportionately more affected by this change than higher-cost ones. Some manufacturers of very high-priced pianos have opted not to take this allowance. A special allowance for duty and freight has also been factored into the wholesale price of those brands ordered by the dealer F.O.B. factory from Europe.

Style and Finish

Unless otherwise indicated, the cabinet style is assumed to be "traditional" and is not stated. Exactly what "traditional" means varies from brand to brand. In general, it is a "classic" styling with minimal embellishment and straight legs. The vertical pianos have front legs, which are free-standing on smaller verticals and attached to the cabinet with toe blocks on larger verticals, the latter often called "institutional-style." "Continental" or European styling refers to vertical pianos without decorative trim and usually without front legs. Other furniture styles (Chippendale, French Provincial, Queen Anne, etc.) are as noted. The manufacturer's own trademarked style name is used when an appropriate generic name could not be determined.

"Satin" finishes reflect light but not images. "Polished" finishes, also known as "high-gloss" or "high-polish," are mirror-like. "Oiled" finishes are usually matte (not shiny). "Open-pore" finishes, common on some European pianos, are slightly grainier satin finishes due to the wood pores not being filled in prior to finishing. In fact, many finishes labeled "satin" on European pianos are actually open-pore. "Ebony" is a black finish.

Special-order–only styles and finishes are in italics.

Some descriptions of style and finish may be slightly different from the manufacturer's own for the purpose of clarity, consistency, saving space, or other reason.

Size

The height of a vertical piano is measured from the floor to the top of the piano. The length of a grand piano is measured from the very front (keyboard end) to the very back (tail end), usually with the lid closed.

Actual Selling or "Street" Price

Buying a piano is something like buying a car—the list price is deliberately set high in anticipation of negotiating.* But sometimes this is carried to extremes, as when the salesperson reduces the price three times in the first fifteen minutes to barely half the sticker price. In situations like this, the customer, understandably confused, is bound to ask in exasperation, "What is the *real* price of this piano?"

Unfortunately, there *is* no "real" price. In theory, the dealer pays a wholesale price and then marks it up by an amount sufficient to cover the overhead and produce a profit. In practice, however, the markup can vary considerably from sale to sale depending on such factors as:

- how long the inventory has been sitting around, racking up finance charges for the dealer
- how much of a discount the dealer received at the wholesale level for buying in quantity or for paying cash
- the dealer's cash flow situation
- the ease of comparison shopping in that geographic area
- the competition in that geographic area for a particular brand or type of piano
- special piano sales events taking place in the area
- how the salesperson sizes up your situation and your willingness to pay
- the level of pre- and post-sale service the dealer seeks to provide
- the dealer's other overhead expenses

One way some manufacturers assist dealers in overcoming downward price pressure is to publish wholesale price lists that are less than honest. That is, dealers are routinely offered large discounts (ten to thirty percent) from the published wholesale price if they buy in sufficient quantity, or for certain models, or for any other reason the manufacturer can think of. Since the prices in this *Supplement* are calculated from the published wholesale prices, this practice results in over-inflated list prices in this book for those particular companies, allowing dealers of those brands to advertise larger "discounts" without losing profit. This practice is especially common among some Chinese and Korean companies, but has also spread to some high-end makers, too. The problem for the consumer is that these wholesale discounts are not given out uniformly by manufacturers or among dealers, one reason why an appropriate "street" price figured from the price information presented here will have to remain a rough estimate.

---

* A relatively small number of dealers have non-negotiable prices.

Discounts from "standard" list price for Yamaha pianos are usually limited to about twenty percent in most cases. Kawai dealers tend to discount a little more than Yamaha; twenty-five percent off is not uncommon in a competitive environment. Inexpensive Chinese pianos tend to be service intensive and it's not cost-effective to sell them at a steep discount. On the other hand, the wholesale (and therefore retail) prices are sometimes vastly inflated. Therefore, discounts can vary a lot — from ten to thirty percent. Some dealers just use them as "loss leaders," that is, just to get people into the store, whereupon the customer is sold on a more expensive piano. Discounts on other Asian pianos vary a lot, too, from twenty to perhaps thirty percent.

The Boston piano, although manufactured in Asia, is generally viewed as being a little more "exclusive" due to its association with Steinway, so deep discounting is much less likely. Discounts in the range of ten to fifteen percent or so are common. Selling-price information is scarce on Baldwin products because of the company's re-establishment and the sharp trimming of its dealerships, but fifteen to twenty-five percent would probably be a safe bet, with larger discounts possible on some of the more expensive U.S.-made Baldwin products.

Western European instruments tend to be extremely expensive here due to their high quality, the high European cost of doing business, additional middlemen/importers and, recently, unfavorable exchange rates. Discounts generally range from twenty-five to thirty percent, but can go as high as forty percent if the piano has gone unsold for an extended period of time. Eastern European brands like Petrof and Estonia are already seen as being a good deal for the money, so expect moderate discounts—perhaps fifteen to twenty percent on Petrof and twenty to twenty-five percent on Estonia.

Steinway pianos have always been in a class by themselves, historically the only expensive piano to continually command high profit margins. Except for older Steinways and the occasional Mason & Hamlin, Steinway has little competition and only about seventy-five dealers in the United States. Service requirements can be quite high, at least in part because of the higher standards often required to satisfy a fussier clientele. Historically, Steinway pianos have sold at or near full list price. (Some dealers even sell *above* list!) This is still true in some places, but in recent years I have seen a little more discounting than in the past. Five percent is most common in the largest metropolitan areas (except New York, where there is no discounting). Ten to fifteen percent is not unusual in some less populated areas. As much as twenty percent would be rare, and is usually limited to institutional purchases of larger instruments. Mason & Hamlin pianos are typically sold at discounts of twenty-five percent or more.

For brands not mentioned or implied in the above discussion, it's usually a safe bet to figure a discount of fifteen to twenty-five percent from the prices in this *Supplement*, with greater discounts possible in selected situations.

There is no "fair" price for a piano except the one the buyer and seller agree on. The dealer is no more obligated to sell you a piano at a deep discount than you are obligated to pay the list price. Many dealers are simply not able to sell at the low end of the range consistently and still stay in business. It's understandable that you would like to pay the lowest price possible, and there's no harm in asking, but remember that piano shopping is not just about chasing the lowest price. Be sure you are getting the instrument that best suits your needs and preferences and that the dealer is committed to providing the proper pre- and post-sale service.

(Note: Remember that the "street" price discounts suggested above should be subtracted from the "standard" list prices in this *Supplement*, not from the manufacturer's suggested retail price.)

For more information on shopping for a new piano and on how to save money, please see pages 60–75 in *The Piano Book* (fourth edition).

Model	**Size**	**Style and Finish**	**Price***

Altenburg

Grands

AG160	5' 3"	Polished Ebony	10,360.
AG160	5' 3"	Wood Finish	10,760.
AG170	5' 7"	Polished Ebony	11,160.
AG170	5' 7"	Wood Finish	11,560.
AG185	6' 1"	Polished Ebony	13,160.
AG185	6' 1"	Wood Finish	13,560.
All models		With Round or Curved Legs, add'l	200.

Astin-Weight

Verticals

U-500	50"	Oiled Oak	14,180.
U-500	50"	Santa Fe Oiled Oak	15,580.
U-500	50"	Lacquer Oak	14,580.
U-500	50"	Oiled Walnut	14,780.
U-500	50"	Lacquer Walnut	15,180.

Grands

———	5' 9"	Satin Ebony	36,500.

Model	Size	Style and Finish	Price*

Baldwin

Verticals

Model	Size	Style and Finish	Price*
660E	43½"	Satin Mahogany	5,398.
662E	43½"	French Provincial Satin Cherry	5,398.
667E	43½"	Country French Satin Oak	5,398.
2090E	43½"	Satin Mahogany	6,120.
2095E	43½"	Satin Oak	6,120.
2096E	43½"	French Provincial Satin Cherry	6,120.
243E	45"	Satin Ebony/Oak/Walnut	6,312.
243Elvis	45"	Elvis Presley Signature	12,134.
BBK 243	45"	BB King Polished Ebony	14,820.
GSV10	45"	Gibson Les Paul Signature	17,160.
5050E	45"	Satin Mahogany	12,030.
5052E	45"	Satin Cherry	12,030.
5057E	45"	Satin Oak	12,030.
5062E	45"	Queen Anne Distressed Satin Cherry	12,690.
248E	48"	Satin Walnut	9,190.
6000E	52"	Satin Ebony/Mahogany	16,420.
6000E	52"	Satin Cherry with Gold Trim	17,950.

Grands

Model	Size	Style and Finish	Price*
M1	5' 2"	Satin Ebony	31,806.
M1	5' 2"	Polished Ebony	33,872.
M1	5' 2"	Satin Mahogany/Walnut	34,832.
M1	5' 2"	Polished Mahogany/Walnut/Cherry	36,912.
225E	5' 2"	French Provincial Satin Cherry	41,552.
R1	5' 8"	Satin Ebony	35,706.
R1	5' 8"	Polished Ebony	38,032.
R1	5' 8"	Satin Mahogany/Walnut/Cherry	39,372.
R1	5' 8"	Polished Mahogany/Walnut	41,624.
226E	5' 8"	French Provincial Satin and Polished Cherry	46,272.
227E	5' 8"	Louis XVI Satin Mahogany	46,272.
BBK 58L	5' 8"	BB King (includes Lucille Guitar)	48,800.
L1	6' 3"	Satin Ebony	40,146.
L1	6' 3"	Polished Ebony	42,588.
L1	6' 3"	Satin Mahogany/Walnut	44,336.
L1	6' 3"	Polished Mahogany/Walnut/Cherry	46,784.
SF10E	7'	Satin Ebony	55,986.
SF10E	7'	Polished Ebony	60,608.
SD10	9'	Satin Ebony	87,636.
SD10	9'	Polished Ebony	99,920.

Model	Size	Style and Finish	Price*

ConcertMaster (approximate, including installation by factory or dealer)

Grands		ConcertMaster CD	5,406.
		ConcertMaster with Playback only	7,024.
		ConcertMaster with Performance Option	8,058.
		With stop rail, add $314	

Note: Discounts may apply, especially as an incentive to purchase the piano.

Baldwin, D.H.

Verticals

562	43½"	Satin Cherry	3,700.
569	43½"	Satin Ebony	3,700.
E100	43½"	Polished Ebony/Mahogany/Cherry	4,798.

Bechstein, (C.)

Models beginning with "A" say only "Bechstein" on the fallboard. Others say "C. Bechstein."

Bechstein Verticals

A-3	45½"	Polished Ebony	17,000.
A-3	45½"	Satin Mahogany/Walnut/Cherry	17,000.
A-3	45½"	Polished Mahogany/Walnut/Cherry/White	18,000.
A-3	45½"	Satin Alder/Beech	16,200.
A-2	47½"	Polished Ebony	18,000.
A-2	47½"	Satin Mahogany/Walnut/Cherry	18,000.
A-2	47½"	Polished Mahogany/Walnut/Cherry	19,000.
A-2	47½"	Polished White	18,800.
A-2	47½"	Polished Blue	19,600.
A-1	49½"	Polished Ebony	19,400.
A-1	49½"	Satin Mahogany/Walnut/Cherry	19,400.
A-1	49½"	Polished Mahogany/White	20,800.
A-1	49½"	Polished Walnut/Cherry	21,200.

C. Bechstein Verticals

Balance	45½"	Continental Polished Ebony	26,600.
Classic 118	46½"	Polished Ebony	22,600.
Classic 118	46½"	Satin Beech	21,200.
Classic 118	46½"	Satin Cherry	22,800.
Classic 118	46½"	Polished Walnut/Cherry/Mahogany	24,400.
Contur 118	46½"	Polished Ebony	24,000.
Contur 118	46½"	Satin Cherry	24,000.
Contur 118	46½"	Polished Cherry	25,600.
Contur 118	46½"	Satin Alder	22,400.
Avance	46½"	Polished Ebony	33,000.
Classic 124	49"	Polished Ebony	30,200.

*For explanation of terms and prices, please see pages 113–117.

Model	Size	Style and Finish	Price*

Bechstein, C. (continued)

Model	Size	Style and Finish	Price*
Classic 124	49"	Satin Walnut/Mahogany/Cherry	30,200.
Classic 124	49"	Polished Walnut/Mahogany/Cherry	31,800.
Elegance 124	49"	Polished Ebony	32,400.
Elegance 124	49"	Satin Walnut/Cherry	32,400.
Elegance 124	49"	Polished Walnut/Mahogany/Cherry	35,800.
Ars Nova	49"	Polished Ebony	37,000.
Concert 8	51½"	Polished Ebony	45,600.
Concert 8	51½"	Satin Walnut/Mahogany/Cherry	45,600.
Concert 8	51½"	Polished Walnut/Mahogany	47,800.
Concert 8	51½"	Special Woods	56,200.

Bechstein Grands

Model	Size	Style and Finish	Price*
A-160	5' 3"	Polished Ebony	45,600.
A-160	5' 3"	Polished Mahogany	48,000.
A-160	5' 3"	Polished White	50,000.
A-160	5' 3"	Special Woods	55,200.
A-190	6' 3"	Polished Ebony	53,800.
A-190	6' 3"	Polished Mahogany	55,800.
A-190	6' 3"	Polished White	58,200.
A-190	6' 3"	Special Woods	65,400.
A-208	6' 10"	Polished Ebony	60,200.
A-208	6' 10"	Polished Mahogany	63,200.
A-208	6' 10"	Polished White	65,600.
A-208	6' 10"	Special Woods	72,200.
A-228	7' 5"	Polished Ebony	70,600.

C. Bechstein Grands

Model	Size	Style and Finish	Price*
L-167	5' 6"	Ebony and Polished Ebony	82,600.
L-167	5' 6"	Satin Mahogany/Walnut/Cherry	82,000.
L-167	5' 6"	Polished Mahogany/Walnut/Cherry/White	87,200.
L-167	5' 6"	Special Woods	98,200.
M/P 192	6' 4"	Satin and Polished Ebony	95,800.
M/P 192	6' 4"	Satin Mahogany/Walnut/Cherry	95,800.
M/P 192	6' 4"	Polished Mahogany/Walnut/Cherry/White	101,000.
M/P 192	6' 4"	Special Woods	113,000.
B-210	6' 11"	Satin and Polished Ebony	114,400.
C-234	7' 8"	Polished Ebony	143,400.
D-280	9' 2"	Polished Ebony	186,600.

Bergmann

Verticals

Model	Size	Style and Finish	Price*
BT-109	43"	Continental Polished Ebony	3,716.
BT-109	43"	Continental Polished Mahogany	3,796.
BT-109	43"	Continental Polished Ivory	3,716.

Model	Size	Style and Finish	Price*
BAF-108	43"	Satin Mahogany	4,196.
BAF-108	43"	Queen Anne Satin Oak/Cherry	4,196.
BAF-108	43"	Mediterranean Satin Oak	4,196.
BAF-108	43"	French Provincial Satin Cherry	4,196.
BT-116	46½"	Satin Oak/Walnut	4,396.
BT-116E	46½"	Polished Ebony with Chrome	4,396.
BT-116E	46½"	Polished Mahogany with Chrome	4,476.
BT-121	48"	Polished Ebony	4,356.
BT-121	48"	Polished Mahogany	4,476.
BT-131	52"	Polished Ebony	4,596.
BT-131	52"	Polished Mahogany	4,716.

Grands

Model	Size	Style and Finish	Price*
BTG-150	4' 11"	Polished Ebony/Ivory	9,636.
BTG-150	4' 11"	Polished Mahogany	9,836.
BTG-150	4' 11"	Satin Walnut/Cherry	9,836.
BTG-150C	4' 11"	French Provicial Satin Cherry	9,916.
BTG-157	5' 2"	Satin and Polished Ebony	10,676.
BTG-157	5' 2"	Polished Mahogany	10,796.
BTG-157	5' 2"	Satin Walnut/Cherry	10,796.
BTG-157	5' 2"	Polished Ivory/White	10,676.
BTG-175	5' 9"	Satin and Polished Ebony	11,916.
BTG-175	5' 9"	Polished Mahogany	12,116.
BTG-185	6' 1"	Satin and Polished Ebony	12,796.
BTG-185	6' 1"	Polished Mahogany	13,116.

Blüthner

Prices do not include bench.

Verticals

Model	Size	Style and Finish	Price*
I	45"	Satin and Polished Ebony	23,770.
I	45"	Satin and Polished Walnut	25,024.
I	45"	Satin and Polished Mahogany	24,898.
I	45"	Satin and Polished Cherry	24,892.
I	45"	Satin and Polished White	25,024.
C	46"	Satin and Polished Ebony	25,128.
C	46"	Satin and Polished Walnut	26,588.
C	46"	Satin and Polished Mahogany	26,334.
C	46"	Satin and Polished Cherry	26,454.
C	46"	Satin and Polished White	26,588.
C	46"	Satin/Polished Bubinga/Yew/Rosewd/Macassar	28,056.
C	46"	Saxony Polished Pyramid Mahogany	33,154.
C	46"	Saxony Pol. Burl Walnut Inlay/Camphor	33,472.
A	49"	Satin and Polished Ebony	32,004.
A	49"	Satin and Polished Walnut	33,856.

*For explanation of terms and prices, please see pages 113–117.

Model	Size	Style and Finish	Price*

Blüthner (continued)

Model	Size	Style and Finish	Price*
A	49"	Satin and Polished Mahogany	33,534.
A	49"	Satin and Polished Cherry	33,696.
A	49"	Satin and Polished White	33,856.
A	49"	Satin/Polished Bubinga/Yew/RosewdMacassar	35,732.
A	49"	Saxony Polished Pyramid Mahogany	42,224.
A	49"	Saxony Polished Burl Walnut Inlay/Camphor	42,632.
B	52"	Satin and Polished Ebony	35,548.
B	52"	Satin and Polished Walnut	38,652.
B	52"	Satin and Polished Mahogany	38,294.
B	52"	Satin and Polished Cherry	38,468.
B	52"	Satin and Polished White	38,652.
B	52"	Satin/Polished Bubinga/Yew/RosewdMacassar	40,792.
B	52"	Saxony Polished Pyramid Mahogany	48,212.
B	52"	Saxony Polished Burl Walnut Inlay/Camphor	48,680.
—	—	*Sostenuto pedal on vertical piano, add'l*	2,484.

Grands

Model	Size	Style and Finish	Price*
11	5' 1"	Satin and Polished Ebony	64,802.
11	5' 1"	Satin and Polished Walnut	68,552.
11	5' 1"	Satin and Polished Mahogany	67,898.
11	5' 1"	Satin and Polished Cherry	68,230.
11	5' 1"	Satin and Polished White	68,552.
11	5' 1"	Satin/Polished Bubinga/Yew/Rosewd/Macassar	72,346.
11	5' 1"	Saxony Polished Pyramid Mahogany	85,502.
11	5' 1"	Saxony Polished Burl Walnut Inlay/Camphor	86,318.
11	5' 1"	"President" Polished Ebony	72,346.
11	5' 1"	"President" Polished Mahogany	75,246.
11	5' 1"	"President" Polished Walnut	75,964.
11	5' 1"	"President" Polished Bubinga	79,580.
11	5' 1"	Louis XVI Satin and Polished Ebony	75,636.
11	5' 1"	Louis XVI Satin and Polished Mahogany	79,416.
11	5' 1"	Louis XVI Satin and Polished Walnut	78,660.
11	5' 1"	"Kaiser Wilhelm II" Polished Ebony	76,292.
11	5' 1"	"Kaiser Wilhelm II" Polished Mahogany	79,344.
11	5' 1"	"Kaiser Wilhelm II" Polished Walnut	80,104.
11	5' 1"	"Kaiser Wilhelm II" Polished Cherry	79,724.
11	5' 1"	"Ambassador" Satin East Indian Rosewood	88,788.
11	5' 1"	"Ambassador" Satin Walnut	82,214.
11	5' 1"	"Nicolas II" Satin Walnut with Burl Inlay	88,788.
11	5' 1"	Louis XIV Rococo Satin White with Gold	95,366.
11	5' 1"	"Alexandra" Polished Ebony	73,662.
11	5' 1"	"Alexandra" Polished Mahogany	77,342.
11	5' 1"	"Alexandra" Polished Walnut	76,608.
11	5' 1"	Julius Blüthner Edition	88,788.

Model	Size	Style and Finish	Price*
10	5' 5"	Satin and Polished Ebony	74,704.
10	5' 5"	Satin and Polished Walnut	79,026.
10	5' 5"	Satin and Polished Mahogany	78,268.
10	5' 5"	Satin and Polished Cherry	78,648.
10	5' 5"	Satin and Polished White	79,026.
10	5' 5"	Satin/Polished Bubinga/Yew/Rosewd Macassar	83,398.
10	5' 5"	Saxony Polished Pyramid Mahogany	98,560.
10	5' 5"	Saxony Polished Burl Walnut Inlay/Camphor	99,508.
10	5' 5"	"President" Polished Ebony	83,398.
10	5' 5"	"President" Polished Mahogany	86,734.
10	5' 5"	"President" Polished Walnut	87,568.
10	5' 5"	"President" Polished Bubinga	91,738.
10	5' 5"	"Senator" French Satin Walnut with Leather	90,982.
10	5' 5"	"Senator" Jacaranda Satin Rosewood w/Leather	97,046.
10	5' 5"	Louis XVI Satin and Polished Ebony	87,190.
10	5' 5"	Louis XVI Satin and Polished Mahogany	91,550.
10	5' 5"	Louis XVI Satin and Polished Walnut	90,678.
10	5' 5"	"Kaiser Wilhelm II" Polished Ebony	87,946.
10	5' 5"	"Kaiser Wilhelm II" Polished Mahogany	91,466.
10	5' 5"	"Kaiser Wilhelm II" Polished Walnut	92,344.
10	5' 5"	"Kaiser Wilhelm II" Polished Cherry	91,904.
10	5' 5"	"Ambassador" Satin East Indian Rosewood	102,348.
10	5' 5"	"Ambassador" Satin Walnut	94,772.
10	5' 5"	"Nicolas II" Satin Walnut with Burl Inlay	102,348.
10	5' 5"	Louis XIV Rococo Satin White with Gold	109,936.
10	5' 5"	"Alexandra" Polished Ebony	84,916.
10	5' 5"	"Alexandra" Polished Mahogany	89,160.
10	5' 5"	"Alexandra" Polished Walnut	88,310.
10	5' 5"	Julius Blüthner Edition	102,348.
6	6' 3"	Satin and Polished Ebony	81,478.
6	6' 3"	Satin and Polished Walnut	86,194.
6	6' 3"	Satin and Polished Mahogany	85,364.
6	6' 3"	Satin and Polished Cherry	85,778.
6	6' 3"	Satin and Polished White	86,194.
6	6' 3"	Satin/Polished Bubinga/Yew/RosewdMacassar	90,964.
6	6' 3"	Saxony Polished Pyramid Mahogany	107,500.
6	6' 3"	Saxony Polished Burl Walnut Inlay/Camphor	108,536.
6	6' 3"	"President" Polished Ebony	90,964.
6	6' 3"	"President" Polished Mahogany	94,600.
6	6' 3"	"President" Polished Walnut	95,508.
6	6' 3"	"President" Polished Bubinga	100,056.
6	6' 3"	"Senator" French Satin Walnut with Leather	99,230.
6	6' 3"	"Senator" Jacaranda Satin Rosewood w/Leather	105,846.
6	6' 3"	Louis XVI Satin and Polished Ebony	95,094.
6	6' 3"	Louis XVI Satin and Polished Mahogany	99,852.

*For explanation of terms and prices, please see pages 113–117.

Model	Size	Style and Finish	Price*

Blüthner (continued)

Model	Size	Style and Finish	Price*
6	6' 3"	Louis XVI Satin and Polished Walnut	98,902.
6	6' 3"	"Kaiser Wilhelm II" Polished Ebony	95,924.
6	6' 3"	"Kaiser Wilhelm II" Polished Mahogany	99,758.
6	6' 3"	"Kaiser Wilhelm II" Polished Walnut	100,716.
6	6' 3"	"Kaiser Wilhelm II" Polished Cherry	100,244.
6	6' 3"	"Ambassador" Satin East Indian Rosewood	111,636.
6	6' 3"	"Ambassador" Satin Walnut	103,362.
6	6' 3"	"Nicolas II" Satin Walnut with Burl Inlay	111,636.
6	6' 3"	Louis XIV Rococo Satin White with Gold	119,902.
6	6' 3"	"Alexandra" Polished Ebony	92,614.
6	6' 3"	"Alexandra" Polished Mahogany	97,244.
6	6' 3"	"Alexandra" Polished Walnut	96,320.
6	6' 3"	Julius Blüthner Edition	111,636.
6	6' 3"	*Jubilee Edition Plate, add'l*	5,980.
4	6' 10"	Satin and Polished Ebony	96,636.
4	6' 10"	Satin and Polished Walnut	102,222.
4	6' 10"	Satin and Polished Mahogany	101,258.
4	6' 10"	Satin and Polished Cherry	101,740.
4	6' 10"	Satin and Polished White	102,226.
4	6' 10"	Satin/Polished Bubinga/Yew/Rosewd/Macassar	107,882.
4	6' 10"	Saxony Polished Pyramid Mahogany	127,498.
4	6' 10"	Saxony Polished Burl Walnut Inlay/Camphor	128,726.
4	6' 10"	"President" Polished Ebony	107,884.
4	6' 10"	"President" Polished Mahogany	112,202.
4	6' 10"	"President" Polished Walnut	113,276.
4	6' 10"	"President" Polished Bubinga	118,674.
4	6' 10"	"Kaiser Wilhelm II" Polished Ebony	113,768.
4	6' 10"	"Kaiser Wilhelm II" Polished Mahogany	118,322.
4	6' 10"	"Kaiser Wilhelm II" Polished Walnut	119,458.
4	6' 10"	"Kaiser Wilhelm II" Polished Cherry	118,886.
4	6' 10"	"Ambassador" Satin East Indian Rosewood	132,402.
4	6' 10"	"Ambassador" Satin Walnut	122,602.
4	6' 10"	"Alexandra" Polished Ebony	109,846.
4	6' 10"	"Alexandra" Polished Mahogany	115,336.
4	6' 10"	"Alexandra" Polished Walnut	114,238.
4	6' 10"	Julius Blüthner Edition	132,402.
2	7' 8"	Satin and Polished Ebony	108,008.
2	7' 8"	Satin and Polished Walnut	114,252.
2	7' 8"	Satin and Polished Mahogany	113,160.
2	7' 8"	Satin and Polished Cherry	113,712.
2	7' 8"	Satin and Polished White	114,252.
2	7' 8"	Satin/Polished Bubinga/Yew/Rosewd/Macassar	120,578.
2	7' 8"	Saxony Polished Pyramid Mahogany	142,506.

Model	Size	Style and Finish	Price*
2	7' 8"	Saxony Polished Burl Walnut Inlay/Camphor	143,876.
2	7' 8"	"President" Polished Ebony	120,578.
2	7' 8"	"President" Polished Mahogany	125,396.
2	7' 8"	"President" Polished Walnut	126,604.
2	7' 8"	"President" Polished Bubinga	132,640.
2	7' 8"	"Kaiser Wilhelm II" Polished Ebony	127,154.
2	7' 8"	"Kaiser Wilhelm II" Polished Mahogany	132,250.
2	7' 8"	"Kaiser Wilhelm II" Polished Walnut	133,512.
2	7' 8"	"Kaiser Wilhelm II" Polished Cherry	132,882.
2	7' 8"	"Ambassador" Satin East Indian Rosewood	147,982.
2	7' 8"	"Ambassador" Satin Walnut	137,024.
2	7' 8"	Julius Blüthner Edition	147,982.
1	9' 2"	Satin and Polished Ebony	140,116.
1	9' 2"	Satin and Polished Walnut	148,224.
1	9' 2"	Satin and Polished Mahogany	146,808.
1	9' 2"	Satin and Polished Cherry	147,522.
1	9' 2"	Satin and Polished White	148,224.
1	9' 2"	"President" Polished Ebony	156,424.
1	9' 2"	"President" Polished Mahogany	162,692.
1	9' 2"	"President" Polished Walnut	164,242.
1	9' 2"	"President" Polished Bubinga	172,074.

Bohemia

Adjustable Artist Bench included with all pianos.

Verticals

Model	Size	Style and Finish	Price*
113	45"	Satin and Polished Ebony	6,520.
113	45"	Satin and Polished Mahogany/Walnut	6,720.
113	45"	Open-pore Mahogany/Walnut/Cherry	6,540.
113	45"	Polished White	7,100.
121A	48"	Satin and Polished Ebony	7,380.
122A	48"	Demi-Chippendale Satin Walnut/Mahogany	8,600.
122A	48"	Demi-Chippendale Polished Walnut/Mahogany	8,600.
122A	48"	Demi-Chippendale Polished Pomele	9,180.
122A	48"	Chippendale Satin Walnut/Mahogany	8,780.
122A	48"	Chippendale Polished Walnut/Mahogany	8,780.
122A	48"	"Romance" Satin Ebony with Mahogany Oval	9,040.
123A	48"	Satin and Polished Ebony	7,840.
123A	48"	Open-pore Walnut/Mahogany/Cherry	8,000.
123A	48"	Satin and Polished Walnut/Mahogany	8,380.
123A	48"	Polished Pomele	8,780.
123A	48"	Polished White	8,540.
123A	48"	"Exclusive" Satin Ebony with Mahogany Oval	8,240.
122A-123A	48"	With Bohemia/Renner Action, add'l	1,100.
122A-123A	48"	With Full Renner Action, add'l	2,100.

*For explanation of terms and prices, please see pages 113–117.

Model	Size	Style and Finish	Price*
Bohemia (continued)			
125A	49"	Satin and Polished Ebony	8,560.
125A	49"	Satin and Polished Walnut/Mahogany	9,140.
125A	49"	Polished Pomele	9,560.
125A	49"	Polished White	9,320.
125A-BR	49"	125A with Bohemia/Renner Action, add'l	1,200
132	52"	Satin and Polished Ebony	9,500.
132	52"	Polished Mahogany	10,380.
132BR	52"	132 with Bohemia/Renner Action, add'l	1,400.
Grands			
150-B	4' 11"	Satin and Polished Ebony	20,600.
150-B	4' 11"	Polished Mahogany	22,600.
156A-B	5' 2"	Satin and Polished Ebony	25,380.
156A-B	5' 2"	Satin and Polished Walnut/Mahogany	27,800.
156A-B	5' 2"	Hand-Rubbed Satin Ebony/Walnut/Mahogany	29,200.
156A-B	5' 2"	Polished Pomele	33,800.
156A-B	5' 2"	Polished White	27,800.
156A-B	5' 2"	Demi-Chip. Satin and Pol. Walnut/Mahogany	30,740.
156A-B	5' 2"	Chippendale Satin and Pol. Walnut/Mahogany	31,660.
156A-BR	5' 2"	156A-B with Bohemia/Renner Action, add'l	2,000.
170-B	5' 7"	Satin and Polished Ebony	23,000.
170-B	5' 7"	Polished Mahogany	25,200.
170-B	5' 7"	Polished Bubinga	28,200.
173-B	5' 8"	Satin and Polished Ebony	28,780.
173-B	5' 8"	Satin and Polished Walnut/Mahogany	31,200.
173-B	5' 8"	Demi-Chippendale Satin and Polished Ebony	31,180.
173-B	5' 8"	Demi-Chip. Satin and Pol. Walnut/Mahogany	32,200.
173-B	5' 8"	Chippendale Satin and Pol. Walnut/Mahogany	35,180.
185A-B	6' 1"	Satin and Polished Ebony	30,780.
185A-B	6' 1"	Satin and Polished Walnut/Mahogany	33,600.
185A-B	6' 1"	Hand-Rubbed Satin Ebony/Walnut/Mahogany	35,300.
185A-B	6' 1"	Polished White	33,600.
185A-BR	6' 1"	185A-B with Bohemia/Renner Action, add'l	2,400.
185AE-B	6' 1"	Empire Satin and Polished Ebony	32,400.
185AE-B	6' 1"	Empire Satin and Polished Walnut/Mahogany	35,600.
185AE-BR	6' 1"	185AE-B w/ Bohemia/Renner Action, add'l	2,400.
225R	7' 4"	Satin and Polished Ebony (Full Renner)	44,780.
272R	8' 11"	Satin and Polished Ebony (Full Renner)	56,780.

Bösendorfer

Verticals

Model	Size	Style and Finish	Price*
130	52"	Satin and Polished Ebony	45,334.
130	52"	Satin and Polished White, other colors	48,734.

Model	Size	Style and Finish	Price*
130	52"	Polished, Satin, Open-pore: Walnut, Cherry, Mahogany, Pomele, Bubinga, Wenge	50,774.
130	52"	Polished, Satin, Open-pore: Pyramid Mahogany, Amboyna, Rio Rosewood, Burl Walnut, Birdseye Maple, Yew, Macassar	51,774.

Grands

Model	Size	Style and Finish	Price*
170	5' 8"	Satin and Polished Ebony	89,934.
170	5' 8"	Satin and Polished White, other colors	96,678.
170	5' 8"	Polished, Satin, Open-pore: Walnut, Cherry, Mahogany, Pomele, Bubinga, Wenge	99,184.
170	5' 8"	Polished, Satin, Open-pore: Pyramid Mahogany, Amboyna, Rio Rosewood, Burl Walnut, Birdseye Maple, Yew, Macassar	105,020.
170	5' 8"	"Johann Strauss" Satin and Polished Ebony	95,578.
170	5' 8"	"Johann Strauss," other finish	111,320.
170	5' 8"	"Franz Schubert" Satin and Polished Ebony	95,578.
170	5' 8"	"Franz Schubert," other finish	111,320.
170	5' 8"	"Vienna"	146,146.
170	5' 8"	"Senator"	107,590.
170	5' 8"	"Chopin"	131,560.
170	5' 8"	"Liszt"	125,826.
170	5' 8"	"Yacht"	117,742.
170	5' 8"	"Artisan," Satin and Polished	168,570.
170	5' 8"	"Edge"	100,726.
170	5' 8"	Louis XVI & Baroque, add'l	21,624.
185	6' 1"	Satin and Polished Ebony	92,230.
185	6' 1"	Satin and Polished White, other colors	99,148.
185	6' 1"	Polished, Satin, Open-pore: Walnut, Cherry, Mahogany, Pomele, Bubinga, Wenge	103,798.
185	6' 1"	Polished, Satin, Open-pore: Pyramid Mahogany, Amboyna, Rio Rosewood, Burl Walnut, Birdseye Maple, Yew, Macassar	109,984.
185	6' 1"	"Johann Strauss" Satin and Polished Ebony	101,874.
185	6' 1"	"Johann Strauss," other finish	116,502.
185	6' 1"	"Franz Schubert" Satin and Polished Ebony	101,874.
185	6' 1"	"Franz Schubert," other finish	116,502.
185	6' 1"	"Vienna"	146,146.
185	6' 1"	"Senator"	113,462.
185	6' 1"	"Chopin"	134,708.
185	6' 1"	"Porsche Design," Satin and Polished	130,750.
185	6' 1"	"Porsche Design," Polished Colors	139,792.
185	6' 1"	"Liszt"	129,040.
185	6' 1"	"Yacht"	120,750.
185	6' 1"	"Artisan," Satin and Polished	175,802.
185	6' 1"	"Edge"	103,298.

*For explanation of terms and prices, please see pages 113–117.

Model	Size	Style and Finish	Price*

Bösendorfer (continued)

Model	Size	Style and Finish	Price*
185	6' 1"	Louis XVI & Baroque, add'l	21,624.
200CS	6' 7"	"Conservatory" Satin Ebony	73,154.
200	6' 7"	Satin and Polished Ebony	101,718.
200	6' 7"	Satin and Polished White, other colors	109,346.
200	6' 7"	Polished, Satin, Open-pore: Walnut, Cherry, Mahogany, Pomele, Bubinga, Wenge	110,986.
200	6' 7"	Polished, Satin, Open-pore: Pyramid Mahogany, Amboyna, Rio Rosewood, Burl Walnut, Birdseye Maple, Yew, Macassar	116,060.
200	6' 7"	"Johann Strauss" Satin and Polished Ebony	110,986.
200	6' 7"	"Johann Strauss," other finish	130,212.
200	6' 7"	"Franz Schubert" Satin and Polished Ebony	110,986.
200	6' 7"	"Franz Schubert," other finish	130,212.
200	6' 7"	"Vienna"	146,146.
200	6' 7"	"Senator"	121,666.
200	6' 7"	"Chopin"	146,178.
200	6' 7"	"Liszt"	142,316.
200	6' 7"	"Yacht"	137,724.
200	6' 7"	"Artisan," Satin and Polished	180,326.
200	6' 7"	"Edge"	113,924.
200	6' 7"	Louis XVI & Baroque, add'l	21,624.
214CS	7'	"Conservatory" Satin Ebony	79,770.
214	7'	Satin and Polished Ebony	118,488.
214	7'	Satin and Polished White, other colors	127,374.
214	7'	Polished, Satin, Open-pore: Walnut, Cherry, Mahogany, Pomele, Bubinga, Wenge	130,606.
214	7'	Polished, Satin, Open-pore: Pyramid Mahogany, Amboyna, Rio Rosewood, Burl Walnut, Birdseye Maple, Yew, Macassar	135,188.
214	7'	"Johann Strauss" Satin and Polished Ebony	128,188.
214	7'	"Johann Strauss," other finish	143,420.
214	7'	"Franz Schubert" Satin and Polished Ebony	128,188.
214	7'	"Franz Schubert," other finish	143,420.
214	7'	"Vienna"	163,470.
214	7'	"Senator"	132,208.
214	7'	"Chopin"	161,696.
214	7'	"Porsche Design," Satin and Polished	152,544.
214	7'	"Porsche Design," Polished Colors	167,798.
214	7'	"Liszt"	165,776.
214	7'	"Yacht"	155,126.
214	7'	"Artisan," Satin and Polished	205,868.
214	7'	"Edge"	132,706.
214	7'	Louis XVI & Baroque, add'l	21,624.
225	7' 4"	Satin and Polished Ebony	124,224.

Model	Size	Style and Finish	Price*
225	7' 4"	Satin and Polished White, other colors	133,540.
225	7' 4"	Polished, Satin, Open-pore: Walnut, Cherry, Mahogany, Pomele, Bubinga, Wenge	135,256.
225	7' 4"	Polished, Satin, Open-pore: Pyramid Mahogany, Amboyna, Rio Rosewood, Burl Walnut, Birdseye Maple, Yew, Macassar	140,994.
225	7' 4"	"Johann Strauss" Satin and Polished Ebony	135,256.
225	7' 4"	"Johann Strauss," other finish	158,098.
225	7' 4"	"Franz Schubert" Satin and Polished Ebony	135,256.
225	7' 4"	"Franz Schubert," other finish	158,098.
225	7' 4"	"Vienna"	175,668.
225	7' 4"	"Senator"	138,964.
225	7' 4"	"Chopin"	168,442.
225	7' 4"	"Liszt"	173,804.
225	7' 4"	"Yacht"	162,636.
225	7' 4"	"Artisan," Satin and Polished	221,408.
225	7' 4"	"Edge"	139,130.
225	7' 4"	Louis XVI & Baroque, add'l	21,624.
280	9' 2"	Satin and Polished Ebony	161,072.
280	9' 2"	Satin and Polished White, other colors	173,152.
280	9' 2"	Polished, Satin, Open-pore: Walnut, Cherry, Mahogany, Pomele, Bubinga, Wenge	179,410.
280	9' 2"	Polished, Satin, Open-pore: Pyramid Mahogany, Amboyna, Rio Rosewood, Burl Walnut, Birdseye Maple, Yew, Macassar	186,284.
280	9' 2"	"Johann Strauss" Satin and Polished Ebony	176,088.
280	9' 2"	"Johann Strauss," other finish	200,152.
280	9' 2"	"Franz Schubert" Satin and Polished Ebony	176,088.
280	9' 2"	"Franz Schubert," other finish	200,152.
280	9' 2"	"Vienna"	222,026.
280	9' 2"	"Senator"	180,938.
280	9' 2"	"Chopin"	215,444.
280	9' 2"	"Porsche Design," Satin and Polished	202,612.
280	9' 2"	"Porsche Design," Polished Colors	222,874.
280	9' 2"	"Liszt"	225,358.
280	9' 2"	"Yacht"	210,878.
280	9' 2"	"Artisan," Satin and Polished	255,414.
280	9' 2"	Louis XVI & Baroque, add'l	25,948.
290	9' 6"	Satin and Polished Ebony	183,136.
290	9' 6"	Satin and Polished White, other colors	196,872.
290	9' 6"	Polished, Satin, Open-pore: Walnut, Cherry, Mahogany, Pomele, Bubinga, Wenge	202,782.
290	9' 6"	Polished, Satin, Open-pore: Pyramid Mahogany, Amboyna, Rio Rosewood, Burl Walnut, Birdseye Maple, Yew, Macassar	210,114.
290	9' 6"	"Johann Strauss" Satin and Polished Ebony	199,028.

*For explanation of terms and prices, please see pages 113–117.

Model	Size	Style and Finish	Price*

Bösendorfer (continued)

Model	Size	Style and Finish	Price*
290	9' 6"	"Johann Strauss," other finish	222,640.
290	9' 6"	"Franz Schubert" Satin and Polished Ebony	199,028.
290	9' 6"	"Franz Schubert," other finish	222,640.
290	9' 6"	"Vienna"	246,424.
290	9' 6"	"Senator"	203,666.
290	9' 6"	"Chopin"	242,880.
290	9' 6"	"Liszt"	256,228.
290	9' 6"	"Yacht"	239,766.
290	9' 6"	"Artisan," Satin and Polished	269,724.
290	9' 6"	Louis XVI & Baroque, add'l	25,948.
170–280	5' 8"–9' 2"	"CEUS" Computer Grand, add'l	61,402.
290	9' 6"	"CEUS" Computer Grand, add'l	67,682.

Boston

Verticals

Model	Size	Style and Finish	Price*
UP-118E	46"	Satin and Polished Ebony	10,620.
UP-118E	46"	Satin Walnut	11,790.
UP-118E	46"	Polished Walnut/Mahogany	12,020.
UP-118E	46"	Polished White	11,860.
UP-118A	46"	Art Deco Satin Aniegre	8,790.
UP-118S	46"	Open-Pore Honey Oak/Black Oak/Red Oak	6,940.
UP-118S	46"	Satin Mahogany	8,400.
UP-126E	50"	Satin and Polished Ebony	12,720.
UP-126E	50"	Polished Mahogany	14,560.
UP-132E	52"	Polished Ebony	13,900.

Grands

Model	Size	Style and Finish	Price*
GP-156	5' 1"	Satin and Polished Ebony	17,990.
GP-163	5' 4"	Satin Ebony	21,340.
GP-163	5' 4"	Polished Ebony	21,900.
GP-163	5' 4"	Satin Mahogany	23,280.
GP-163	5' 4"	Polished Mahogany	23,900.
GP-163	5' 4"	Satin Walnut	23,480.
GP-163	5' 4"	Polished Walnut	24,160.
GP-163	5' 4"	Polished White/Ivory	22,480.
GP-178	5' 10"	Satin Ebony	24,500.
GP-178	5' 10"	Polished Ebony	25,100.
GP-178	5' 10"	Satin Mahogany	26,140.
GP-178	5' 10"	Polished Mahogany	26,840.
GP-178	5' 10"	Satin Walnut	26,440.
GP-178	5' 10"	Polished Walnut	27,320.
GP-178	5' 10"	Polished White/Ivory	25,620.
GP-193	6' 4"	Satin Ebony	30,920.

Model	Size	Style and Finish	Price*
GP-193	6' 4"	Polished Ebony	31,700.
GP-193	6' 4"	Satin Walnut	34,360.
GP-193	6' 4"	Polished Mahogany	34,600.
GP-193	6' 4"	Polished White	33,320.
GP-215	7' 1"	Satin Ebony	39,720.
GP-215	7' 1"	Polished Ebony	40,700.

Breitmann

Verticals

B110	44"	Polished Ebony	4,220.
B110	44"	Polished Mahogany/Walnut	4,280.
B120	47¼"	Polished Ebony	4,510.
B120	47¼"	Polished Mahogany/Walnut	4,580.
B122	48"	Polished Ebony	4,850.
B122	48"	Polished Mahogany/Walnut	4,940.
B130	52"	Polished Ebony	5,190.
B130	52"	Polished Mahogany/Walnut	5,530.
B130	52"	Polished White	5,480.

Grands

B16	5' 2"	Polished Ebony	10,550.
B16	5' 2"	Polished White	10,700.
B17	5' 8"	Polished Ebony	11,450.

Brodmann

Verticals

BU 116	45"	Polished Ebony	5,100.
BU 121	47"	Polished Ebony	5,500.
BU 123C	48"	Italian Provincial Satin Cherry	6,190.
BU 123M	48"	French Provincial Satin Mahogany	6,190.
BU 123W	48"	Satin Walnut	6,190.
BU 125	49"	Polished Ebony	6,100.
BU 128	50"	Polished Ebony	7,480.
BU 132	52"	Polished Ebony	8,580.

"European Premium" Verticals

SB 121	47"	Polished Ebony	15,060.
SB 121	47"	Polished Mahogany/Walnut	15,590.
VE 125	48"	Polished Ebony with Exotic Wood Panels	14,995.
VE 125	48"	Polished Mahogany	15,995.
VE 125	48"	Polished Pyramid Mahogany	15,995.
VE 125	48"	Polished Bubinga/Pommele	15,995.
VE 125	48"	Polished Rosewood	15,995.

*For explanation of terms and prices, please see pages 113–117.

Model	Size	Style and Finish	Price*

Brodmann (continued)

Grands

BG 150	4' 11"	Polished Ebony	12,580.
BG 162	5' 4"	Polished Ebony	13,780.
BG 187	6' 2"	Polished Ebony	14,780.
BG 212	7'	Polished Ebony	24,780.
BG 228	7' 5"	Polished Ebony	30,780.
BG 275	9'	Polished Ebony *(available 2008)*	

Cable, Hobart M. — see "Sejung"

Cable-Nelson

Verticals

CN 116	45"	Polished Ebony	4,190.
CN 216	45"	Satin Walnut	3,990.

Chase, A. B.

Verticals

EV-112	44"	Continental Polished Ebony	3,380.
EV-112	44"	Continental Polished Mahogany	3,500.
EV-113	45"	Polished Ebony	3,580.
EV-113	45"	Polished Mahogany	3,700.
EV-115CB	45"	Chippendale Polished Mahogany	3,900.
EV-121	48"	Polished Ebony	3,980.
EV-121	48"	Polished Mahogany	4,100.

Grands

EV-152	5'	Polished Ebony	8,780.
EV-152	5'	Polished Mahogany/Walnut	9,280.
EV-152	5'	Polished Sapele	9,480.
EV-152	5'	Polished White	9,280.
EV-165	5' 5"	Polished Ebony	9,780.
EV-165	5' 5"	Polished Mahogany/Walnut	10,280.
EV-185	6' 1"	Polished Ebony	11,780.
EV-185	6' 1"	Polished Mahogany	12,280.

Conover Cable

Verticals

CC-142	42"	Continental Polished Ebony	3,990.
CC-142	42"	Continental Satin Walnut/Cherry	3,990.
CC-142	42"	Continental Polished Mahogany/Walnut/Ivory	4,090.
CC-043F	43"	French Provincial Satin Cherry	4,390.

Model	Size	Style and Finish	Price*
CC-043T	43"	Satin Mahogany	4,390.
CC-145	45"	Polished Ebony	4,490.
CC-145	45"	Satin Walnut/Cherry	4,490.
CC-145	45"	Polished Mahogany/Walnut/Ivory	4,590.
CC-247	46½"	Satin and Polished Ebony	6,190.
CC-247	46½"	Satin Walnut/Mahogany	6,190.
CC-247	46½"	Polished Walnut/Mahogany	6,190.
CC-121M	48"	Mediterranean Polished Ebony	5,190.
CC-121M	48"	Mediterranean Polished Mahogany	5,290.
CC-131	52"	Polished Ebony	5,890.
CC-132	52"	Polished Mahogany	5,990.

Grands

Model	Size	Style and Finish	Price*
CCIG-50	4' 11½"	Satin Ebony	11,790.
CCIG-50	4' 11½"	Polished Ebony	11,090.
CCIG-50	4' 11½"	Satin Mahogany/Walnut	11,790.
CCIG-50	4' 11½"	Polished Mahogany/Walnut	11,790.
CCIG-54	5' 3"	Satin Ebony	12,490.
CCIG-54	5' 3"	Polished Ebony	11,790.
CCIG-54	5' 3"	Satin Mahogany/Walnut	12,490.
CCIG-54	5' 3"	Polished Mahogany/Walnut	12,490.
CCIG-57	5' 7"	Satin Ebony	14,190.
CCIG-57	5' 7"	Polished Ebony	13,290.
CCIG-57	5' 7"	Satin Mahogany/Walnut	14,190.
CCIG-57	5' 7"	Polished Mahogany/Walnut	14,190.
CCIG-61	6' 1"	Satin Ebony	15,390.
CCIG-61	6' 1"	Polished Ebony	14,490.
CCIG-61	6' 1"	Satin Mahogany/Walnut	15,390.
CCIG-61	6' 1"	Polished Mahogany/Walnut	15,390.

Cristofori

Verticals

Model	Size	Style and Finish	Price*
CRV430C	43"	Continental Polished Ebony	3,598.
CRV430C	43"	Continental Polished Mahogany/Walnut	3,798.
CRV430C	43"	Continental Satin Walnut/Oak	3,798.
CRV440P	44"	Satin Ebony	4,298.
CRV440P	44"	Polished Ebony	4,198.
CRV440P	44"	Polished Mahogany/Walnut	4,398.
CRV440P	44"	Satin Walnut/Oak	4,398.
CRV445F	44½"	French Provincial Satin Cherry	4,598.
CRV445T	44½"	Satin Cherry	4,598.
CRV445M	44½"	Mediterranean Satin Oak	4,598.
CRV460F	46"	French Provincial Satin Cherry	5,198.

*For explanation of terms and prices, please see pages 113–117.

Model	Size	Style and Finish	Price*
Cristofori (continued)			
CRV460CF	46"	Country French Satin Oak	5,198.
CRV460R	46"	Regency Satin Cherry	5,398.
CRV460SP	46"	School Satin Ebony	4,598.
CRV460SP	46"	School Satin Walnut/Oak	4,798.
CRV470P	47"	Satin Ebony	4,898.
CRV470P	47"	Polished Ebony	4,798.
CRV470P	47"	Polished Mahogany/Walnut	4,998.
CRV470P	47"	Satin Walnut/Oak	4,998.
CRV480P	48"	Satin Ebony	5,698.
CRV480P	48"	Polished Ebony	5,598.
CRV480P	48"	Polished Mahogany/Walnut	5,798.
CRV480P	48"	Satin Walnut/Oak	5,798.
Grands			
G42/CRG48L	4' 8"	"Vivace" Satin Ebony	7,648.
G42/CRG48L	4' 8"	"Vivace" Polished Ebony	7,398.
G42/CRG48L	4' 8"	"Vivace" Polished Mahogany/Walnut	7,748.
G42/CRG48L	4' 8"	"Vivace" Satin Walnut/Oak	7,748.
G42/CRG48L	4' 8"	"Vivace" French Provincial Satin Cherry	8,098.
G42/CRG48L	4' 8"	"Vivace" Satin Bubinga	8,098.
CRG48	4' 8"	Satin Ebony	8,448.
CRG48	4' 8"	Polished Ebony	8,198.
CRG48	4' 8"	Polished Mahogany/Walnut	8,548.
CRG48	4' 8"	Satin Walnut/Oak	8,548.
CRG48	4' 8"	French Provincial Satin Cherry	8,898.
CRG48	4' 8"	Satin Bubinga	8,898.
CRG50	5'	Satin Ebony	9,048.
CRG50	5'	Polished Ebony	8,798.
CRG50	5'	Polished Mahogany/Walnut	9,148.
CRG50	5'	Satin Walnut/Oak	9,148.
CRG50	5'	French Provincial Satin Cherry	9,498.
CRG50	5'	Satin Bubinga	9,498.
CRG54	5' 4"	Satin Ebony	10,248.
CRG54	5' 4"	Polished Ebony	9,998.
CRG54	5' 4"	Polished Mahogany/Walnut	10,348.
CRG54	5' 4"	Satin Walnut/Oak	10,348.
CRG54	5' 4"	French Provincial Satin Cherry	10,698.
CRG54	5' 4"	Satin Bubinga	10,698.
CRG58	5' 8"	Satin Ebony	11,048.
CRG58	5' 8"	Polished Ebony	10,798.
CRG58	5' 8"	Polished Mahogany/Walnut	11,148.
CRG58	5' 8"	Satin Walnut/Oak	11,148.
CRG58	5' 8"	French Provincial Satin Cherry	11,498.
CRG58	5' 8"	Satin Bubinga	11,498.

Model	Size	Style and Finish	Price*
CRG62	6' 2"	Satin Ebony	12,448.
CRG62	6' 2"	Polished Ebony	12,198.
CRG62	6' 2"	Polished Mahogany/Walnut	12,548.
CRG62	6' 2"	Satin Walnut/Oak	12,548.
CRG62	6' 2"	French Provincial Satin Cherry	12,898.
CRG62	6' 2"	Satin Bubinga	12,898.

Ebel, Carl

Verticals
115	45"	Polished Ebony	5,990.
115	45"	Polished Mahogany/Walnut/Oak	6,190.
121	48"	Polished Ebony	6,350.
121	48"	Polished Mahogany/Walnut	6,580.

Grands
G-151	4' 11½"	Polished Ebony	11,790.
G-151	4' 11½"	Polished Mahogany/Walnut/Oak/White	12,290.
G-151	4' 11½"	Satin Finishes	12,290.
G-151	4' 11½"	Polished Ebony (round leg)	12,090.
G-151	4' 11½"	Polished Mahogany/Walnut (round leg)	12,590.
G-151	4' 11½"	Satin Finishes (round leg)	12,590.
G-151	4' 11½"	Polished Ebony (curved leg)	12,090.
G-151	4' 11½"	Polished Mahogany/Walnut (curved leg)	12,590.
G-151	4' 11½"	Satin Finishes (curved leg)	12,590.
G-151	4' 11½"	Ebony w/Sapeli Fallboard Front	12,290.
G-151	4' 11½"	Ebony w/Bubinga Fallbrd. & Lid Underside	14,290.
G-151	4' 11½"	Ebony w/Sapeli Fallboard & Lid Underside	12,590.

Essex

Verticals
EUP-108C	43"	Continental Polished Ebony	4,570.
EUP-111E	44"	Polished Ebony	4,910.
EUP-111E	44"	Polished Sapele Mahogany	5,010.
EUP-111E	44"	Polished Walnut	5,030.
EUP-111E	44"	Polished White	4,940.
EUP-111F	44"	French Provincial Satin Cherry	5,050.
EUP-111M	44"	Modern Satin Walnut	4,870.
EUP-111R	44"	English Regency Satin Sapele Mahogany	4,770.
EUP-111T	44"	Transitional Satin Ash	4,810.
EUP-116E	45"	Polished Ebony	5,290.
EUP-116E	45"	Polished Sapele Mahogany	5,390.
EUP-116E	45"	Polished Walnut	5,390.
EUP-116E	45"	Polished White	5,290.
EUP-116FC	45"	French Country Satin Cherry	5,390.

*For explanation of terms and prices, please see pages 113–117.

Model	Size	Style and Finish	Price*

Essex (continued)

Model	Size	Style and Finish	Price*
EUP-116CT	45"	Contemporary Satin Sapele Mahogany	5,590.
EUP-116IP	45"	Italian Provincial Satin Cherry	5,590.
EUP-116IP	45"	Italian Provincial Satin Walnut	5,590.
EUP-116QA	45"	Queen Anne Satin Cherry	5,590.
EUP-116ST	45"	Sheraton Traditional Satin Sapele Mahogany	5,590.
EUP-116EC	45"	English Country Satin Walnut	5,790.
EUP-116ET	45"	English Traditional Satin Sapele Mahogany	5,790.
EUP-116FF	45"	Formal French Satin Brown Cherry	5,790.
EUP-116FF	45"	Formal French Satin Red Cherry	5,790.
EUP-123E	48"	Polished Ebony	5,690.
EUP-123E	48"	Satin Sapele Mahogany	5,890.
EUP-123E	48"	Polished Sapele Mahogany	5,790.
EUP-123E	48"	Satin Walnut	5,790.
EUP-123CL	48"	French Satin Walnut	6,190.
EUP-123CL	48"	French Satin Sapele Mahogany	6,300.
EUP-123FL	48"	Empire Satin Walnut	6,190.
EUP-123FL	48"	Empire Satin Sapele Mahogany	6,300.

Grands

Model	Size	Style and Finish	Price*
EGP-155	5' 1"	Polished Ebony	11,790.
EGP-155	5' 1"	Polished Walnut	11,990.
EGP-155	5' 1"	Polished Sapele Mahogany	12,190.
EGP-155	5' 1"	Polished Cherry	12,390.
EGP-155	5' 1"	Polished Kewazinga Bubinga	12,590.
EGP-155T	5' 1"	Polished Ebony	12,190.
EGP-155R	5' 1"	Renaissance Polished Ebony	12,390.
EGP-155T	5' 1"	Polished Walnut	12,590.
EGP-155R	5' 1"	Renaissance Polished Sapele Mahogany	12,790.
EGP-161	5' 3"	Satin Ebony	13,190.
EGP-161	5' 3"	Polished Ebony	12,990.
EGP-161	5' 3"	Satin Sapele Mahogany	14,790.
EGP-161	5' 3"	Polished Sapele Mahogany	14,590.
EGP-161	5' 3"	Satin Walnut	14,790.
EGP-161	5' 3"	Satin Cherry	15,190.
EGP-161	5' 3"	Satin Kewazinga Bubinga	15,390.
EGP-161	5' 3"	Polished White	13,190.
EGP-161N	5' 3"	Neo-Classic Satin Sapele Mahogany	15,790.
EGP-161N	5' 3"	Neo-Classic Polished Sapele Mahogany	15,590.
EGP-161N	5' 3"	Neo-Classic Satin Cherry	16,390.
EGP-161F	5' 3"	French Provincial Satin Walnut	16,190.
EGP-161F	5' 3"	French Provincial Polished Walnut	15,990.
EGP-161F	5' 3"	French Provincial Satin Brown Cherry	16,390.
EGP-161F	5' 3"	French Provincial Satin Red Cherry	16,390.
EGP-173	5' 8"	Polished Ebony	15,190.

Model	Size	Style and Finish	Price*
EGP-173	5' 8"	Polished Walnut	15,590.
EGP-173	5' 8"	Polished Sapele Mahogany	15,790.
EGP-173	5' 8"	Polished Cherry	15,990.
EGP-173	5' 8"	Polished Kewazinga Bubinga	16,590.
EGP-173	5' 8"	Polished White	16,190.
EGP-183	6'	Satin Ebony	18,900.
EGP-183	6'	Polished Ebony	18,640.
EGP-183	6'	Polished Sapele Mahogany	19,850.
EGP-183	6'	Satin Walnut	20,650.

Estonia

The Estonia factory can make custom-designed finishes with exotic veneers; prices upon request. Prices here include Jansen adjustable artist bench.

Grands

Model	Size	Style and Finish	Price*
L168	5' 6"	Satin and Polished Ebony	29,345.
L168	5' 6"	Satin and Polished Mahogany	31,845.
L168	5' 6"	Satin and Polished Walnut	31,845.
L168	5' 6"	Satin and Polished Bubinga	34,615.
L168	5' 6"	"Hidden Beauty" Polished Ebony w/Bubinga	32,605.
L168	5' 6"	"Hidden Beauty" Polished Ebony w/Karelia	34,235.
L168	5' 6"	Satin and Polished White	31,845.
L190	6' 3"	Satin and Polished Ebony	35,865.
L190	6' 3"	Satin and Polished Mahogany	38,650.
L190	6' 3"	Polished Pyramid Mahogany	46,370.
L190	6' 3"	Victorian Satin Pyramid Mahogany	51,500.
L190	6' 3"	Satin and Polished Rosewood	46,370.
L190	6' 3"	Victorian Satin Rosewood	51,500.
L190	6' 3"	Satin and Polished Walnut	38,650.
L190	6' 3"	Satin and Polished Bubinga	41,735.
L190	6' 3"	Satin or Polished White	38,650.
L190	6' 3"	"Hidden Beauty" Polished Ebony w/Bubinga	38,205.
L190	6' 3"	"Hidden Beauty" Polished Ebony w/Karelia	39,100.
L273	9'	Satin and Polished Ebony	87,000.
L273	9'	Satin and Polished Walnut	104,350.
	All sizes	Queen Anne Mahogany, Walnut, White, add'l	3,200.
	All sizes	Victorian Satin Ebony, add'l	3,200.

Everett

Verticals

Model	Size	Style and Finish	Price*
EV-112	44"	Continental Polished Ebony	3,380.
EV-112	44"	Continental Polished Mahogany	3,500.
EV-113	45"	Polished Ebony	3,580.
EV-113	45"	Polished Mahogany	3,700.

*For explanation of terms and prices, please see pages 113–117.

Model	Size	Style and Finish	Price*

Everett (continued)

Model	Size	Style and Finish	Price
EV-115CB	45"	Chippendale Polished Mahogany	3,900.
EV-121	48"	Polished Ebony	3,980.
EV-121	48"	Polished Mahogany	4,100.

Grands

Model	Size	Style and Finish	Price
EV-146	4' 9"	Polished Ebony	7,980.
EV-146	4' 9"	Polished Mahogany	8,480.
EV-152	5'	Polished Ebony	8,780.
EV-152	5'	Polished Mahogany/Walnut	9,280.
EV-152	5'	Polished Sapele	9,480.
EV-152	5'	Polished White	9,280.
EV-165	5' 5"	Polished Ebony	9,780.
EV-165	5' 5"	Polished Mahogany/Walnut	10,280.
EV-185	6' 1"	Polished Ebony	11,780.
EV-185	6' 1"	Polished Mahogany	12,380.

Falcone — see "Sejung"

Fandrich & Sons

Verticals

Model	Size	Style and Finish	Price
126V	50"	Polished Ebony	13,760.
132V	52"	Polished Ebony	14,700.

Grands

Model	Size	Style and Finish	Price
165HGS	5' 5"	Polished Ebony	19,990.
165S	5' 5"	Polished Ebony	15,560.
185HGS	6' 1"	Polished Ebony	20,990.
185S	6' 1"	Polished Ebony	16,560.
215HGS	7'	Polished Ebony	31,900.
215S	7'	Polished Ebony	22,260.

Fazioli

Fazioli is willing to make custom-designed cases with exotic veneers, marquetry, and other embellishments. Prices on request to Fazioli.

Grands

Model	Size	Style and Finish	Price
F156	5' 2"	Satin and Polished Ebony	84,400.
F156	5' 2"	Satin Walnut/Palisander	89,500.
F156	5' 2"	Polished Walnut/Palisander	91,200.
F156	5' 2"	Polished Pyramid Mahogany	94,500.
F156	5' 2"	Polished Burl Woods	101,300.
F156	5' 2"	Solid Colors, Satin or Polished	85,200.
F183	6'	Satin and Polished Ebony	97,500.

Model	Size	Style and Finish	Price*
F183	6'	Satin Walnut/Palisander	103,300.
F183	6'	Polished Walnut/Palisander	105,300.
F183	6'	Polished Pyramid Mahogany	109,200.
F183	6'	Polished Burl Woods	117,000.
F183	6'	Solid Colors, Satin or Polished	98,500.
F212	6' 11"	Satin and Polished Ebony	112,360.
F212	6' 11"	Satin Walnut/Palisander	119,100.
F212	6' 11"	Polished Walnut/Palisander	121,300.
F212	6' 11"	Polished Pyramid Mahogany	125,800.
F212	6' 11"	Polished Burl Woods	134,800.
F212	6' 11"	Solid Colors, Satin or Polished	113,500.
F228	7' 6"	Satin and Polished Ebony	138,840.
F228	7' 6"	Satin Walnut/Palisander	147,200.
F228	7' 6"	Polished Walnut/Palisander	149,900.
F228	7' 6"	Polished Pyramid Mahogany	155,500.
F228	7' 6"	Polished Burl Woods	166,600.
F228	7' 6"	Solid Colors, Satin or Polished	140,200.
F278	9' 2"	Satin and Polished Ebony	167,200.
F278	9' 2"	Satin Walnut/Palisander	177,200.
F278	9' 2"	Polished Walnut/Palisander	180,600.
F278	9' 2"	Polished Pyramid Mahogany	187,300.
F278	9' 2"	Polished Burl Woods	200,600.
F278	9' 2"	Solid Colors, Satin or Polished	168,900.
F308	10' 2"	Satin and Polished Ebony	198,400.
F308	10' 2"	Satin Walnut/Palisander	210,300.
F308	10' 2"	Polished Walnut/Palisander	214,300.
F308	10' 2"	Polished Pyramid Mahogany	222,200.
F308	10' 2"	Polished Burl Woods	238,000.
F308	10' 2"	Solid Colors, Satin or Polished	200,400.
F308	10' 2"	Fourth pedal and two lyres included in price of F308	
All other models		*Fourth pedal, add'l*	10,400.

Feurich

Prices do not include bench

Verticals

F 123	49"	Satin Ebony	25,200.
F 123	49"	Polished Ebony	26,800.
F 123	49"	Polished Mahogany/Walnut	31,240.
F 123	49"	With Fandrich Action, add'l	3,100.

Grands

F 172	5' 8"	Polished Ebony	73,640.
F 172	5' 8"	Polished Sapeli Mahogany/Walnut	78,300.
F 172	5' 8"	Satin Cherry	69,720.

*For explanation of terms and prices, please see pages 113–117.

Model	Size	Style and Finish	Price*

Feurich (continued)

Model	Size	Style and Finish	Price
F 172 ADF	5' 8"	"Old German Style" Satin Ebony	75,160.
F 172 ADF	5' 8"	"Old German Style" Polished Ebony	84,380.
F 172 ADF	5' 8"	"Old German Style" Satin Cherry	75,160.
F 172 C	5' 8"	Classic Polished Ebony	77,530.
F 172 C	5' 8"	Classic Polished Ebony w/Pyramid Mahog.	81,240.
F 172 R	5' 8"	Rococco Polished Walnut	105,840.
F 172 S	5' 8"	Sheraton Polished Mahogany	86,400.
F 227	7' 5"	Polished Ebony	94,240.
F 227	7' 5"	Polished Mahogany/Walnut	101,280.
F 227 ADF	7' 5"	"Old German Style" Satin Ebony	92.890.
F 227 ADF	7' 5"	"Old German Style" Polished Ebony	102,800.
F 227 R	7' 5"	Rococco Polished Walnut	129,860.

Förster, August

Prices do not include bench. Euro=$1.35

Verticals

Model	Size	Style and Finish	Price
116C	46"	Chippendale Polished Ebony	23,362.
116C	46"	Chippendale Satin and Polished Walnut	24,425.
116C	46"	Chippendale Satin and Polished Mahogany	23,447.
116C	46"	Chippendale Polished White	23,858.
116D	46"	Continental Polished Ebony	18,684.
116D	46"	Continental Satin and Polished Walnut	19,846.
116D	46"	Continental Satin and Polished Mahogany	18,755.
116D	46"	Continental Polished White	19,208.
116E	46"	Polished Ebony	22,129.
116E	46"	Satin and Polished Walnut	23,206.
116E	46"	Satin and Polished Mahogany	22,214.
116E	46"	Polished White	22,625.
125G	49"	Polished Ebony	23,801.
125G	49"	Satin and Polished Walnut	24,978.
125G	49"	Satin and Polished Mahogany	23,872.
125G	49"	Polished White	24,326.

Grands

Model	Size	Style and Finish	Price
170	5' 8"	Polished Ebony	50,607.
170	5' 8"	Satin and Polished Walnut	52,450.
170	5' 8"	Satin and Polished Mahogany	50,763.
170	5' 8"	Polished White	52,890.
170	5' 8"	*Satin Pyramid Mahogany*	57,794.
170	5' 8"	"Classic" Polished Ebony	57,397.
170	5' 8"	"Classic" Satin and Polished Walnut	65,179.
170	5' 8"	"Classic" Satin and Polished Mahogany	58,531.
170	5' 8"	"Classic" Polished White	61,947.

Model	Size	Style and Finish	Price*
170	5' 8"	*Chippendale, additional*	13,495.
190	6' 4"	Polished Ebony	58,531.
190	6' 4"	Satin and Polished Walnut	60,558.
190	6' 4"	Satin and Polished Mahogany	58,701.
190	6' 4"	Polished White	60,884.
190	6' 4"	*Satin Pyramid Mahogany*	65,718.
190	6' 4"	"Classic" Polished Ebony	64,428.
190	6' 4"	"Classic" Satin and Polished Walnut	72,366.
190	6' 4"	"Classic" Satin and Polished Mahogany	65,562.
190	6' 4"	"Classic" Polished White	68,978.
190	6' 4"	*Chippendale, additional*	13,495.
215	7' 2"	Polished Ebony	65,959.
275	9' 1"	Polished Ebony	123,708.

Grotrian

Prices do not include bench. Other woods available on request. Euro=$1.35

Verticals

Model	Size	Style and Finish	Price
Fried. Grotrian	43½"	Polished Ebony	15,103.
Cristal	44"	Satin Ebony	17,885.
Cristal	44"	Polished Ebony	18,381.
Cristal	44"	Open-pore Oak/Walnut/Beech	17,885.
Cristal	44"	Polished Walnut/White	19,866.
Carat	45½"	Polished Ebony	22,506.
Carat	45½"	Open-pore Oak/Walnut	21,845.
Carat	45½"	Polished Walnut/White	24,320.
College	48"	Satin Ebony	22,778.
College	48"	Polished Ebony	24,924.
College	48"	Open-pore Beech	22,778.
Classic	49"	Polished Ebony	29,706.
Classic	49"	Open-pore Oak/Walnut	27,563.
Classic	49"	Polished Walnut/White	32,181.
Concertino	52"	Polished Ebony	35,107.
	48"–52"	*Sostenuto pedal, add'l*	1,049.

Grands

Model	Size	Style and Finish	Price
Chambre	5' 5"	Satin Ebony	51,665.
Chambre	5' 5"	Polished Ebony	57,272.
Chambre	5' 5"	Open-pore Oak/Walnut	53,479.
Chambre	5' 5"	Polished Walnut/White	62,387.
Cabinet	6' 3"	Satin Ebony	59,087.
Cabinet	6' 3"	Polished Ebony	66,180.
Cabinet	6' 3"	Open-pore Oak/Walnut	62,551.
Cabinet	6' 3"	Polished Walnut/White	71,294.
Charis	6' 3"	Satin Ebony	66,146.

***For explanation of terms and prices, please see pages 113–117.**

Model	Size	Style and Finish	Price*

Grotrian (continued)

Charis	6' 10"	Polished Ebony	74,152.
Concert	7' 4"	Satin Ebony	78,660.
Concert	7' 4"	Polished Ebony	83,879.
Concert Royal	9' 1"	Polished Ebony	104,033.
All models		*Chippendale/Empire, add'l*	3,119.
All models		*CS Style, add'l*	3,969.
All models		*Rokoko, add'l*	11,198.

Gulbransen

Verticals

87050	45"	Satin Oak	4,190.
87058	45"	Satin Cherry	4,190.
87162	47"	Polished Ebony	4,590.
87170	47"	Polished Mahogany	4,590.

Grands

80462	4' 7"	Polished Ebony	8,300.
80462PM	4' 7"	Polished Ebony w/Pianomation CD2000+	12,590.
80662	5'	Polished Ebony	8,900.
80662PM	5'	Polished Ebony w/Pianomation CD2000+	13,590.

Haessler

Prices do not include bench.

Verticals

115 K	45"	Satin and Polished Ebony	16,302.
115 K	45"	Satin Beech/Ash/Waxed Alder	16,016.
115 K	45"	Satin and Polished White	16,918.
118 K	47"	Satin and Polished Ebony	17,874.
118 K	47"	Satin Ebony with Walnut Accent	19,240.
118 K	47"	Satin and Polished Mahogany	18,854.
118 K	47"	Satin and Polished Walnut	18,854.
118 K	47"	Satin and Polished Cherry	20,208.
118 K	47"	Cherry with Yew Inlay, Satin and Polish	20,208.
118 K	47"	Satin Oak	17,094.
118 K	47"	Polished Bubinga	20,438.
118 K	47"	Satin and Polished White	18,624.
118 KM	47"	Satin and Polished Ebony	18,766.
118 KM	47"	Satin and Polished White	19,470.
118 CH	47"	Chippendale Satin and Polished Mahogany	20,164.
118 CH	47"	Chippendale Satin and Polished Walnut	20,164.
124 K	49"	Satin and Polished Ebony	18,986.
124 K	49"	Satin Ebony with Walnut Accent	19,976.

Model	Size	Style and Finish	Price*
124 K	49"	Satin and Polished Mahogany	20,416.
124 K	49"	Satin and Polished Walnut	20,416.
124 K	49"	Satin and Polished Cherry	20,922.
124 K	49"	Cherry with Yew Inlay, Satin and Polish	21,868.
124 K	49"	Satin and Polished White	19,712.
124 KM	49"	Satin and Polished Ebony	19,426.
124 KM	49"	Satin and Polished White	20,130.
132	52"	Satin and Polished Ebony	25,828.

Grands

Model	Size	Style and Finish	Price*
175	5' 8"	Satin and Polished Ebony	49,192.
175	5' 8"	Satin and Polished Mahogany	51,162.
175	5' 8"	Satin and Polished Walnut	51,656.
175	5' 8"	Satin and Polished Cherry	51,414.
175	5' 8"	Polished Bubinga	54,120.
175	5' 8"	Satin and Polished White	57,870.
175	5' 8"	Saxony Polished Pyramid Mahogany	64,912.
175	5' 8"	Saxony Polished Burl Walnut	65,538.
175	5' 8"	"President" Polished Ebony	54,924.
175	5' 8"	"President" Polished Mahogany	57,124.
175	5' 8"	"President" Polished Walnut	57,672.
175	5' 8"	"President" Polished Bubinga	60,412.
175	5' 8"	Louis XV Ebony, Satin and Polished	57,420.
175	5' 8"	Louis XV Mahogany, Satin and Polished	60,292.
175	5' 8"	Louis XV Walnut, Satin and Polished	59,718.
175	5' 8"	Kaiser Wilhelm II Polished Ebony	57,914.
175	5' 8"	Kaiser Wilhelm II Polished Mahogany	60,236.
175	5' 8"	Kaiser Wilhelm II Polished Walnut	60,820.
175	5' 8"	Kaiser Wilhelm II Polished Cherry	60,522.
175	5' 8"	Ambassador Satin East Indian Rosewood	67,408.
175	5' 8"	Ambassador Satin Walnut	62,414.
175	5' 8"	Nicolas II Satin Walnut w/Burl Inlay	67,408.
175	5' 8"	Louis XVI Rococo Satin White w/Gold	72,402.
175	5' 8"	Classic Alexandra Polished Ebony	55,924.
175	5' 8"	Classic Alexandra Polished Mahogany	58,718.
175	5' 8"	Classic Alexandra Polished Walnut	58,158.
186	6' 1"	Satin and Polished Ebony	55,430.
186	6' 1"	Satin and Polished Mahogany	57,640.
186	6' 1"	Satin and Polished Walnut	58,200.
186	6' 1"	Satin and Polished Cherry	57,926.
186	6' 1"	Polished Bubinga	60,972.
186	6' 1"	Satin and Polished White	58,200.
186	6' 1"	Saxony Polished Pyramid Mahogany	73,128.
186	6' 1"	Saxony Polished Burl Walnut	73,832.
186	6' 1"	"President" Polished Ebony	61,876.

*For explanation of terms and prices, please see pages 113–117.

Model	Size	Style and Finish	Price*

Haessler (continued)

Model	Size	Style and Finish	Price*
186	6' 1"	"President" Polished Mahogany	64,350.
186	6' 1"	"President" Polished Walnut	64,978.
186	6' 1"	"President" Polished Bubinga	68,066.
186	6' 1"	Louis XV Ebony, Satin and Polished	64,690.
186	6' 1"	Louis XV Mahogany, Satin and Polished	67,924.
186	6' 1"	Louis XV Walnut, Satin and Polished	67,276.
186	6' 1"	Kaiser Wilhelm II Polished Ebony	65,252.
186	6' 1"	Kaiser Wilhelm II Polished Mahogany	67,860.
186	6' 1"	Kaiser Wilhelm II Polished Walnut	68,518.
186	6' 1"	Kaiser Wilhelm II Polished Cherry	68,190.
186	6' 1"	Ambassador Satin East Indian Rosewood	75,944.
186	6' 1"	Ambassador Satin Walnut	70,312.
186	6' 1"	Nicolas II Satin Walnut w/Burl Inlay	75,944.
186	6' 1"	Louis XVI Rococo Satin White w/Gold	81,566.
186	6' 1"	Classic Alexandra Polished Ebony	63,006.
186	6' 1"	Classic Alexandra Polished Mahogany	66,154.
186	6' 1"	Classic Alexandra Polished Walnut	65,526.

Hailun

Verticals

Model	Size	Style and Finish	Price*
110	43½"	Polished Ebony	3,580.
110	43½"	Polished Mahogany/Walnut	3,780.
116	45½"	Satin Ebony/Walnut (school piano)	4,580.
121	48"	Polished Ebony	4,990.
121	48"	Polished Mahogany/Walnut	5,190.
121C	48"	Polished Ebony (curved legs)	5,190.
121C	48"	Polished Mahogany/Walnut (curved legs)	5,390.
H1	48"	"Estate" Polished Ebony w/Mahogany Trim	4,990.
123	49"	Polished Ebony	5,190.
123	49"	Polished Mahogany/Walnut	5,390.
125	50"	Polished Ebony	5,390.
125	50"	Polished Mahogany/Walnut	5,590.
131	52"	Polished Ebony	5,780.
131	52"	Polished Mahogany/Walnut	6,100.

Grands

Model	Size	Style and Finish	Price*
151	4' 11½"	Polished Ebony	9,990.
151	4' 11½"	Polished Mahogany/Walnut	10,390.
151C	4' 11½"	Polished Ebony (curved legs)	10,390.
151C	4' 11½"	Polished Mahogany/Walnut (curved legs)	10,590.
161	5' 4"	Polished Ebony	10,990.
161	5' 4"	Polished Mahogany/Walnut	11,390.
161	5' 4"	"Georgian" Polished Ebony	10,790.

Model	Size	Style and Finish	Price*
161	5' 4"	"Georgian" Polished Mahogany/Walnut	11,390.
178	5' 10"	Polished Ebony	12,790.
178	5' 10"	Polished Mahogany/Walnut	13,190.
178	5' 10"	"Baroque" Polished Ebony w/Birds-Eye Maple	12,790.
198	6' 5"	Polished Ebony	14,580.
198	6' 5"	Polished Mahogany/Walnut	15,380.
198	6' 5"	"Symphony" Polished Ebony w/Mahog/Walnut	15,380.
218	7' 2"	Polished Ebony	19,380.
277	9'	Polished Ebony	39,980.

Hallet, Davis & Co.

Model numbers ending in "I" use imported veneers from around the world.

Verticals

Model	Size	Style and Finish	Price
H-111GD	44"	Continental Polished Ebony	3,420.
H-111GD	44"	Continental Polished Mahogany/Walnut/White	3,480.
H-111GD I	44"	Continental Polished American Walnut	3,680.
H-115GC	45"	Chippendale Polished Ebony	3,680.
H-115GC	45"	Chippendale Polished Mahogany/Walnut/White	3,720.
H-115GC I	45"	Chippendale Polished American Walnut	3,920.
H-115WH	46"	Polished Ebony	3,720.
H-115WH	46"	Polished Mahogany/Walnut	3,770.
H-115WH I	46"	Polished Walnut	3,970.
H-121WH	48"	Polished Ebony	3,940.
H-121WH	48"	Polished Mahogany/Walnut	4,050.
H-121WH I	48"	Polished American Walnut	4,250.
H-126WH	50"	Polished Ebony	4,590.
H-126WH	50"	Polished Mahogany	4,700.
H-131WH	52"	Polished Ebony	5,700.

Grands

Model	Size	Style and Finish	Price
H-143	4' 8"	Satin and Polished Ebony	7,590.
H-143	4' 8"	Satin and Polished Mahogany	7,990.
H-143	4' 8"	Polished Walnut/White	7,990.
H-143F	4' 8"	Queen Anne Polished Ebony	7,990.
H-143F	4' 8"	Queen Anne Satin and Polished Mahogany	8,390.
H-143F	4' 8"	Queen Anne Polished Walnut/White	8,390.
H-143R	4' 8"	Victorian Polished Mahogany	8,390.
H-152C	5'	Satin Ebony	9,590.
H-152C	5'	Polished Ebony	9,190.
H-152C	5'	Satin Mahogany	9,790.
H-152C	5'	Polished Mahogany/White	9,590.
H-152C	5'	Polished Brown Sapeli Mahogany	9,590.
H-152C I	5'	"Metropolitan" Polished Ebony with Silver	9,590.
H-152C I	5'	Satin Mahogany/Walnut	10,190.

*For explanation of terms and prices, please see pages 113–117.

Model	Size	Style and Finish	Price*

Hallet, Davis & Co. (continued)

Model	Size	Style and Finish	Price*
H-152C I	5'	Polished Mahogany/Walnut	9,990.
H-152D	5'	Victorian Polished Ebony	9,790.
H-152D	5'	Victorian Satin Mahogany	10,390.
H-152D	5'	Victorian Polished Mahogany/Walnut	10,190.
H-152D	5'	Victorian Polished Brown Sapeli Mahogany	10,190.
H-152D I	5'	Victorian Satin Mahogany/Walnut	10,790.
H-152D I	5'	Victorian Polished Mahogany/Walnut	10,590.
H-152S	5'	Queen Anne Polished Ebony	9,790.
H-152S I	5'	Queen Anne Satin Mahogany/Walnut	10,790.
H-152S I	5'	Queen Anne Polished Mahogany/Walnut	10,590.
H-165C	5' 5"	Satin Ebony	10,390.
H-165C	5' 5"	Polished Ebony	9,990.
H-165C	5' 5"	Polished Mahogany/Walnut/White	10,390.
H-165C	5' 5"	Polished Brown Sapeli Mahogany	10,390.
H-165C I	5' 5"	Satin Mahogany/Walnut	10,990.
H-165C I	5' 5"	Polished Mahogany/Walnut	10,790.
H-165D	5' 5"	"Period" Polished Ebony	10,590.
H-165D	5' 5"	"Period" Polished Brown Sapeli Mahogany	10,990.
H-165D I	5' 5"	"Period" Satin Mahogany	11,590.
H-165D I	5' 5"	"Period" Polished Mahogany/Walnut	11,390.
H-185C	6' 1"	Satin Ebony	12,390.
H-185C	6' 1"	Polished Ebony	11,990.
H-185C	6' 1"	Polished Mahogany/Sapeli Mahog./Walnut	12,390.
H-185C I	6' 1"	Satin Mahogany/Walnut	12,990.
H-185C I	6' 1"	Polished Mahogany/Walnut	12,790.
H-185D	6' 1"	"Period" Polished Ebony	12,590.
H-215C	7' 1"	Polished Ebony	18,790.

Hamilton

Verticals

Model	Size	Style and Finish	Price*
W-H100	39"	Continental Polished Ebony (73-note)	2,778.
W-H100	39"	Continental Polished Cherry (73-note)	2,898.
W-H350	42½"	Continental Polished Ebony/Mahogany	3,590.
W-H310	44"	Satin Mahogany/Oak/Cherry	3,790.
W-H360	47"	Classic Polished Ebony/Oak/Mahogany	4,190.
W-H370	47"	Deluxe Console Satin Oak/Mahogany/Cherry	4,590.

Grands

Model	Size	Style and Finish	Price*
W-H391	4' 7"	Polished Ebony/White	8,550.
W-H391	4' 7"	Polished Mahogany	8,750.
W-H396	5' 1"	Satin Ebony	10,090.
W-H396	5' 1"	Polished Ebony/White	9,790.
W-H396	5' 1"	Polished Mahogany	10,090.

Model	Size	Style and Finish	Price*
W-H398	5' 4"	Satin Ebony	10,850.
W-H398	5' 4"	Polished Ebony	10,500.
W-H398	5' 4"	Polished Mahogany	10,850.
W-H399	5' 8"	Satin Ebony	11,598.
W-H399	5' 8"	Polished Ebony	11,198.
W-H399	5' 8"	Polished Mahogany	11,598.
W-H401	6' 2"	Satin Ebony	12,300.
W-H401	6' 2"	Polished Ebony	11,900.
W-H401	6' 2"	Polished Mahogany	12,300.

Hansing, Siegfried

Verticals

Model	Size	Style and Finish	Price*
F 123	49"	Polished Ebony w/ Silver Fittings and Plate	18,030.

Grands

Model	Size	Style and Finish	Price*
F 172	5' 8"	Polished Ebony w/ Silver Fittings and Plate	33,390.

Heintzman & Co.

Verticals

Model	Size	Style and Finish	Price*
121D	47½"	Satin Ebony	5,984.
121D	47½"	Polished Ebony	5,784.
121D	47½"	Satin White	5,984.
121D	47½"	Polished White	5,784.
121D	47½"	Satin Mahogany/Walnut/Cherry	6,028.
121D	47½"	Polished Mahogany/Walnut/Cherry	5,828.
123B	48½"	Satin Ebony	6,516.
123B	48½"	Polished Ebony	6,316.
123B	48½"	Satin White	6,516.
123B	48½"	Polished White	6,316.
123B	48½"	Satin Mahogany/Walnut/Cherry	6,562.
123B	48½"	Polished Mahogany/Walnut/Cherry	6,362.
123E	48½"	Satin Ebony	6,162.
123E	48½"	Polished Ebony	5,962.
123E	48½"	Polished Mahogany	6,006.
123F	48½"	French Polished Ebony	5,962.
123F	48½"	French Polished Mahogany	6,006.
126C	50"	Satin Ebony	6,516.
126C	50"	Polished Ebony	6,316.
126C	50"	Polished Mahogany	6,362.
130A	51"	Satin Ebony	6,856.
130A	51"	Polished Ebony	6,656.
130A	51"	Polished Mahogany	6,700.
132C	52"	Satin Ebony	7,034.
132C	52"	Polished Ebony	6,834.

*For explanation of terms and prices, please see pages 113–117.

Model	Size	Style and Finish	Price*

Heintzman & Co. (continued)

Model	Size	Style and Finish	Price*
132C	52"	Satin Mahogany	7,078.
132C	52"	Polished Mahogany/Walnut/Cherry	6,878.
132E	52"	French Satin Ebony	7,212.
132E	52"	French Polished Ebony	7,012.
132E	52"	French Satin Mahogany	7,256.
132E	52"	French Polished Mahogany/Cherry	7,056.
140CK	52"	Satin Ebony	8,990.
140CK	55"	Polished Ebony	8,790.
140CK	55"	Satin Mahogany	9,036.
140CK	55"	Polished Mahogany/Cherry	8,836.

Grands

Model	Size	Style and Finish	Price*
168A	5' 6"	Satin Ebony	14,850.
168A	5' 6"	Polished Ebony	14,494.
168A	5' 6"	Polished White	14,494.
168A	5' 6"	Satin Mahogany	15,240.
168A	5' 6"	Polished Mahogany	15,028.
168A	5' 6"	Polished Sapele Mahogany	15,400.
203A	6' 8"	Satin Ebony	17,700.
203A	6' 8"	Polished Ebony	17,320.
203A	6' 8"	Polished White	17,320.
203A	6' 8"	Satin Mahogany	18,400.
203A	6' 8"	Polished Mahogany	18,000.
203A	6' 8"	Polished Sapele Mahogany	19,200.
274A	*9'*	*Satin and Polished Ebony*	*on request*

Howard

Grands

Model	Size	Style and Finish	Price*
H52	5' 2"	Satin Ebony	22,550.
H52	5' 2"	Polished Ebony	24,000.
H58	5' 8"	Satin Ebony	25,550.
H58	5' 8"	Polished Ebony	27,200.

Ibach

Verticals

Model	Size	Style and Finish	Price*
B-114	45"	"Classic/Tradition" Open-Pore Beech	16,754.
B-114	45"	"Classic/Tradition" Open-Pore Alder	16,754.
B-114	45"	"Classic/Tradition" Open-Pore Oak	16,754.
B-114	45"	"Classic/Tradition" Open-Pore Maple	17,115.
B-114	45"	"Classic/Tradition" Open-Pore Cherry	17,115.
C-118	46½"	"Elegance" Open-Pore Beech	18,054.
C-118	46½"	"Elegance" Open-Pore Oak	18,054.

Model	Size	Style and Finish	Price*
C-118	46½"	"Elegance" Open-Pore Cherry	18,460.
C-118	46½"	"Elegance" Polished Ebony	18,517.
C-118	46½"	"Elegance" Polished White	19,155.
C-118	46½"	"Elegance" Polished Walnut	19,910.
C-118	46½"	"Elegance" Polished Mahogany	19,910.
C-118	46½"	"Elegance" Polished Cherry	19,910.
C-118	46½"	"Elegance" Polished Burr Walnut	22,057.
C-118	46½"	"Edition (Bruno Paul 1911)" Polished Ebony	21,651.
C-118	46½"	"Edition (Bruno Paul 1911)" Polished White	22,436.
C-118	46½"	"Edition (Bruno Paul1911)" Oiled Oak	22,436.
C-118	46½"	"Antik" Polished Ebony	on request
K-122	48"	"Exclusive" Polished Ebony	on request
H-128	50"	"Edition" Swiss Pear-Tree	on request
L-132	52"	"Tradition" Polished Ebony	26,060.

Grands

Model	Size	Style and Finish	Price*
F-II 183	6'	Polished Ebony	53,731.
F-II 183	6'	Polished Mahogany	59,474.
F-II 183	6'	Polished Burr Walnut	60,912.
F-II 183	6'	*"Edition Ibach Design 1913"*	56,318.
F-II 183	6'	*"Eigenentwurf Ibach Design 1908"*	55,680.
F-II 183	6'	*"Ausfuhrung Art Design"*	66,873.
F-III 215	7' 1"	"Richard Strauss" Polished Ebony	68,064.
F-III 215	7' 1"	*"Klassifizismus"*	115,767.
F-III 215	7' 1"	*"Richard Meier"*	on request
F-IV 240	7' 10½"	"Richard Wagner" Polished Ebony	74,168.

Irmler

Verticals

Model	Size	Style and Finish	Price*
M113E	44½"	Polished Ebony	8,830.
M113E	44½"	Satin Walnut/Beech/Alder	8,560.
M113E	44½"	Satin Mahogany/Cherry	8,750.
M113E	44½"	Polished Walnut/Mahogany/Cherry	8,950.
M113E	44½"	Polished White	9,340.
M122E	48"	Polished Ebony	9,390.
M122E	48"	Polished Ebony with Burl Oval	10,150.
M122E	48"	Satin Walnut	9,140.
M122E	48"	Polished Walnut	9,350.
M122E	48"	Satin Mahogany/Cherry	9,340.
M122E	48"	Polished Mahogany	9,560.
M122E	48"	Polished Cherry	9,530.
M122E	48"	Polished Cherry with Inlay	10,310.
M122E	48"	Satin Beech/Alder	8,950.
M122E	48"	Polished Bubinga	11,020.

*For explanation of terms and prices, please see pages 113–117.

Model	Size	Style and Finish	Price*
Irmler (continued)			
M122E	48"	Polished White	9,920.
Grands			
F16E	5' 5"	Polished Ebony	29,610.
F16E	5' 5"	Satin Walnut/Mahogany	30,500.
F16E	5' 5"	Polished Walnut/Mahogany	31,300.
F16E	5' 5"	Satin Cherry	29,620.
F16E	5' 5"	Polished Cherry	31,910.
F16E	5' 5"	Polished White	30,360.
F18E	5' 11"	Polished Ebony	36,060.
F22E	7' 5"	Polished Ebony	45,210.
F22E	7' 5"	Polished Walnut/Mahogany	48,450.
F22E	7' 5"	Polished White	47,270.

Kawai

Model	Size	Style and Finish	Price*
Verticals			
K-15	44"	Continental Polished Ebony	4,190.
K-15	44"	Continental Polished Mahogany	4,390.
506N	44½"	Satin Ebony	4,390.
506N	44½"	Satin Mahogany/Oak	4,390.
508	44½"	Satin Mahogany/Oak	4,990.
607	44½"	Satin American Oak	5,390.
607	44½"	French Provincial Satin Cherry	5,490.
607	44½"	Queen Anne Satin Mahogany	5,490.
K-2	45"	Satin and Polished Ebony	5,390.
K-2	45"	Satin and Polished Mahogany	5,990.
UST-9	46"	Satin Ebony/Oak/Walnut/Cherry	6,590.
907	46"	English Regency Satin Mahogany	7,790.
907	46"	French Provincial Satin Cherry	7,790.
VT-118	46"	Vari-Touch Satin Ebony/Oak	6,990.
K-3	48"	Satin and Polished Ebony	6,990.
K-3	48"	Satin and Polished Mahogany	7,590.
K-3	48"	Polished White	7,390.
K-5	49"	Satin and Polished Ebony	9,190.
K-5	49"	Polished Sapeli Mahogany	9,790.
K-5	49"	French Provincial Polished Mahogany	10,590.
K-6	52"	Polished Ebony	11,990.
K-8	52"	Satin and Polished Ebony	14,390.
Grands			
GM-10K	5'	Satin and Polished Ebony	10,990.
GM-10K	5'	Polished Mahogany	11,990.
GM-12	5'	Satin and Polished Ebony	13,590.
GM-12	5'	Polished Mahogany/Snow White	14,790.

Model	Size	Style and Finish	Price*
GE-20	5' 1"	Satin and Polished Ebony	15,690.
GE-20	5' 1"	Satin Walnut	17,190.
GE-20	5' 1"	Polished Mahogany/Sapeli Mahogany	17,390.
GE-20	5' 1"	Polished Snow White	16,790.
GE-20	5' 1"	French Provincial Polished Mahogany	18,790.
GE-30	5' 5"	Satin and Polished Ebony	17,790.
GE-30	5' 5"	Satin Mahogany	19,690.
GE-30	5' 5"	Polished Mahogany	19,790.
GE-30	5' 5"	Polished Sapeli Mahogany	19,690.
GE-30	5' 5"	Satin Walnut	19,490.
GE-30	5' 5"	Polished Snow White	18,990.
RX-1	5' 5"	Satin and Polished Ebony	21,190.
RX-1	5' 5"	Satin Walnut	23,590.
RX-1	5' 5"	Polished Walnut/Sapeli Mahogany	24,390.
RX-1	5' 5"	Polished Snow White	23,590.
RX-2	5' 10"	Satin and Polished Ebony	23,790.
RX-2	5' 10"	Satin Walnut/Cherry/Oak	26,790.
RX-2	5' 10"	Polished Walnut/Mahogany	27,790.
RX-2	5' 10"	Polished Sapeli Mahogany	27,790.
RX-2	5' 10"	Polished Rosewood	30,790.
RX-2	5' 10"	Polished Snow White	25,790.
RX-2	5' 10"	French Provincial Polished Mahogany	30,790.
RX-3	6' 1"	Satin and Polished Ebony	30,790.
RX-3	6' 1"	Satin Walnut	34,790.
RX-3	6' 1"	Polished Sapeli Mahogany	36,790.
RX-3	6' 1"	Polished Snow White	32,790.
CR40N	6' 1"	Plexiglass	76,090.
RX-5	6' 6"	Satin and Polished Ebony	34,790.
RX-5	6' 6"	Satin Walnut	38,790.
RX-5	6' 6"	Polished Sapeli Mahogany	40,790.
RX-5	6' 6"	Polished Snow White	36,790.
RX-6	7'	Satin and Polished Ebony	38,790.
RX-7	7' 6"	Satin and Polished Ebony	44,790.
EX	9'	Polished Ebony	111,590.
EXG	9'	Polished Ebony	116,790.

Kawai, Shigeru

Grands

Model	Size	Style and Finish	Price*
SK2	5' 10"	Polished Ebony	37,500.
SK2	5' 10"	Polished Sapeli Mahogany	39,500.
SK2	5' 10"	Polished Pyramid Mahogany	59,500.
SK2	5' 10"	Polished Honduran Mahogany	44,700.
SK2	5' 10"	"Classic Noblesse" w/Burl Walnut Inlay	57,300.
SK3	6' 1"	Satin Ebony	45,700.

*For explanation of terms and prices, please see pages 113–117.

Model	Size	Style and Finish	Price*
Kawai, Shigeru (continued)			
SK3	6' 1"	Polished Ebony	43,700.
SK3	6' 1"	Polished Sapeli Mahogany	46,100.
SK5	6' 6"	Polished Ebony	50,100.
SK5	6' 6"	Polished Sapeli Mahogany	53,100.
SK6	7'	Satin Ebony	58,500.
SK6	7'	Polished Ebony	56,500.
SK7	7' 6"	Polished Ebony	62,500.
SK7	7' 6"	Polished Pyramid Mahogany	93,700.
SK7	7' 6"	"Classic Noblesse" w/Burl Walnut Inlay	85,700.
SK-EX	9'	Polished Ebony	144,800.

Kemble

Verticals

Model	Size	Style and Finish	Price*
Cambridge 12	44"	Continental Polished Ebony	8,250.
Cambridge 12	44"	Continental Satin Mahogany/Walnut	8,050.
Oxford	44"	Satin Walnut	8,250.
Oxford	44"	Satin Mahogany with Inlay	8,690.
Oxford	44"	Polished Mahogany	9,040.
Classic-T	45"	Polished Ebony/Mahogany	9,540.
Classic-T	45"	Polished Ebony and Chrome	9,840.
Classic-T	45"	Satin Mocha Oak	9,440.
Empire	46½"	Empire Polished Mahogany	11,540.
Prestige	46½"	Satin Cherry with Yew Inlay	11,540.
K121CL	48"	Polished Ebony/Mahogany/Walnut	11,050.
K121CL	48"	Satin Walnut	10,780.
K121CLM	48"	"Mozart" Polished Ebony with Oval	12,050.
K121CLM	48"	"Mozart" Polished Mahogany with Inlay	12,050.
Vermont	48"	Satin Cherry	13,050.
Conservatoire	49"	Polished Ebony	12,050.
K131SN	52"	Polished Ebony/Mahogany	15,050.

Grands

Model	Size	Style and Finish	Price*
KC173	5' 8"	Polished Ebony	27,040.

Kimball

Grands

Model	Size	Style and Finish	Price*
K1	5' 1"	Polished Ebony	16,790.
K1	5' 1"	Polished Mahogany	17,390.
K2	5' 9"	Polished Ebony	18,790.
K2	5' 9"	Polished Mahogany	19,590.
K3	6' 2"	Polished Ebony	22,790.

Model	Size	Style and Finish	Price*

Knabe, Wm.

Verticals

Model	Size	Style and Finish	Price*
WKV-118F	46½"	French Prov. Lacquer Semi-Gloss Cherry	9,200.
WKV-118R	46½"	Renaissance Lacquer Polished Ebony	9,100.
WKV-118R	46½"	Renaissance Lacquer Semi-Gloss Walnut	9,200.
WKV-118R	46½"	Renaissance Lacquer Satin American Oak	8,900.
WKV-118T	46½"	Lacquer Semi-Gloss Mahogany	9,200.
WKV-121	48"	Satin Ebony	9,500.
WKV-121	48"	Polished Ebony	9,100.
WKV-121	48"	Polished Mahogany	10,400.
SMR-2200	48"	Contemporary Art Case	11,800.
WKV-131	52"	Satin Ebony	10,400.
WKV-131	52"	Polished Ebony	10,000.
WKV-131	52"	Polished Mahogany	11,400.

Grands

Model	Size	Style and Finish	Price*
WKG-53	5' 3"	Satin Ebony	21,200.
WKG-53	5' 3"	Polished Ebony	20,600.
WKG-53	5' 3"	Lacquer Semi-Gloss Wood Finishes	22,600.
WKG-53	*5' 3"*	*Polished Bubinga/Pommele*	*22,600.*
WKG-58	5' 8"	Satin Ebony	24,600.
WKG-58	5' 8"	Polished Ebony	23,900.
WKG-58	5' 8"	Lacquer Semi-Gloss Wood Finishes	26,000.
WKG-58	*5' 8"*	*Polished Bubinga/Pommele*	*26,000.*
WKG-58A	5' 8"	170th Anniv. Lacquer Semi-Gloss Walnut	30,800.
WKG-58F	5' 8"	French Prov. Lacquer Semi-Gloss Woods	29,200.
WKG-58M	5' 8"	Empire Satin Ebony	25,300.
WKG-58M	5' 8"	Empire Polished Ebony	24,600.
WKG-58M	5' 8"	Empire Lacquer Semi-Gloss Wood Finishes	26,700.
WKG-58M	*5' 8"*	*Empire Polished Bubinga/Pommele*	*26,700.*
WKG-64	6' 4"	Satin Ebony	29,700.
WKG-64	6' 4"	Polished Ebony	29,000.
WKG-64	6' 4"	Lacquer Semi-Gloss Wood Finishes	31,100.
WKG-70	7'	Satin Ebony	37,600.
WKG-70	7'	Polished Ebony	36,800.
WKG-70	7'	Lacquer Semi-Gloss Wood Finishes	37,000.

Kohler & Campbell

Verticals

Model	Size	Style and Finish	Price*
KC-142	42"	Continental Polished Ebony	4,190.
KC-142	42"	Continental Satin Cherry/Walnut	4,190.
KC-142	42"	Continental Polished Mahogany/Walnut/Ivory	4,190.
KC-244F	44"	French Provincial Satin Cherry	5,250.
KC-244M	44"	Mediterranean Satin Brown Oak	5,250.

*For explanation of terms and prices, please see pages 113–117.

Model	Size	Style and Finish	Price*

Kohler & Campbell (continued)

Model	Size	Style and Finish	Price*
KC-244T	44"	Satin Mahogany	5,250.
KC-245	45"	Polished Ebony	4,790.
KC-245	45"	Satin Cherry/Walnut	4,790.
KC-245	45"	Polished Mahogany/Walnut/Ivory	4,890.
KC-247	46½"	Satin and Polished Ebony	6,790.
KC-247	46½"	Satin Mahogany/Walnut	6,790.
KC-247	46½"	Polished Mahogany/Walnut	6,790.
KC-647F	46½"	French Provincial Satin Cherry	5,590.
KC-647R	46½"	Renaissance Satin Walnut	5,590.
KC-647T	46½"	Satin Mahogany	5,590.
KM-647F	46½"	French Provincial Satin Cherry	6,700.
KM-647R	46½"	Renaissance Satin Walnut	6,700.
KM-647T	46½"	Satin Mahogany	6,700.
KC-121M	48"	Satin Ebony	5,290.
KC-121M	48"	Polished Ebony	5,190.
KC-121M	48"	Polished Mahogany	5,290.
KMV-48SD	48"	Satin Ebony	10,100.
KMV-48SD	48"	Polished Ebony	9,700.
KMV-48SD	48"	Polished Mahogany	11,200.
KC-131	52"	Polished Ebony	5,890.
KC-131	52"	Polished Mahogany	5,990.
KMV-52MD	52"	Polished Ebony	10,800.
KMV-52MD	52"	Polished Mahogany	10,800.

Grands

Model	Size	Style and Finish	Price*
KIG-47	4' 7"	Polished Ebony	10,090.
KIG-47	4' 7"	Polished Mahogany	10,790.
KCG-450	4' 9"	Satin Ebony	11,590.
KCG-450	4' 9"	Polished Ebony	10,790.
KCG-450	4' 9"	Lacquer Satin Mahogany/Walnut	11,590.
KCG-450	4' 9"	Polished Mahogany/Walnut	11,590.
KCG-500	5' 1½"	Satin Ebony	12,790.
KCG-500	5' 1½"	Polished Ebony	12,090.
KCG-500	5' 1½"	Lacquer Satin Mahogany and Pol. Mahogany	12,790.
KCG-500	5' 1½"	Lacquer Satin Walnut and Polished Walnut	12,790.
KCG-500KBF	5' 1½"	French Provincial Polished Mahogany/Cherry	15,790.
KCM-500	5' 1½"	Satin Ebony	15,000.
KCM-500	5' 1½"	Polished Ebony	14,300.
KCM-500	5' 1½"	Lacquer Satin Mahogany/Walnut	15,000.
KCM-500	5' 1½"	Polished Mahogany/Walnut	15,000.
KCG-600	5' 9"	Satin Ebony	14,690.
KCG-600	5' 9"	Polished Ebony	13,790.
KCG-600	5' 9"	Lacquer Satin Mahogany and Pol. Mahogany	13,790.
KCG-600	5' 9"	Lacquer Satin Walnut and Polished Walnut	13,790.

Model	Size	Style and Finish	Price*
KCM-600	5' 9"	Satin Ebony	16,300.
KCM-600	5' 9"	Polished Ebony	15,400.
KCM-600	5' 9"	Lacquer Satin Mahogany/Walnut	16,300.
KCM-600	5' 9"	Polished Mahogany/Walnut	16,300.
KCG-650	6' 1"	Satin Ebony	15,990.
KCG-650	6' 1"	Polished Ebony	15,090.
KCG-650	6' 1"	Lacquer Satin Mahogany/Walnut	15,990.
KCG-650	6' 1"	Polished Mahogany/Walnut	15,990.
KCM-650	6' 1"	Satin Ebony	17,400.
KCM-650	6' 1"	Polished Ebony	16,500.
KCM-650	6' 1"	Lacquer Satin Mahogany/Walnut	17,400.
KCM-650	6' 1"	Polished Mahogany/Walnut	17,400.
KFM-700	6' 8"	Polished Ebony	32,800.
KFM-850	7' 4"	Polished Ebony	34,800.

Mason & Hamlin

Verticals

Model	Size	Style and Finish	Price*
50	50"	Satin and Polished Ebony	18,756.
50	50"	Satin Mahogany	19,076.

Grands

Model	Size	Style and Finish	Price*
A	5' 8"	Satin Ebony	47,636.
A	5' 8"	Polished Ebony	50,942.
A	5' 8"	Satin Mahogany/Walnut	51,220.
A	5' 8"	Polished Pyramid Mahogany	62,262.
A	5' 8"	Satin Rosewood/Bubinga	56,492.
A	5' 8"	Polished Bubinga	58,840.
A	5' 8"	Satin Macassar Ebony	60,156.
A	5' 8"	Polished Macassar Ebony	62,262.
A	5' 8"	"Monticello" Polished Ebony	54,266.
A	5' 8"	"Monticello" Satin Mahogany	54,526.
A	5' 8"	"Monticello" Satin Walnut/Rosewood	66,102.
AA	6' 4"	Satin Ebony	54,962.
AA	6' 4"	Polished Ebony	56,744.
AA	6' 4"	Satin Mahogany/Walnut	57,856.
AA	6' 4"	Polished Pyramid Mahogany	66,462.
AA	6' 4"	Satin Rosewood/Bubinga	61,052.
AA	6' 4"	Polished Bubinga	63,040.
AA	6' 4"	Satin Macassar Ebony	64,356.
AA	6' 4"	Polished Macassar Ebony	66,462.
AA	6' 4"	"Monticello" Polished Ebony	60,702.
AA	6' 4"	"Monticello" Satin Mahogany	61,162.
AA	6' 4"	"Monticello" Satin Walnut/Rosewood	74,656.
BB	7'	Satin Ebony	62,288.

*For explanation of terms and prices, please see pages 113–117.

Model	Size	Style and Finish	Price*

Mason & Hamlin (continued)

Model	Size	Style and Finish	Price*
BB	7'	Polished Ebony	64,080.
BB	7'	Satin Mahogany/Walnut	64,494.
BB	7'	Polished Pyramid Mahogany	76,786.
BB	7'	Satin Rosewood/Bubinga	72,196.
BB	7'	Polished Bubinga	73,988.
BB	7'	Satin Macassar Ebony	74,928.
BB	7'	Polished Macassar Ebony	76,786.
BB	7'	"Monticello" Polished Ebony	67,140.
BB	7'	"Monticello" Satin Mahogany	67,800.
BB	7'	"Monticello" Satin Walnut/Rosewood	83,208.
CC	9' 4"	Satin Ebony	92,610.
CC	9' 4"	Polished Ebony	96,810.

May Berlin

Verticals

Model	Size	Style and Finish	Price*
M 114 T	45"	Polished Ebony	5,180.
M 121 T	47½"	Polished Ebony	5,380.
M 121 T	47½"	Satin Beech/Cherry/Walnut	5,380.
M 121 T	47½"	Polished White	5,380.
M 126 N	49½"	Polished Ebony	5,780.

Grands

Model	Size	Style and Finish	Price*
M 162 T	5' 4"	Polished Ebony	14,780.

Meister, Otto

Verticals

Model	Size	Style and Finish	Price*
C-45	45"	Satin Cherry/Oak	3,680.
C-45	45"	French Provincial Satin Cherry/Oak	3,680.
C-45	45"	Italian Provincial Satin Cherry	3,680.
OU-115	45"	Polished Ebony	3,530.
OU-115	45"	Polished Mahogany	3,530.
OU-123K	49"	Polished Ebony	4,790.
OU-123K	49"	Polished Mahogany	4,880.
OU-131K	52"	Polished Ebony	4,990.
OU-131K	52"	Polished Mahogany	5,080.

Grands

Model	Size	Style and Finish	Price*
G-143	4' 8"	Polished Ebony	7,120.
G-143	4' 8"	Polished Mahogany	7,480.
G-143	4' 8"	Empire Polished Ebony	7,480.
G-143	4' 8"	Empire Polished Mahogany	7,560.
G-143	4' 8"	French Provincial Polished Mahogany	7,560.
G-158	5' 2"	Polished Ebony	7,580.

Model	Size	Style and Finish	Price*
G-158	5' 2"	Polished Mahogany	7,980.
G-158	5' 2"	Empire Polished Ebony	7,990.
G-158	5' 2"	French Provincial Polished Mahogany	8,190.
G-168	5' 7"	Polished Ebony	7,880.
G-168	5' 7"	Polished Mahogany	8,280.
G-185	6' 1"	Polished Ebony	9,780.

Miller, Henry F.

Verticals

Model	Size	Style and Finish	Price*
HMV-043	42½"	Continental Polished Ebony	4,100.
HMV-043	42½"	Continental Polished Mahogany	4,200.
HMV-045	43½"	French Provincial Satin Cherry	5,000.
HMV-045	43½"	Italian Provincial Satin Cherry	5,020.
HMV-045	43½"	Mediterranean Satin Oak	5,020.
HMV-047	46½"	Satin Ebony	4,832.
HMV-047	46½"	Polished Ebony	4,738.
HMV-047	46½"	Polished Mahogany	4,832.
HMV-048	48"	Satin Cherry	5,520.

Grands

Model	Size	Style and Finish	Price*
HMG-058S	4' 10"	Satin Ebony	10,410.
HMG-058S	4' 10"	Polished Ebony	10,310.
HMG-058S	4' 10"	Polished Mahogany	10,610.
HMG-063S	5' 3"	Satin Ebony	11,830.
HMG-063S	5' 3"	Polished Ebony	11,580.
HMG-063S	5' 3"	Polished Mahogany	12,030.

Nordiska

Verticals

Model	Size	Style and Finish	Price*
109-CM	43"	Continental Polished Ebony/Mahogany	3,480.
114-MC	45"	French Satin Walnut/Mahogany	4,580.
114-MCH	45"	Satin Walnut/Mahogany	4,580.
116-CB	46"	Chippendale Polished Ebony	4,580.
116-CB	46"	Chippendale Polished Walnut/Mahogany	4,780.
116-MC	46"	Satin Ebony/Walnut	4,580.
118-C GT	47"	Polished Ebony	4,480.
118-MC	47"	Satin Walnut/Mahogany/Oak	4,780.
120-CA	47"	Polished Ebony	4,780.
120-CA	47"	Polished Walnut/Mahogany	4,980.
126-PRO	50"	Polished Ebony	5,580.
126-PRO	50"	Satin Walnut	5,580.
126-PRO	50"	Satin Mahogany	5,780.
131	52"	Polished Ebony	6,180.

*For explanation of terms and prices, please see pages 113–117.

Model	Size	Style and Finish	Price*

Nordiska (continued)

Model	Size	Style and Finish	Price*
131	52"	Satin Mahogany	6,380.

Grands

Model	Size	Style and Finish	Price*
B	4' 8"	Polished Ebony	8,980.
B	4' 8"	Polished Walnut/Mahogany	9,390.
D	5'	Satin and Polished Ebony	9,590.
D	5'	Satin Walnut	10,180.
D	5'	Polished Walnut/Mahogany	10,180.
D	5'	Polished Sapeli Mahogany/White	9,980.
D	5'	Demi-Chippendale Polished Ebony	10,500.
D	5'	Demi-Chippendale Satin Mahogany	11,100.
D	5'	Demi-Chippendale Polished Mahogany/Walnut	11,100.
D	5'	Demi-Chippendale Polished Sapeli Mahogany	10,780.
G	5' 5"	Polished Ebony	10,780.
G	5' 5"	Polished Sapeli Mahogany	11,100.
G	5' 5"	Polished Walnut/Mahogany	11,380.
G	5' 5"	Demi-Chippendale Polished Ebony	11,780.
G	5' 5"	Demi-Chippendale Polished Walnut/Mahogany	12,380.
G	5' 5"	Regency Polished Ebony	11,380.
G	5' 5"	Regency Polished Walnut/Mahogany	11,980.
G	5' 5"	Satin Ebony with Acrylic	24,600.
K	6' 1"	Polished Ebony	12,580.
K	6' 1"	Polished Walnut/Mahogany	13,180.
K	6' 1"	Empire Polished Ebony	13,980.
K	6' 1"	Empire Polished Walnut/Mahogany	14,580.
K	6' 1"	Imperial Polished Ebony	13,180.
K	6' 1"	Imperial Polished Walnut/Mahogany	13,780.
O	7'	Polished Ebony	21,180.
Y	9'	Polished Ebony	53,000.

Palatino

Verticals

Model	Size	Style and Finish	Price*
PUP-121T	48"	Satin Ebony/Brown Mahogany	3,890.
PUP-121T	48"	Polished Ebony	3,690.
PUP-121T	48"	Polished Dark Walnut	3,890.
PUP-121Y	48"	Satin Cherry	3,940.
PUP-123F	48½"	French Polished Ebony	4,398.
PUP-123F	48½"	French Polished Mahogany/Walnut/White	4,598.
PUP-123JH	48½"	French legs w/ Chysanthemum Engraving	4,798.
PUP-123SXH	48½"	French legs with Elodea Vine Engraving	4,798.
PUP-123T	48½"	Satin Ebony/Brown Mahogany/Cherry	4,598.
PUP-123T	48½"	Polished Ebony	4,398.
PUP-123T	48½"	Polished Mahogany/Dark Walnut	4,598.

Model	Size	Style and Finish	Price*
PUP-123T	48½"	Polished White/Red/Wine Red	4,598.
PUP-123TU	48½"	Polished Ebony w/Decorated Wood Panel	5,000.
PUP-123Y	48½"	Polished Ebony	4,398.
PUP-123Y	48½"	Polished Mahogany/Cherry/White/Red	4,598.
PUP-123Y	48½"	Polished Wine Red	4,598.
PUP-126C	50"	French Legs with Carvings	5,198.
PUP-126T	50"	Satin Ebony	4,998.
PUP-126T	50"	Polished Ebony	4,798.
PUP-126T	50"	Polished Mahogany/Cherry/Dark Walnut	4,998.

Grands

Model	Size	Style and Finish	Price*
PGD-46F	4' 6"	French Satin Ebony	8,740.
PGD-46F	4' 6"	French Polished Ebony	8,340.
PGD-46F	4' 6"	French Polished Mahogany/White/Red	8,740.
PGD-46T	4' 6"	Satin Ebony	8,490.
PGD-46T	4' 6"	Polished Ebony	8,090.
PGD-46T	4' 6"	Polished Mahogany/White/Red	8,490.
PGD-50F	5'	French Satin Ebony	9,490.
PGD-50F	5'	French Polished Ebony	9,090.
PGD-50F	5'	French Satin Mahogany/White/Red	9,490.
PGD-50T	5'	Satin Ebony	9,290.
PGD-50T	5'	Polished Ebony	8,890.
PGD-50T	5'	Polished Mahogany/White/Red	9,290.
PGD-59F	5' 9"	French Satin Ebony	11,540.
PGD-59F	5' 9"	French Polished Ebony	11,140.
PGD-59F	5' 9"	French Satin Mahogany/White/Red	11,540.
PGD-59T	5' 9"	Satin Ebony	11,290.
PGD-59T	5' 9"	Polished Ebony	10,890.
PGD-59T	5' 9"	Polished Mahogany/White/Red	11,290.

Pearl River

Verticals

Model	Size	Style and Finish	Price*
UP-108D3	42½"	Continental Polished Ebony	3,660.
UP-108D3	42½"	Continental Polished Mahogany	3,760.
UP-108M2	42½"	Demi-Chippendale Polished Ebony	4,080.
UP-108M2	42½"	Demi-Chippendale Polished Mahogany	4,170.
UP-110P2	43½"	French Provincial Satin Cherry	4,700.
UP-110P5	43½"	Italian Provincial Satin Walnut/Cherry	4,760.
UP-110P6	43½"	French Classic Satin Cherry	5,080.
UP-115E	45"	Satin Ebony/Oak/Walnut	4,500.
UP-115M	45"	Polished Ebony	4,330.
UP-115M	45"	Polished Mahogany	4,370.
UP-115P1	45"	Satin Walnut	5,330.
UP-118E	47"	Polished Ebony	4,560.
UP-118E	47"	Polished Mahogany	4,650.

*For explanation of terms and prices, please see pages 113–117.

Model	Size	Style and Finish	Price*

Pearl River (continued)

Model	Size	Style and Finish	Price
UP-120S	48"	Polished Ebony	5,190.
UP-120S	48"	Polished Mahogany	5,300.
UP-125M1	49"	Polished Ebony (with Yamaha)	6,410.
UP-130T2	51½"	Polished Mahogany w/Burl Oval Inlay	6,900.

Grands

Model	Size	Style and Finish	Price
GP-142	4' 7"	Polished Ebony	9,300.
GP-142	4' 7"	Polished Mahogany	9,850.
GP-142D	4' 7"	French Provincial Satin Cherry	10,430.
GP-142P1	4' 7"	Satin Walnut	10,620.
GP-150	5'	Satin and Polished Ebony	9,810.
GP-150	5'	Satin Cherry	10,340.
GP-150D	5'	Satin Walnut	10,630.
GP-150D	5'	Polished Mahogany	10,630.
GP-159	5' 3"	Satin and Polished Ebony	11,910.
GP-159	5' 3"	Satin and Polished Mahogany	12,230.
GP-170	5' 7"	Satin and Polished Ebony	14,210.
GP-170	5' 7"	Polished Mahogany	15,130.
GP-170D	5' 7"	French Provincial Satin Cherry	15,260.
GP-183	6'	Polished Ebony	15,520.
GP-186	6' 1"	Euro-style Polished Ebony (Silver Plate & Trim)	17,490.
GP-188	6' 4"	Polished Ebony	18,460.
GP-198	6' 6"	Butterfly Lid Blue & Pink/Silver	25,380.
GP-213	7'	Polished Ebony	20,530.
GP-275	9'	Polished Ebony	57,960.

Perzina, Gebr.

Verticals

Model	Size	Style and Finish	Price
GP-112	44"	Continental Polished Ebony	6,190.
GP-112	44"	Continental Polished Mahogany/Walnut/Oak	6,350.
GP-112	44"	Continental Polished White	6,350.
GP-112	44"	Continental Satin Finishes	6,350.
GP-112	44"	Polished Ebony	6,350.
GP-112	44"	Polished Mahogany/Walnut/Oak	6,550.
GP-112	44"	Polished White	6,550.
GP-112	44"	Satin Finishes	6,550.
GP-112	44"	Queen Anne Polished Ebony	6,550.
GP-112	44"	Queen Anne Polished Mahogany/Walnut	6,740.
GP-112	44"	Queen Anne Satin Walnut	6,740.
GP-118	46½"	Continental Satin Ebony	8,590.
GP-118	46½"	Continental Polished Ebony	8,190.
GP-118	46½"	Continental Polished Mahogany/Walnut	8,590.
GP-122	48"	Polished Ebony	7,990.

Model	Size	Style and Finish	Price*
GP-122	48"	Polished Ebony with Pommele Center	8,390.
GP-122	48"	Polished Mahogany/Walnut/Oak/White	8,520.
GP-122	48"	Satin Finishes	8,520.
GP-122	48"	Deco Leg Polished Ebony	8,420.
GP-122	48"	Deco Leg Polished Ebony w/Oak Trim	8,790.
GP-122	48"	Deco Leg Polished Mahogany/Oak/White	8,790.
GP-122	48"	Deco Leg Polished Ebony w/Bubinga Front	8,790.
GP-122	48"	Deco Leg Polished Bubinga	9,220.
GP-122	48"	Queen Anne Polished Ebony	8,420.
GP-122	48"	Queen Anne Polished Mahogany/Walnut	8,790.
GP-122	48"	Queen Anne Satin Walnut	8,790.
GP-122	48"	Queen Anne Polished Ebony w/Molding	8,520.
GP-122	48"	Queen Anne Pol. Mahogany/Walnut w/Molding	9,030.
GP-122	48"	Queen Anne Satin Walnut w/Molding	9,030.
GP-129	51"	Polished Ebony	9,220.
GP-129	51"	Polished Ebony w/Pommele Center	9,450.
GP-129	51"	Polished Mahogany/Walnut/Oak/White	9,750.
GP-129	51"	Satin Finishes	9,750.
GP-129	51"	Queen Anne Polished Ebony	9,450.
GP-129	51"	Queen Anne Polished Mahogany/Walnut	10,020.
GP-129	51"	Queen Anne Satin Walnut	10,020.
GP-129	51"	Queen Anne Pol. Mahogany/Walnut w/Molding	10,370.
GP-129	51"	Queen Anne Satin Walnut w/Molding	10,370.
All models		With slow-fall fallboard, add'l	290.

Grands

On E-series grands, other leg styles and finishes available by special order.

Model	Size	Style and Finish	Price*
E-160	5' 3"	Polished Ebony	25,550.
E-160	5' 3"	Polished Mahogany/Walnut	26,900.
EX-160	5' 3"	Upgrade to Renner AA hammers, etc., add'l	1,050.
G-160	5' 3"	Polished Ebony	18,650.
G-160	5' 3"	Polished Mahogany/Walnut/Oak/White	19,340.
G-160	5' 3"	Satin Finishes	19,340.
G-160	5' 3"	Polished Ebony (round leg)	19,010.
G-160	5' 3"	Satin Mahogany/Walnut (round leg)	19,690.
G-160	5' 3"	Polished Mahogany/Walnut (round leg)	19,690.
G-160	5' 3"	Queen Anne Polished Ebony	19,010.
G-160	5' 3"	Queen Anne Satin Mahogany/Walnut	19,690.
G-160	5' 3"	Queen Anne Polished Mahogany/Walnut	19,690.
G-160	5' 3"	Designer Ebony w/Sapeli Fallboard Front	19,690.
G-160	5' 3"	Designer Ebony w/Bubinga Fallboard/Lid	20,030.
G-160	5' 3"	Designer Ebony w/Sapeli Fallboard/Lid	20,030.
G-160	5' 3"	Designer Satin Bubinga	21,490.
GX-160	5' 3"	Upgrade to Renner AA hammers, etc., add'l	1,050.
E-187	6' 1"	Polished Ebony	28,130.

*For explanation of terms and prices, please see pages 113–117.

Model	Size	Style and Finish	Price*

Perzina, Gebr. (continued)

Model	Size	Style and Finish	Price*
E-187	6' 1"	Polished Mahogany/Walnut	29,510.
EX-187	6' 1"	Upgrade to Renner AA hammers, etc., add'l	1,050.
G-187	6' 1"	Polished Ebony	20,720.
G-187	6' 1"	Polished Mahogany/Walnut/Oak/White	21,760.
G-187	6' 1"	Satin Finishes	21,760.
G-187	6' 1"	Polished Ebony (round leg)	21,070.
G-187	6' 1"	Satin Mahogany/Walnut (round leg)	22,100.
G-187	6' 1"	Polished Mahogany/Walnut (round leg)	22,100.
G-187	6' 1"	Queen Anne Polished Ebony	21,070.
G-187	6' 1"	Queen Anne Satin Mahogany/Walnut	22,100.
G-187	6' 1"	Queen Anne Polished Mahogany/Walnut	22,100.
G-187	6' 1"	Designer Ebony w/Sapeli Fallboard Front	22,100.
G-187	6' 1"	Designer Ebony w/Bubinga Fallboard/Lid	22,430.
G-187	6' 1"	Designer Ebony w/Sapeli Fallboard/Lid	22,430.
G-187	6' 1"	Designer Satin Bubinga	24,430.
GX-187	6' 1"	Upgrade to Renner AA hammers, etc., add'l	1,050.

Petrof

Prices below do not include bench. Add from $220 to $630 (most are under $400), depending on choice of bench.

Verticals

Model	Size	Style and Finish	Price*
P 116 E1	45"	Continental Polished Ebony	7,760.
P 118 C1	46"	Chippendale Polished Walnut/Mahogany	8,780.
P 118 D1	46"	Demi-Chip. Designer Pol. Walnut/Mahogany	8,780.
P 118 G1	46"	Polished Ebony/Walnut/Mahogany	8,380.
P 118 H1	46"	Contemporary Pol. Ebony/Walnut/Mahogany	7,980.
P 118 H1	46"	Polished Walnut with Marquetry	8,380.
P 118 H1	46"	Designer Polished Walnut/Mahogany	8,380.
P 118 H2	46"	Polished Ebony with Brass Trim	8,180.
P 118 P1	46"	Classic Polished Ebony/Walnut/Mahogany	8,580.
P 125 F1	50"	Polished Walnut/Mahogany	9,780.
P 125 F1	50"	Polished Walnut/Mahogany w/Fan Panels	9,980.
P 125 G1	50"	Polished Ebony	9,900.
P 125 H2	50"	Polished Ebony w/Burl Walnut/Brass Trim	10,380.
P 131 E1	52"	Polished Ebony/Walnut/Mahogany	13,180.
P 135 K1	53"	Polished Ebony	17,780.

Grands

Model	Size	Style and Finish	Price*
VI	4' 10"	Polished Ebony/Walnut/Mahogany	22,780.
VI DC	4' 10"	Demi-Chip. Polished Ebony/Walnut/Mahogany	26,000.
V	5' 3"	Polished Ebony/Walnut/Mahogany	24,000.
V DC	5' 3"	Demi-Chip. Polished Ebony/Walnut/Mahogany	26,780.
IV	5' 8"	Polished Ebony/Walnut/Mahogany	25,800.

Model	Size	Style and Finish	Price*
IV C	5' 8"	Chippendale Polished Ebony/Walnut/Mahogany	31,800.
IV DC	5' 8"	Demi-Chip. Polished Ebony/Walnut/Mahogany	27,800.
IV	5' 8"	"Klasik" Polished Ebony/Walnut/Mahogany	30,780.
III	6' 4"	Polished Ebony/Walnut/Mahogany	31,000.
III	6' 4"	"Majestic" Polished Ebony/Walnut/Mahogany	32,780.
Pasat B	6' 10½"	Polished Ebony	43,800.
II	7' 9"	Polished Ebony/Walnut	48,200.
I	9' 3"	"Mistral" Polished Ebony	72,780.
III, IV, V		With Sterling Original Action, add'l approx.	3,000.

PianoDisc

Prices for PianoDisc and QuietTime systems vary by piano manufacturer and installer. The following are suggested retail prices from PianoDisc. The usual dealer discounts may apply, especially as an incentive to purchase a piano.

Opus7 "Opulence," factory-installed or retrofitted	18,357.
Opus7 "Luxury," factory-installed or retrofitted	14,276.
Opus7 Performance Package option	2,733.
228CFX System, factory-installed or retrofitted:	
Playback only	6,635.
Add for MX (Music Expansion) Platinum	1,758.
Add for MX (Music Expansion) Basic	1,171.
Add for SymphonyPro Sound Module	1,115.
Add for TFT MIDI Record system	1,627.
Add for PianoMute Rail	664.
Add for amplified speakers, pair	735.
PianoCD System	5,995.
QuietTime GT-2 System (Control unit w/ Piano and Organ sounds, MIDI Strip, MIDI interface board, pedal switches, cable, headphones, power supply, PianoMute rail)	2,362.
MIDI Controller (TFT MIDI Strip, MIDI interface board, pedal switches, cable, power supply)	1,816.
AudioForte	2,447.

Pleyel

Verticals

Model	Size	Style and Finish	Price
P 118	47"	Polished Ebony	15,424.
P 118	47"	Polished Mahogany	18,078.
P 118	47"	Satin Cherry with Marquetry	17,098.
P 118	47"	*Satin Walnut*	17,098.
P 118	47"	Satin Walnut with Leather	22,000.
P 118	47½"	"Romantica Noyer" Satin Walnut	16,568.

*For explanation of terms and prices, please see pages 113–117.

Model	Size	Style and Finish	Price*
Pleyel (continued)			
P 124	49"	Polished Ebony	18,058.
P 124	49"	Satin Cherry with Marquetry	19,878.
P 124	49"	*Satin Walnut with Marquetry*	19,878.
P 131	51½"	Polished Ebony	23,928.
P 131	51½"	Polished Mahogany	25,582.
P 131	51½"	*With Sostenuto, add'l*	970.
Grands			
P 170	5' 7"	Polished Ebony	55,378.
P 170	5' 7"	Polished Mahogany	61,602.
P 170	5' 7"	Satin Walnut	78,300.
P 190	6' 3"	Polished Ebony	66,756.
P 190	6' 3"	Polished Mahogany	78,492.
P 190	6' 3"	Satin Cherry with Marquetry	78,492.
P 190	6' 3"	Satin Poplar Burl	126,156.
P 280	9' 2½"	Polished Ebony	179,990.

Pramberger

J. Pramberger Signature Series Verticals

Model	Size	Style and Finish	Price
PV-110F	43"	French Provincial Satin Cherry	5,790.
PV-110R	43"	Renaissance Satin Walnut	5,590.
PV-110T	43"	Satin Mahogany	5,590.
PV-118S	46½"	Satin and Polished Ebony	6,190.
PV-118S	46½"	Lacquer Satin Mahogany/Walnut	6,190.
PV-121	48"	Polished Ebony	6,090.
PV-121	48"	Polished Mahogany	6,190.
PV-131	52"	Polished Ebony	6,290.
PV-131	52"	Polished Mahogany	6,390.

J.P. Pramberger Platinum Series Verticals

Model	Size	Style and Finish	Price
JP-116	45"	Satin Ebony	10,700.
JP-116	45"	Polished Ebony	10,400.
JP-116	45"	Lacquer Semi-Gloss Mahogany/Walnut	11,600.
JP-118F	46½"	French Provincial Lacquer Semi-Gloss Cherry	8,900.
JP-118T	46½"	Lacquer Semi-Gloss Mahogany	8,900.
JP-125	49"	Satin Ebony	11,100.
JP-125	49"	Polished Ebony	10,700.
JP-125	49"	Lacquer Semi-Gloss Mahogany/Walnut	11,900.
JP-125	49"	Lacquer Semi-Gloss Bubinga	16,800.
JP-131	52"	Satin Ebony	12,200.
JP-131	52"	Polished Ebony	11,800.
JP-131	52"	Lacquer Semi-Gloss Mahogany/Walnut	13,200.
JP-131	52"	Lacquer Semi-Gloss Bubinga	17,200.

Model	Size	Style and Finish	Price*
J. Pramberger Signature Series Grands			
PS-150	5'	Satin Ebony	14,190.
PS-150	5'	Polished Ebony	13,790.
PS-150	5'	Lacquer Satin Mahogany/Walnut	14,790.
PS-150	5'	Polished Mahogany/Walnut	14,390.
PS-157	5' 2"	Satin Ebony	14,990.
PS-157	5' 2"	Polished Ebony	14,290.
PS-157	5' 2"	Lacquer Satin Mahogany/Walnut	14,990.
PS-157	5' 2"	Polished Satin Mahogany/Walnut	14,990.
PS-175	5' 9"	Satin Ebony	15,990.
PS-175	5' 9"	Polished Ebony	15,090.
PS-175	5' 9"	Lacquer Satin Mahogany/Walnut	16,290.
PS-175	5' 9"	Polished Mahogany/Walnut	15,990.
PS-185	6' 1"	Satin Ebony	16,890.
PS-185	6' 1"	Polished Ebony	15,990.
PS-185	6' 1"	Lacquer Satin Mahogany/Walnut	16,890.
PS-185	6' 1"	Polished Mahogany/Walnut	16,890.
J.P. Pramberger Platinum Series Grands			
JP-160S	5' 3"	Satin Ebony	24,300.
JP-160S	5' 3"	Polished Ebony	23,600.
JP-160S	5' 3"	Lacquer Semi-Gloss Mahogany/Walnut	25,600.
JP-179F	5' 10"	Fr. Prov. Lacquer S-G Mahogany/Wal./Cherry	32,400.
JP-179L	5' 10"	Satin Ebony	27,700.
JP-179L	5' 10"	Polished Ebony	27,000.
JP-179L	5' 10"	Lacquer Semi-Gloss Mahogany/Walnut	29,000.
JP-179L	*5' 10"*	*Polished Bubinga/Pommele*	*29,000.*
JP-190A	6' 3"	Satin Ebony	31,900.
JP-190A	6' 3"	Polished Ebony	31,200.
JP-190A	6' 3"	Lacquer Semi-Gloss Mahogany/Walnut	33,200.
JP-190A	*6' 3"*	*Polished Bubinga/Pommele*	*33,600.*
JP-208B	6' 10"	Satin Ebony	34,500.
JP-208B	6' 10"	Polished Ebony	33,800.
JP-208B	6' 10"	Lacquer Semi-Gloss Mahogany/Walnut	35,800.
JP-228C	7' 6"	Satin Ebony	37,400.
JP-228C	7' 6"	Polished Ebony	36,800.

QRS / Pianomation

Prices for Pianomation systems vary by piano manufacturer, installer, and accessories. The following are approximate retail prices for installed systems and accessories from QRS. The usual dealer discounts may apply, especially as an incentive to purchase a piano.

*For explanation of terms and prices, please see pages 113–117.

Model	Size	Style and Finish	Price*

QRS / Pianomation (continued)

Pianomation 2000C with pedal solenoid and sostenuto trapwork		5,995.
Pianomation 2000CD+ with pedal solenoid, sostenuto trapwork, and amplified speaker		6,640.
Pianomation Petine with pedal solenoid, sostenuto trapwork, and amplified speaker		7,130.
Pianomation Ancho with pedal solenoid, sostenuto trapwork, and amplified speaker		7,470.
Amplified Speaker, each		350.
PNOscan, installed		1,995.
SilentPNO, installed		2,995.
Grand Piano Mute Rail (alone), installed		399.
NetPiano, Lifetime Subscription, Pianomation Owner		2,280.
Qtouch Tablet		3,200.
Qsync		n/a
Playola with 2000C		6,000.
Playola with 2000CD+		6,750.

Remington

Verticals

Model	Size	Style and Finish	Price
RV-108	42"	Continental Polished Ebony	4,090.
RV-108	42"	Continental Polished Mahogany/Ivory	4,190.
RV-43F	43"	French Provincial Satin Cherry/Brown Oak	4,990.
RV-43T	43"	Satin Mahogany/Walnut	4,990.
RV-118	45"	Polished Ebony/Mahogany	4,990.
RV-121	48"	Polished Ebony	4,990.
RV-121	48"	Polished Mahogany	5,090.
RV-131	52"	Polished Ebony	5,790.
RV-131	52"	Polished Mahogany	5,890.

Grands

Model	Size	Style and Finish	Price
RG-140	4' 7"	Polished Ebony	10,090.
RG-140	4' 7"	Polished Mahogany	10,790.
RG-150	4' 11½"	Polished Ebony	11,090.
RG-150	4' 11½"	Polished Mahogany	11,790.
RG-157	5' 2"	Polished Ebony	11,790.
RG-157	5' 2"	Polished Mahogany	12,490.
RG-175	5' 9"	Polished Ebony	13,990.
RG-175	5' 9"	Polished Mahogany	14,790.
RG-185	6' 1"	Polished Ebony	15,190.
RG-185	6' 1"	Polished Mahogany	15,990.

Model	Size	Style and Finish	Price*

Ritmüller

Verticals

Model	Size	Style and Finish	Price*
UP-110R2	43½"	Continental Polished Ebony	4,480.
UP-110R2	43½"	Continental Polished Mahogany/Walnut	4,520.
UP-110R4	43½"	French Provincial Satin Cherry	4,760.
UP-110R5	43½"	Satin Walnut	4,760.
UP-110R6	43½"	Satin American Country Oak	4,760.
UP-118R2	46½"	"Scandinavian Design" Polished Ebony	5,190.
UP-118R2	46½"	"Scandinavian Design" Polished Mahogany	5,260.
UP-118R3	46½"	Satin Cherry	6,240.
UP-120R	48"	Polished Ebony	5,830.
UP-120R	48"	Polished Mahogany/Walnut/White	5,900.
UP-120R1	48"	"European Decorator" Pol. Ebony w/Mahogany	5,940.
UP-120R2	48"	Chippendale Satin Walnut/Mahogany	6,080.
UP-120R3	48"	"Euro-Modern" Continental Polished Ebony	6,450.
UP-120R4	48"	French Provincial Satin Cherry	6,290.
UP-120R6	48"	Queen Anne Satin Cherry	6,620.
UP-120R7	48"	Italian Provincial Satin Walnut	6,620.
UP-120R8	48"	American Classic Satin Walnut	6,620.
UP-123R	48"	"Classic Euro" Polished Ebony	7,040.
UP-123R	48"	"Classic Euro" Polished Mahogany/Walnut	7,100.
UP-123R1	48"	"Deluxe European" Polished Ebony	7,050.
UP-125R	49"	"European" Polished Ebony w/Walnut Burl	7,520.
UP-125R2	49"	"Deluxe European" Pol. Ebony w/Mahogany	7,730.
UP-126R	49"	Polished Ebony w/Mahogany Trim	7,570.
UP-130R	51"	Polished Ebony (movable front)	7,720.
UP-130R	51"	Satin Walnut (movable front)	7,770.
UP-130R	51"	Satin Mahogany (movable front)	7,770.
UP-130R1	51"	Polished Ebony	7,660.
UP-130R2	51"	Polished Ebony	8,090.

Grands

Model	Size	Style and Finish	Price*
GP-148R	4' 10"	Hand-rubbed Satin Ebony (round leg, brass trim)	10,980.
GP-148R	4' 10"	Polished Ebony (round leg, brass trim)	10,760.
GP-148R	4' 10"	Polished Mahogany (round leg, brass trim)	11,190.
GP-148R1	4' 10"	Polished Ebony (tapered leg, brass trim)	10,600.
GP-159R	5' 3"	Hand-rubbed Satin Ebony (round leg, brass trim)	14,700.
GP-159R	5' 3"	Polished Ebony (round leg, brass trim)	14,370.
GP-159R	5' 3"	Satin Mahogany (round leg, brass trim)	14,950.
GP-159R	5' 3"	Pol. Mahogany/Walnut (round leg, brass trim)	14,700.
GP-159R1	5' 3"	Hand-rubbed Sat. Ebony (tapered leg, brass trim)	14,330.
GP-159R1	5' 3"	Polished Ebony (tapered leg, brass trim)	14,360.
GP-159R1	5' 3"	Polished Mahogany (tapered leg, brass trim)	14,330.
GP-159R2	5' 3"	Louis XV Satin Cherry	14,300.
GP-183R	6'	Hand-rubbed Satin Ebony (round leg, brass trim)	18,730.

*For explanation of terms and prices, please see pages 113–117.

Model	Size	Style and Finish	Price*

Ritmüller (continued)

Model	Size	Style and Finish	Price
GP-183R	6'	Polished Ebony (round leg, brass trim)	18,230.
GP-183R1	6'	Hand-rubbed Sat. Ebony (tapered leg, brass trim)	18,300.
GP-183R1	6'	Polished Ebony (tapered leg, brass trim)	18,090.
GP-213R1	7'	Polished Ebony	25,240.
GP-275R1	9'	Polished Ebony	78,290.

Samick

Verticals

Model	Size	Style and Finish	Price
JS-042	42"	Continental Polished Ebony	3,990.
JS-042	42"	Continental Polished Mahogany/Walnut/Ivory	3,990.
JS-042	42"	Continental Satin Cherry/Walnut	4,090.
JS-143F	43"	French Provincial Satin Cherry	5,090.
JS-143M	43"	Mediterranean Satin Brown Oak	5,090.
JS-143T	43"	Satin Mahogany	5,090.
JS-115	45"	Satin Ebony/Mahogany/Walnut/Cherry	4,590.
JS-115	45"	Polished Ebony/Mahogany	4,490.
JS-247	46½"	Satin Ebony/Mahogany/Walnut	6,190.
JS-247	46½"	Polished Ebony/Mahogany/Walnut	6,190.
JS-121M	48"	Satin Ebony	5,290.
JS-121M	48"	Polished Ebony	5,190.
JS-121M	48"	Polished Mahogany	5,290.
JS-131	52"	Satin Ebony	5,990.
JS-131	52"	Polished Ebony	5,890.
JS-131	52"	Polished Mahogany	5,990.

Grands

Model	Size	Style and Finish	Price
SIG-47	4' 7"	Polished Ebony	10,090.
SIG-47	4' 7"	Polished Mahogany	10,790.
SIG-50	4' 11½"	Satin Ebony	11,790.
SIG-50	4' 11½"	Polished Ebony	11,090.
SIG-50	4' 11½"	Lacquer Satin Mahogany and Pol. Mahogany	11,790.
SIG-50	4' 11½"	Lacquer Satin Walnut and Polished Walnut	11,790.
SIG-54	5' 3"	Satin Ebony	12,490.
SIG-54	5' 3"	Polished Ebony	11,790.
SIG-54	5' 3"	Lacquer Satin Mahogany and Pol. Mahogany	12,490.
SIG-54	5' 3"	Lacquer Satin Walnut and Polished Walnut	12,490.
SIG-54 KBF	5' 3"	French Provincial Polished Cherry	15,590.
SIG-57	5' 7"	Satin Ebony	14,190.
SIG-57	5' 7"	Polished Ebony	13,290.
SIG-57	5' 7"	Lacquer Satin Mahogany and Pol. Mahogany	14,190.
SIG-57	5' 7"	Lacquer Satin Walnut and Polished Walnut	14,190.
SIG-57L	5' 7"	Empire Polished Ebony	14,190.
SIG-57L	5' 7"	Empire Lacquer Satin Mahog. and Pol. Mahog.	15,690.

Model	Size	Style and Finish	Price*
SIG-61	6' 1"	Satin Ebony	15,390.
SIG-61	6' 1"	Polished Ebony	14,490.
SIG-61	6' 1"	Lacquer Satin Mahogany/Walnut	15,390.
SIG-61	6' 1"	Polished Mahogany/Walnut	15,390.

Sauter

Verticals

Model	Size	Style and Finish	Price*
122	48"	"Ragazza" Polished Ebony	23,660.
122	48"	"Ragazza" Satin Cherry	23,420.
122	48"	"Ragazza" Polished Cherry/Yew	27,620.
122	48"	"Vista" Polished Ebony	25,720.
122	48"	"Vista" Satin Maple	24,560.
122	48"	"Vista" Satin Cherry	25,600.
122	48"	School Piano Satin Ebony/Beech Bright	20,720.
122	48"	"M-Line M2" Polished Ebony	30,220.
122	48"	Peter Maly "Artes" Polished Ebony	35,200.
122	48"	Peter Maly "Artes" Polished Palisander	36,280.
122	48"	Peter Maly "Artes" Polished White	35,840.
122	48"	Peter Maly "Cura" Satin Walnut	33,200.
122	48"	Peter Maly "Cura" Satin Cherry	34,260.
122	48"	Peter Maly "Imago" Swiss Pearwood &Grey	30,220.
122	48"	Peter Maly "Pure 2000 Noble" Polished Ebony	32,260.
122	48"	Peter Maly "Pure 2000 Noble" Pol. Ebony & Zebrano	32,260.
122	48"	Peter Maly "Pure 2000 Noble" Polished White	33,100.
122	48"	Peter Maly "Pure 2000 Noble" Polished Red	33,100.
122	48"	Peter Maly "Pure 2000 Basic" Ebony & Walnut	26,180.
122	48"	Peter Maly "Pure 2000 Basic" Satin White	26,180.
122	48"	Peter Maly "Pure 2000 Basic" Wht & Maple	26,180.
122	48"	Peter Maly "Rondo" Polished Ebony	28,380.
122	48"	Peter Maly "Rondo" Satin Wenge	26,280.
122	48"	Peter Maly "Onda" Satin Maple & Silver	24,400.
122	48"	Peter Maly "Vitrea" Dark Oak with Glass	28,400.
128	51"	"M-Line M1" Polished Ebony	34,200.
128	51"	"Competence" Polished Ebony	29,320.
128	51"	"Competence" Satin Walnut	27,840.

Grands

Standard wood finishes are Walnut, Mahogany, Oak, Ash, and Alder.

Model	Size	Style and Finish	Price*
160	5' 3"	"Alpha" Polished Ebony	61,340.
160	5' 3"	"Alpha" Satin Standard Wood Finishes	56,000.
160	5' 3"	Queen Anne Satin Cherry	63,100.
160	5' 3"	Queen Anne Polished Cherry	71,040.
160	5' 3"	Chippendale Satin Cherry	63,320.

*For explanation of terms and prices, please see pages 113–117.

Model	Size	Style and Finish	Price*

Sauter (continued)

Model	Size	Style and Finish	Price*
160	5' 3"	Chippendale Satin Standard Wood Finishes	60,920.
160	5' 3"	"Noblesse" Satin Cherry	68,000.
160	5' 3"	"Noblesse" Polished Cherry	76,140.
160	5' 3"	"Noblesse" Satin Burl Walnut	71,420.
160	5' 3"	"Noblesse" Satin Standard Wood Finishes	65,600.
160	5' 3"	"Noblesse" Polished Standard Wood Finishes	73,800.
185	6' 1"	"Delta" Polished Ebony	66,540.
185	6' 1"	"Delta" Polished Ebony w/Burl Walnut	68,480.
185	6' 1"	"Delta" Polished Pyramid Mahogany	73,520.
185	6' 1"	"Delta" Polished Bubinga/Rio Palisander	73,520.
185	6' 1"	"Delta" Satin Maple with Silver	62,680.
185	6' 1"	"Delta" Polished White	68,900.
185	6' 1"	"Delta" Satin Standard Wood Finishes	60,820.
185	6' 1"	Chippendale Satin Cherry	68,000.
185	6' 1"	Chippendale Satin Standard Wood Finishes	65,600.
185	6' 1"	"Noblesse" Satin Cherry	72,900.
185	6' 1"	"Noblesse" Polished Cherry	81,860.
185	6' 1"	"Noblesse" Satin Burl Walnut	76,100.
185	6' 1"	"Noblesse" Satin Standard Wood Finishes	70,500.
185	6' 1"	"Noblesse" Polished Standard Wood Finishes	79,660.
185	6' 1"	"Amadeus" French Satin Walnut	86,880.
210	6' 11"	Peter Maly "Vivace" Polished Ebony	94,080.
210	6' 11"	Peter Maly "Vivace" Satin Maple	87,700.
210	6' 11"	Peter Maly "Vivace" Polished White	95,540.
220	7' 3"	"Omega" Polished Ebony	84,220.
220	7' 3"	"Omega" M-Line Version, Polished Ebony	89,360.
220	7' 3"	"Omega" Polished Pyramid Mahogany	92,240.
220	7' 3"	"Omega" Satin Standard Wood Finishes	79,420.
230	7' 6"	Peter Maly "Ambiente" Polished Ebony	112,400.
275	9'	"Concert" Polished Ebony	131,680.

Schimmel

When not mentioned, satin finish available on special order at same price as high-polish finish.

Verticals

Model	Size	Style and Finish	Price*
C 112 S	44"	Open-Pore Ebony/Oak/Walnut	15,780.
C 116 T	46"	Polished Ebony	16,180.
C 116 T	46"	Open-Pore Alder	16,780.
C 116 T	46"	Open-Pore Beech	15,780.
C 116 T	46"	Open-Pore Walnut	16,180.
C 116 T	46"	Satin Cherry	17,180.
C 116 T	46"	Polished Mahogany	17,180.

Model	Size	Style and Finish	Price*
C 116 T	46"	Polished White	16,780.
C 120 I	47"	"International" Polished Ebony	16,780.
C 120 I	47"	"International" Polished White	17,380.
C 120 S	47"	Open-Pore Ebony/Oak (school studio)	15,980.
C 120 T	47"	Polished Ebony	17,580.
C 120 T	47"	Open-Pore Alder/Beech	17,580.
C 120 T	47"	Open-Pore Walnut	17,980.
C 120 T	47"	Satin Cherry	19,980.
C 120 T	47"	Polished Mahogany	19,320.
C 120 T	47"	Polished White	18,780.
C 120 TA	47"	"Akademie" Polished Ebony	16,780.
K 122 E	48"	"Elegance" Polished Ebony	22,780.
K 122 MC	48"	"Modern Cubus" Polished Ebony	23,980.
K 122 MC	48"	"Modern Cubus" Satin Swiss Pear	23,980.
K 122 MC	48"	"Modern Cubus" Polished White	24,380.
K 122 TA	48"	"Akademie" Polished Ebony	22,780.
C 124 R	49"	"Royal" Polished Ebony	20,780.
C 124 R	49"	"Royal" Polished Mahogany	23,380.
C 124 RI	49"	"Royale Intarsia Flora" Polished Mahogany	24,380.
C 124 T	49"	Polished Ebony	18,580.
C 124 T	49"	Polished Ebony w/Oval Decoration	19,380.
C 124 T	49"	Polished Mahogany	20,380.
C 124 T	49"	Polished Mahogany w/Oval Decoration	21,380.
C 124 T	49"	Open-Pore Walnut Antique	20,380.
K 125 N	49"	"Noblesse" Polished Ebony	25,380.
K 125 N	49"	"Noblesse" Polished Mahogany	26,780.
K 125 P	49"	"Prestige" Polished Ebony	26,380.
K 125 P	49"	"Prestige" Polished Mahogany	27,980.
C 130 T	51"	Polished Ebony	22,780.
C 130 T	51"	Polished Ebony w/Oval Decoration	23,180.
C 130 T	51"	Open-Pore Walnut	21,180.
C 130 T	51"	Polished Mahogany/Walnut	24,580.
K 132 T	52"	Polished Ebony	27,180.
K 132 T	52"	Polished Mahogany	30,580.
K 132 W	52"	"Wilhelmina" Satin Mahogany/Walnut	36,780.

Grands

Model	Size	Style and Finish	Price*
K 169 AN	5' 7"	"Art Nouveau" Polished Ebony	52,780.
K 169 AN	5' 7"	"Art Nouveau" Polished Mahogany/White	54,780.
K 169 BE	5' 7"	"Belle Epoque" Polished Ebony	49,780.
K 169 R	5' 7"	"Royal" Polished Ebony	46,780.
K 169 R	5' 7"	"Royal" Polished Mahogany/White	48,780.
K 169 RIF	5' 7"	"Royal Intarsie Flora" Polished Mahogany	50,780.
K 169 T	5' 7"	Polished Ebony	44,780.
K 169 T	5' 7"	Polished Mahogany/White/Burl Walnut	46,780.

*For explanation of terms and prices, please see pages 113–117.

Model	Size	Style and Finish	Price*

Schimmel (continued)

Model	Size	Style and Finish	Price*
K 169 T	5' 7"	Polished Flame Mahogany/Macassar	53,780.
K 169 T	5' 7"	Polished Bubinga/Bird's-Eye Maple	52,580.
K 169 TIH	5' 7"	"Intarsie Harp" Polished Ebony	50,780.
K 169 TIV	5' 7"	"Intarsie Vase" Polished Mahogany	50,780.
C 182 AN	6'	"Art Nouveau" Polished Ebony	37,980.
C 182 AN	6'	"Art Nouveau" Polished Mahogany	38,780.
C 182 T	6'	Polished Ebony	34,780.
C 182 T	6'	Polished Mahogany	35,980.
K 189 AN	6' 3"	"Art Nouveau" Polished Ebony	56,780.
K 189 AN	6' 3"	"Art Nouveau" Polished Mahogany/White	58,780.
K 189 BE	6' 3"	"Belle Epoque" Polished Ebony	53,780.
K 189 EP	6' 3"	"Empire" Satin and Polished Mahogany	60,780.
K 189 NWS	6' 3"	"Nikolaus W. Schimmel Special Edition"	58,780.
K 189 R	6' 3"	"Royal" Polished Ebony	50,780.
K 189 R	6' 3"	"Royal" Polished Mahogany/White	52,780.
K 189 RIF	6' 3"	"Royal Intarsie Flora" Polished Mahogany	54,780.
K 189 T	6' 3"	Polished Ebony	48,780.
K 189 T	6' 3"	Polished Walnut/Mahogany/White	50,780.
K 189 T	6' 3"	Polished Burl Walnut	56,580.
K 189 T	6' 3"	Polished Flame Mahogany/Macassar	57,780.
K 189 T	6' 3"	Polished Bubinga/Bird's-Eye Maple	56,580.
K 189 T	6' 3"	Open-Pore Walnut Antique	48,780.
K 189 T	6' 3"	"Red Diamond"	56,780.
K 189 TA	6' 3"	"Akademie" Polished Ebony	48,780.
K 189 TIH	6' 3"	"Intarsie Harp" Polished Ebony	54,780.
K 189 TIV	6' 3"	"Intarsie Vase" Polished Mahogany	54,780.
K 213 G	7'	*"Glas" Clear Acrylic and White*	124,780.
K 213 NWS	7'	"Nikolaus W. Schimmel Special Edition"	62,780.
K 213 OA	7'	*"Otmar Alt" Polished Ebony w/Color Motifs*	142,900.
K 213 R	7'	"Royal" Polished Ebony	53,780.
K 213 R	7'	"Royal" Polished Mahogany/White	55,780.
K 213 T	7'	Polished Ebony	51,780.
K 213 T	7'	Polished Mahogany/Walnut/White	53,780.
K 213 T	7'	Polished Flame Mahogany/Macassar	60,780.
K 213 T	7'	Polished Burl Walnut	59,580.
K 213 T	7'	Polished Bubinga/Bird's-Eye Maple	59,580.
K 213 T	7'	"Red Diamond"	53,780.
K 213 TA	7'	"Akademie" Polished Ebony	51,780.
K 230 T	7' 5"	Polished Ebony	70,780.
K 256 T	8' 4"	Polished Ebony	78,780.
K 280 T	9' 2"	Polished Ebony	102,780.

Model	Size	Style and Finish	Price*

Schulze Pollmann

Verticals

114/P4	45"	Polished Ebony	7,990.
114/P4	45"	Polished Mahogany/Walnut	8,190.
114/P4	45"	Polished Peacock Ebony/Walnut/Mahogany	8,590.
118/P8	46"	Polished Ebony	11,990.
118/P8	46"	Polished Briar Walnut/Mahogany	12,790.
118/P8	46"	Polished Feather or Peacock Mahogany	12,790.
126/P6	50"	Polished Ebony	13,590.
126/P6	50"	Polished Peacock Ebony	14,190.
126/P6	50"	Polished Cherry/Yew	14,190.
126/P6	50"	Polished Peacock Mahogany/Cherry/Walnut	14,190.
126/P6	50"	Polished Briar Mahogany/Walnut	14,190.
126/P6	50"	Polished Feather Mahogany	14,190.

Grands

160/GK	5' 3"	Polished Ebony (spade leg)	30,190.
160/GK	5' 3"	Polished Ebony (round leg)	31,190.
160/GK	5' 3"	Polished Briar Mahogany (spade leg)	33,190.
160/GK	5' 3"	Polished Briar Mahogany (round leg)	35,190.
160/GK	5' 3"	Polished Feather Mahogany (spade leg)	38,790.
160/GK	5' 3"	Polished Feather Mahogany (round leg)	40,790.
190/F	6' 2"	Polished Ebony (spade leg)	40,190.
190/F	6' 2"	Polished Briar Mahogany (spade leg)	43,990.
190/F	6' 2"	Polished Briar Mahogany (round leg)	44,790.
190/F	6' 2"	Polished Feather Mahogany (spade leg)	47,190.
197/G2	6' 7"	Polished Ebony (spade leg)	45,190.
197/G2	6' 7"	Polished Briar Mahogany (spade leg)	49,190.

Seiler

Verticals

116	46"	"Eduard Seiler" Polished Ebony	14,400.
116	46"	"Impuls" Polished Ebony	16,600.
116	46"	"Accent" Polished Ebony	16,600.
116	46"	"Focus" Polished Ebony	16,600.
116	46"	"Clou" Polished Ebony	16,600.
116	46"	"Primus" Polished Ebony	16,600.
116	46"	"Mondial" Open-Pore Ebony/Oak	19,200.
116	46"	"Mondial" Open-Pore Walnut/Mahogany	19,200.
116	46"	"Jubilee" Polished Ebony	18,600.
122	48"	"Primus Eduard Seiler" Polished Ebony	17,000.
122	48"	"Primus" Polished Ebony	21,600.
122	48"	"Konsole" Open-Pore Ebony/Oak	22,000.
122	48"	"Konsole" Open-Pore Walnut/Maple	22,000.

*For explanation of terms and prices, please see pages 113–117.

Model	Size	Style and Finish	Price*

Seiler (continued)

Model	Size	Style and Finish	Price*
122	48"	"Konsole" Polished Ebony	22,000.
122	48"	"Konsole" Polished Mahogany	24,400.
122	48"	"Konsole" Polished Burl Rosewood	26,600.
132	52"	"Primus" Open-Pore Walnut	24,800.
132	52"	"Concert" Polished Ebony	25,800.
132	52"	"Concert" Open-Pore Walnut	25,800.
132	52"	"Concert" Polished Mahogany	29,000.
132	52"	"Concert" Polished Burl Rosewood	30,400.
Grands			
168	5' 6"	"Virtuoso" Polished Ebony	56,800.
168	5' 6"	"Virtuoso" Polished Mahogany	62,800.
186	6' 1"	"Trend" Polished Ebony	46,800.
186	6' 1"	"Maestro" Polished Ebony	58,800.
186	6' 1"	"Maestro" Open-Pore Walnut/Mahogany	58,800.
186	6' 1"	"Maestro" Polished Walnut/Mahogany	64,800.
186	6' 1"	"Maestro" Polished Burl Rosewood	68,600.
186	6' 1"	"Maestro" Polished Flamed Maple	68,740.
186	6' 1"	"Westminster" Polished Mahogany, Intarsia	80,780.
186	6' 1"	"Florenz" Polished Walnut/Myrtle, Intarsia	80,780.
186	6' 1"	"Florenz" Polished Mahog./Myrtle, Intarsia	80,780.
186	6' 1"	"Louvre" Polished Ebony	70,780.
186	6' 1"	"Louvre" Polished Cherry, Intarsia	80,780.
208	6' 10"	Polished Ebony	62,780.
242	8'	Polished Ebony	82,780.
278	9'	Polished Ebony	110,800.

Sejung

Sejung makes pianos under the names Falcone, Hobart M. Cable, and Geo. Steck. The large variety of styles and finishes offered under the three brand names are very similar from one brand to the next, and in most cases the prices are the same. To save space, I have compiled one master list of models for all three brands. Although I have used the generic model prefixes "U" and "C" for the verticals and "G" for grands, each brand actually has its own prefixes: UF, CF, and GF for Falcone; FV and FG for the Falcone Georgian series; UH, CH, and GH for Hobart M. Cable; and US, CS, and GS for Geo. Steck. All the vertical piano prices shown are for models *without* a slow-close fallboard. Models with a slow-close fallboard, where available, have model numbers ending with "D" and cost $120 more than shown. All the grand piano prices shown are for models *with* a slow-close fallboard. Models without a slow-close fallboard, where available, have model numbers omitting the final "D" and cost $120 less than shown. The Falcone Georgian series has upgraded cosmetic and technical features. The Falcone Georgian verticals cost the same as the other-named verticals, but the Falcone Georgian grands cost from $140 to $400 more, depending on size. Not all models, styles, and finishes shown are available under all names.

Model	Size	Style and Finish	Price*
Verticals			
U 09	43"	Continental Polished Ebony	3,790.
U 09	43"	Continental Polished Other Finishes	3,910.
U 09	43"	Continental Satin Finishes	3,850.
U 09A	43"	Continental Polished Ebony (no back posts)	3,590.
U 09A	43"	Continental Pol. Other Finishes (no back posts)	3,710.
U 09L	43"	Polished Ebony	3,850.
U 09L	43"	Polished Other Finishes	3,970.
C 12F	44"	French Provincial Satin Cherry/Brown Oak	4,190.
C 12F1	44"	French Provincial Satin Cherry/Brown Oak	4,090.
C 12IP	44"	Italian Prov. Satin Walnut/Mahogany/Cherry	4,490.
C 12M	44"	Mediterranean Satin Cherry/Brown Oak	4,190.
C 12M1	44"	Mediterranean Satin Cherry/Brown Oak/Sapele	4,090.
U 12F	44"	French Provincial Polished Ebony	4,110.
U 12F	44"	French Provincial Other Polished Finishes	4,230.
U 12F	44"	French Provincial Satin Finishes	4,170.
U 12FC	44"	12F Satin with Decorated Front Panel	4,210.
U 12T	44"	Polished Ebony	3,990.
U 12T	44"	Polished Other Finishes	4,110.
U 12T	44"	Satin Finishes	4,050.
C 13F	44½"	French Provincial Satin Cherry/Mahogany	4,490.
C 13F1	44½"	Fr. Prov. Satin Cherry/Brown Oak/Mahogany	4,690.
C 13M	44½"	Designer Satin Cherry/Dark Cherry/Mahogany	4,490.
C 13M1	44½"	Designer Satin Cherry/Brown Oak/Mahogany	4,690.
C 16AT	45½"	Satin Cherry/Brown Oak	4,690.
C 16F	45½"	Fr. Provincial Satin Cherry/Brown Oak/Walnut	4,390.
C 16FP	45½"	French Provincial Satin Cherry/Brown Oak	4,450.
C 16IP	45½"	Italian Provincial Satin Cherry/Walnut	4,450.
C 16QA	45½"	Queen Anne Satin Cherry/Brown Oak/Mahogany	4,790.
U 16IC	46"	Italian Provincial Polished Ebony	4,050.
U 16IC	46"	Italian Provincial Other Polished Finishes	4,170.
U 16ST	46"	Satin Finishes (school)	4,110.
U 16STL	46"	Polished Ebony (school with lock)	4,130.
U 16STL	46"	Polished Other Finishes (school with lock)	4,250.
U 16STL	46"	Satin Finishes (school with lock)	4,190.
U 16TC	46"	Polished Ebony w/Decorated Front Panel	4,130.
U 16TC	46"	Polished Other Finishes w/Decorated Front Panel	4,250.
U 18MS	46½"	Designer Other Polished Finishes w/Front Inlay	4,230.
C 19F	47"	Country French Satin Cherry/Brown Oak/Mahog.	4,590.
C 19F1	47"	Country French Satin Cherry/Brown Oak	4,590.
C 19M	47"	Mediterranean Satin Brown Oak/Cherry/Mahog.	4,590.
C 19M1	47"	Mediterranean Satin Cherry/Oak/Brown Oak	4,590.
C 19QA	47"	Queen Anne Satin Cherry/Brown Oak	4,990.
C 47CI	47"	Modern Designer C Polished Ebony	5,490.
C 47CI	47"	Modern Designer C Other Polished Finishes	5,610.

*For explanation of terms and prices, please see pages 113–117.

Model	Size	Style and Finish	Price*

Sejung (continued)

Model	Size	Style and Finish	Price*
C 47F	47"	French Provincial Satin Cherry/Mahogany	5,790.
C 47M	47"	Mediterranean Satin Mahogany	5,790.
C 47R	47"	Modern Designer R Other Polished Finishes	5,710.
C 47V	47"	Modern Designer V Polished Ebony	5,990.
U 19F	47"	French Provincial Polished Ebony	4,190.
U 19F	47"	French Provincial Polished Other Finishes	4,310.
U 19F	47"	French Provincial Satin Finishes	4,250.
U 19FC	47"	Polished Other Finishes w/Decorated Front Panel	4,390.
U 19P	47"	Designer Polished Bubinga	4,370.
U 19P	47"	Designer Other Polished Finishes	4,250.
U 19ST	47"	Polished Ebony	4,090.
U 19ST	47"	Polished Other Finishes	4,210.
U 19ST	47"	Satin Finishes	4,150.
U 19T	47"	Polished Ebony	4,090.
U 19T	47"	Polished Other Finishes	4,210.
U 19T	47"	Satin Finishes	4,150.
U 20T	47"	Designer Polished Ebony	4,390.
U 20T	47"	Designer Other Polished Finishes	4,510.
U 210M	47½"	Designer Special Other Polished Finishes	4,390.
U 22F	48"	French Provincial Polished Ebony	4,410.
U 22F	48"	French Provincial Polished Other Finishes	4,530.
U 22IT	48"	Italian Designer Polished Ebony	4,490.
U 22T	48"	Polished Ebony	4,290.
U 22T	48"	Polished Other Finishes	4,410.
U 22T	48"	Satin Finishes	4,350.
U 22WT	48"	Metropolitan Designer Polished Ebony	4,490.
U 23F	48"	French Provincial Polished Ebony	4,590.
U 23F	48"	French Provincial Polished Other Finishes	4,710.
U 23F	48"	French Provincial Satin Finishes	4,650.
U 23T	48"	Designer Polished Ebony	4,470.
U 23T	48"	Designer Polished Other Finishes	4,590.
U 23T	48"	Designer Satin Finishes	4,530.
U 26T	48"	Designer Polished Ebony	4,350.
U 26T	48"	Designer Satin Finishes	4,410.
U 28	48"	Designer Special Polished Bubinga	5,230.
U 28S	48"	Designer Special Polished Bubinga w/Inlay	5,370.
U 230C	48½"	Designer Medieval Special Satin Finishes	5,070.
U 25B	49½"	Designer w/HM on Front Panel Polished Ebony	4,670.
U 25S	49½"	Designer w/BLK Oval Polished Ebony	4,610.
U 25SM	49½"	Designer w/BSP Oval Polished Ebony	4,530.
U 32E	52"	Professional Designer LHM Polished Ebony	5,990.
U 32F	52"	French Provincial Polished Ebony	4,610.
U 32F	52"	French Provincial Polished Other Finishes	4,730.

Model	Size	Style and Finish	Price*
U 32H	52"	Professional Designer Polished Bubinga	5,370.
U 32T	52"	Polished Ebony	4,490.
U 32T	52"	Polished Other Finishes	4,610.
U 32T	52"	Satin Finishes	4,550.
Grands			
G 42D	4' 8"	Satin Ebony	10,110.
G 42D	4' 8"	Polished Ebony	9,910.
G 42D	4' 8"	Satin Wood Finishes	10,510.
G 42D	4' 8"	Polished Wood Finishes	10,310.
G 42D	4' 8"	Polished Bubinga	10,910.
G 42D	4' 8"	Polished Ivory/White	10,110.
G 42FD	4' 8"	French Provincial Polished Ebony	10,390.
G 42FD	4' 8"	French Provincial Satin Wood Finishes	10,990.
G 42FD	4' 8"	French Provincial Polished Wood Finishes	10,790.
G 42LD	4' 8"	Louis XVI Polished Ebony	10,230.
G 52D	5'	Satin Ebony	11,110.
G 52D	5'	Polished Ebony	10,910.
G 52D	5'	Satin Wood Finishes	11,510.
G 52D	5'	Polished Wood Finishes	11,310.
G 52D	5'	Polished Bubinga	11,910.
G 52FD	5'	French Provincial Polished Ebony	11,390.
G 52FD	5'	French Provincial Satin Wood Finishes	11,990.
G 52FD	5'	French Provincial Polished Wood Finishes	11,790.
G 52FD	5'	French Provincial Polished Ivory/White	11,590.
G 52FAD	5'	FrenchAnn Polished Wood Finishes	12,110.
G 52LD	5'	Louis XVI Polished Ebony	11,230.
G 52LD	5'	Louis XVI Polished Wood Finishes	11,630.
G 62D	5' 4"	Satin Ebony	12,110.
G 62D	5' 4"	Polished Ebony	11,910.
G 62D	5' 4"	Satin Wood Finishes	12,510.
G 62D	5' 4"	Polished Wood Finishes	12,310.
G 62D	5' 4"	Polished Bubinga	12,910.
G 62D	5' 4"	Polished Ivory/White	12,110.
G 62FD	5' 4"	French Provincial Satin Ebony	12,590.
G 62FD	5' 4"	French Provincial Satin Wood Finishes	12,990.
G 62FD	5' 4"	French Provincial Polished Wood Finishes	12,790.
G 62FD	5' 4"	French Provincial Polished Ivory/White	12,590.
G 62HLED	5' 4"	Louis XVI Polished Ebony (Hexagonal)	12,630.
G 62HLED	5' 4"	Louis XVI Polished Sapeli (Hexagonal)	13,630.
G 62HLED	5' 4"	Louis XVI Polished Wood Finishes (Hexagonal)	13,630.
G 62PLBD	5' 4"	Louis XVI Polished Bubinga (Octagonal)	13,630.
G 62QAD	5' 4"	Queen Anne Polished Wood Finishes	13,110.
G 72D	5' 8"	Satin Ebony	13,110.
G 72D	5' 8"	Polished Ebony	12,910.

*For explanation of terms and prices, please see pages 113–117.

Model	Size	Style and Finish	Price*

Sejung (continued)

Model	Size	Style and Finish	Price*
G 72D	5' 8"	Satin Wood Finishes	13,510.
G 72D	5' 8"	Polished Wood Finishes	13,310.
G 72D	5' 8"	Polished Bubinga	13,910.
G 72D	5' 8"	Polished Ivory/White	13,110.
G 72FD	5' 8"	French Provincial Polished Ebony	13,390.
G 72FD	5' 8"	French Provincial Satin Wood Finishes	13,990.
G 72FD	5' 8"	French Provincial Polished Wood Finishes	13,790.
G 72FD	5' 8"	French Provincial Polished Ivory/White	13,590.
G 72FFD	5' 8"	Rococo Polished Ivory/White	13,910.
G 72HLD	5' 8"	Louis XVI Satin Wood Finish (Hexagonal)	14,110.
G 72HLD	5' 8"	Louis XVI Polished Bubinga (Hexagonal)	15,710.
G 72LD	5' 8"	Louis XVI Polished Ebony	13,230.
G 72LD	5' 8"	Louis XVI Satin Wood Finishes	13,830.
G 72LD	5' 8"	Louis XVI Polished Wood Finishes	13,630.
G 72PLD	5' 8"	Louis XVI Polished Wood Finishes (Octagonal)	13,910.
G 72PLSD	5' 8"	Louis XVI Polished Wood Finishes (Octagongal)	14,410.
G 72PLSD	5' 8"	Louis XVI Polished Sapeli (Octagonal)	15,010.
G 72QAD	5' 8"	Queen Anne Satin Wood Finishes	14,230.
G 87BCD	6' 2"	Polished Bubinga w/Rim Band/Beveled Lid	15,230.
G 87D	6' 2"	Satin Ebony	14,110.
G 87D	6' 2"	Polished Ebony	13,910.
G 87D	6' 2"	Polished Wood Finishes	14,310.
G 87D	6' 2"	Polished Bubinga	14,910.
G 87FD	6' 2"	French Provincial Polished Ebony	14,390.
G 87FD	6' 2"	French Provincial Satin Wood Finishes	14,990.
G 87FD	6' 2"	French Provincial Polished Wood Finishes	14,790.
G 87FFBD	6' 2"	Rococo Polished Wood Finishes	15,230.
G 87HLBCD	6' 2"	Louis XVI Polished Beech Ebony (Hexagonal)	16,630.
G 87HLD	6' 2"	Louis XVI Satin Wood Finish (Hexagonal)	15,110.
G 87LD	6' 2"	Louis XVI Satin Ebony	14,430.
G 87LD	6' 2"	Louis XVI Polished Ebony	14,230.
G 87LD	6' 2"	Louis XVI Satin Wood Finishes	14,830.
G 87LD	6' 2"	Louis XVI Polished Wood Finishes	14,630.
G 87LD	6' 2"	Louis XVI Polished Ivory/White	14,430.
G 87PLD	6' 2"	Louis XVI Satin Wood Finishes (Octagonal)	15,110.
G 87PLSD	6' 2"	Louis XVI Polished Wood Finishes (Octagonal)	15,510.
G 208D	6' 10"	Satin Ebony	17,010.
G 208D	6' 10"	Polished Ebony	16,790.
G 208D	6' 10"	Satin Wood Finishes	17,390.
G 208D	6' 10"	Polished Wood Finishes	16,790.
G 208HLD	6' 10"	Louis XVI Satin Wood Finish (Hexagonal)	17,990.
G 208HLBCD	6' 10"	Louis XVI Satin Wood Finish (Hexagonal)	18,310.
G 208HLBCD	6' 10"	Louis XVI Polished Wood Finish (Hexagonal)	18,110.

Model	Size	Style and Finish	Price*
G 228D	7' 6"	Polished Ebony	20,790.
G 278D	9' 2"	Polished Ebony	44,790.

Sohmer (Persis International)

Verticals

S-126	50"	Polished Ebony	10,100.
S-126	50"	Polished Mahogany	10,500.

Grands

S-160	5' 3"	Polished Ebony	19,780.
S-160	5' 3"	Polished Mahogany	20,580.
S-180	5' 10"	Polished Ebony	22,780.
S-180	5' 10"	Polished Mahogany	23,580.
S-218	7' 2"	Polished Ebony	32,780.

Sohmer & Co. (SMC)

Verticals

34F	42"	French Provincial Satin Cherry	6,200.
34R	42"	Renaissance Satin Walnut/Cherry	6,200.
34T	42"	Satin Mahogany/Walnut	6,200.
45F	45"	French Provincial Satin Cherry	9,200.
45R	45"	Renaissance Satin Walnut/Cherry	9,200.
45S	45"	Satin Ebony	8,300.
45S	45"	Polished Ebony	7,900.
45T	45"	Satin Mahogany/Walnut	9,200.

Grands

50T	5'	Polished Ebony	13,900.
50T	5'	Satin Mahogany/Walnut/Cherry	14,600.
63E	5' 4"	Empire Semi-Gloss Mahog./Walnut/Cherry	23,000.
63F	5' 4"	Fr. Provincial Semi-Gloss Mahog/Walnut/Cherry	21,500.
63H	5' 4"	Hepplewhite Semi-Gloss Mahog./Walnut/Cherry	20,000.
63T	5' 4"	Satin Ebony	17,400.
63T	5' 4"	Polished Ebony	16,800.
63T	5' 4"	Semi-Gloss Mahogany/Walnut/Cherry	19,000.
77E	5' 9"	Empire Semi-Gloss Mahogany/Walnut/Cherry	23,500.
77F	5' 9"	Fr. Prov. Semi-Gloss Mahogany/Walnut/Cherry	22,100.
77H	5' 9"	Hepplewhite S-G Mahogany/Walnut/Cherry	20,400.
77T	5' 9"	Satin Ebony	18,100.
77T	5' 9"	Polished Ebony	17,400.
77T	5' 9"	Semi-Gloss Mahogany/Walnut/Cherry	19,500.
90H	6' 2"	Hepplewhite S-G Mahogany/Walnut/Cherry	20,900.
90T	6' 2"	Satin Ebony	18,600.
90T	6' 2"	Polished Ebony	17,800.
90T	6' 2"	Semi-Gloss Mahogany	20,000.

*For explanation of terms and prices, please see pages 113–117.

Model	Size	Style and Finish	Price*

Sohmer & Co. (continued)

95T	6' 8"	Satin Ebony	28,600.
95T	6' 8"	Polished Ebony	27,800.
95T	6' 8"	Semi-Gloss Mahogany/Walnut/Cherry	29,800.

Steck, Geo. — see "Sejung"

Steigerman

"Premium Series" model numbers begin with "SP".

Verticals

108SM	42"	Continental Polished Ebony	3,800.
108SM	42"	Continental Polished Dark Walnut/Mahogany	3,900.
C43	43"	Satin Oak/Cherry/Walnut/Mahogany	4,300.
XU110S	43"	Polished Ebony, w/toe blocks	4,100.
XU110S	43"	Polished Mahogany/Walnut, w/toe blocks	4,200.
C45	45"	Satin Oak/Cherry/Walnut/Mahogany	4,500.
115LS	45"	Polished Ebony	4,100.
115LS	45"	Polished Mahogany/Walnut	4,200.
P116	45"	Satin Light Walnut, institutional	4,400.
SPU115	45½"	Polished Ebony	6,400.
SPU115	45½"	Polished Mahogany/Walnut	6,820.
117XK	46"	Polished Mahogany, curved leg	4,200.
118H	46½"	Polished Ebony/Dark Walnut	3,750.
B120LS	47"	Polished Ebony	4,300.
B120LS	47"	Polished Dark Mahogany	4,400.
SPU123	48½"	Polished Ebony	7,860.
SPU123	48½"	Polished Mahogany/Walnut	8,280.
XU132HA	52"	Polished Ebony	4,592.
All models		Color instead of Polished Ebony, add'l	150.

Grands

XG143S	4' 8"	Polished Ebony	9,600.
XG148S	4' 10"	Polished Ebony	10,000.
SPG151	5'	Polished Ebony	14,300.
SPG151	5'	Polished Mahogany/Walnut	14,930.
XG158S	5' 2"	Polished Ebony	11,400.
SPG161	5' 4"	Polished Ebony	15,970.
SPG161	5' 6"	Polished Mahogany/Walnut	16,600.
XG168S	5' 6"	Polished Ebony	12,400.
SPG178	5' 11"	Polished Ebony	18,470.
SPG178	5' 11"	Polished Mahogany/Walnut	19,100.
XG185S	6'	Polished Ebony	13,400.
All models		Color instead of Polished Ebony, add'l	300.
All models		Slow-Close Fallboard, add'l	110.

Model	Size	Style and Finish	Price*

Steinberg, Gerh.

Verticals

Model	Size	Style and Finish	Price*
HM-109	43"	Continental Polished Ebony	5,590.
HM-109	43"	Continental Pol. Mahogany/Walnut/Oak/White	5,790.
HM-109	43"	Continental Satin Finish	5,790.
HM-109	43"	Polished Ebony	5,790.
HM-109	43"	Polished Mahogany/Walnut/Oak/White	5,990.
HM-109	43"	Satin Finish	5,990.
HM-109	43"	Queen Anne Polished Ebony	5,990.
HM-109	43"	Queen Anne Polished Mahogany/Walnut	6,190.
HM-109	43"	Queen Anne Satin Walnut	6,190.
HM-116	46"	Deco Leg Polished Ebony	6,190.
HM-116	46"	Deco Leg Polished Ebony w/Walnut Trim	6,350.
HM-116	46"	Deco Leg Polished Mahogany/Oak/White	6,590.
HM-116	46"	Queen Anne Polished Ebony	6,350.
HM-116	46"	Queen Anne Polished Mahogany/Walnut	6,650.
HM-117	46"	Decorator Cabinet (square leg) Satin Mahogany	7,850.
EV-123	48"	Polished Ebony	6,580.
EV-123	48"	Polished Ebony w/Pommele Center	6,650.
EV-123	48"	Polished Mahogany/Walnut/Oak/White	6,730.
EV-123	48"	Satin Finish	6,730.
EV-123	48"	Queen Anne Polished Ebony	6,730.
EV-123	48"	Queen Anne Polished Mahogany/Walnut	6,950.
EV-125	49"	Polished Ebony	6,950.
EV-125	49"	Polished Ebony w/Pommele Center	7,090.
EV-125	49"	Polished Mahogany/Walnut/White	7,280.
EV-125	49"	Queen Anne Polished Ebony	7,180.
EV-125	49"	Queen Anne Polished Mahogany/Walnut	7,370.
EV-125	49"	Queen Anne Pol. Mahogany/Walnut w/molding	7,580.

Grands

Model	Size	Style and Finish	Price*
S-159	5' 3"	Polished Ebony	18,320.
S-159	5' 3"	Polished Mahogany/Walnut/Oak/White	19,000.
S-159	5' 3"	Satin Finish	19,000.
S-159	5' 3"	Polished Ebony (round leg)	18,650.
S-159	5' 3"	Polished Mahogany/Walnut (round leg)	19,340.
S-159	5' 3"	Satin Finish (round leg)	19,340.
S-159	5' 3"	Queen Anne Polished Ebony	18,650.
S-159	5' 3"	Queen Anne Polished Mahogany/Walnut	19,340.
S-159	5' 3"	Queen Anne Satin Finish	19,340.
S-159	5' 3"	Designer Satin Ebony w/Bubinga Fallboard/Lid	19,690.
S-186	6' 1"	Polished Ebony	20,380.
S-186	6' 1"	Polished Mahogany/Walnut/Oak/White	21,260.
S-186	6' 1"	Satin Finish	21,260.
S-186	6' 1"	Polished Ebony (round leg)	20,720.

*For explanation of terms and prices, please see pages 113–117.

Model	Size	Style and Finish	Price*

Steinberg, Gerh. (continued)

S-186	6' 1"	Polished Mahogany/Walnut (round leg)	21,590.
S-186	6' 1"	Satin Finish (round leg)	21,590.
S-186	6' 1"	Queen Anne Polished Ebony	20,720.
S-186	6' 1"	Queen Anne Polished Mahogany/Walnut	21,590.
S-186	6' 1"	Queen Anne Satin Finish	21,590.
S-186	6' 1"	Designer Satin Ebony w/Bubinga Fallboard/Lid	21,760.

Steinberg, Wilh.

Verticals

IQ 14	45"	Continental Polished Ebony	14,190.
IQ 16	46"	Polished Ebony	15,190.
IQ 16	46"	Satin Beech/Oak/Alder	15,190.
IQ 16	46"	Satin Walnut/Mahogany	15,390.
IQ 16	46"	Satin Cherry	15,590.
IQ 16	46"	Satin Cherry with Yew	16,990.
IQ 24	48½"	Polished Ebony	16,990.
IQ 24	48½"	Satin Beech/Oak/Alder	16,990.
IQ 24	48½"	Satin Walnut/Mahogany	17,590.
IQ 24	48½"	Satin Cherry	17,990.
IQ 24	48½"	Satin Cherry with Yew	18,790.
IQ 24	48½"	"Amadeus" Polished Ebony	18,190.
IQ 24	48½"	"Amadeus" Satin Walnut/Mahogany	18,590.
IQ 28	51"	Polished Ebony	20,390.
IQ 28	51"	Satin Walnut/Mahogany	20,790.
IQ 28	51"	Satin Cherry	21,790.
IQ 28	51"	Satin Cherry with Yew	22,390.
IQ 28	51"	"Amadeus" Polished Ebony	22,790.
IQ 28	51"	"Amadeus" Satin Cherry	22,790.
IQ 28	51"	"Passione" Polished Ebony	24,390.
IQ 28	51"	"Passione" Satin Walnut/Mahogany	24,790.

Grands

IQ 77	5' 8"	Polished Ebony	50,790.
IQ 77	5' 8"	Satin Walnut/Mahogany	54,790.
IQ 77	5' 8"	Satin Cherry	55,390.
IQ 99	6' 4"	Polished Ebony	60,590.
IQ 99	6' 4"	Satin Walnut/Mahogany	68,790.
IQ 99	6' 4"	Satin Cherry	69,790.

Model	Size	Style and Finish	Price*

Steingraeber & Söhne

This list includes only those models most likely to be offered to U.S. customers. Other models, styles, and finishes are available.

Verticals

Model	Size	Style and Finish	Price
122 S	48"	Satin Ebony	25,700.
122 S	48"	Polished Ebony	29,630.
122 S	48"	Polished Sapeli Mahogany	35,420.
130 PS/S	51"	Polished Ebony	38,310.
130 PS/S	51"	Polished Ebony w/Twist & Change Panels	41,672.
130 PS/S	51"	Polished Sapeli Mahogany	39,114.
130 PS/S	51"	Satin Special Veneers	36,376.
130 PS/S	51"	Polished Special Veneers	40,046.
130 PS/R	51"	Polished Ebony with SFM Action	43,784.
130 PS/R	51"	Polished Special Veneers with SFM Action	47,314.
130 K	51"	"Classic" Polished Ebony	38,310.
130 K	51"	"Classic" Polished Ebony w/Twist & Change	41,672.
130 K	51"	"Classic" Polished Sapeli Mahogany	39,114.
130 K	51"	"Classic" Satin Special Veneers	36,376.
130 K	51"	"Classic" Polished Special Veneers	45,516.
138 K	54"	"Classic" Polished Ebony	45,596.
138 K	54"	"Classic" Polished Ebony w/Twist & Change	45,958.
138 K	54"	"Classic" Polished Sapeli Mahogany	46,270.
138 K	54"	"Classic" Satin Special Veneers	42,640.
138 K	54"	"Classic" Polished Special Veneers	48,120.

Grands

Model	Size	Style and Finish	Price
168 N	5' 7"	Polished Ebony	75,522.
168 N	5' 7"	Polished Ebony with Wood Accents	80,934.
168 N	5' 7"	Polished Sapeli Mahogany	83,360.
168 N	5' 7"	Satin Special Veneers	85,436.
168 N	5' 7"	Polished Special Veneers	96,194.
168 K	5' 7"	"Classicism" Polished Ebony	84,440.
168 K	5' 7"	"Classicism" Polished Ebony w/Wood Accents	92,770.
168 K	5' 7"	"Classicism" Polished Sapeli Mahogany	95,330.
168 K	5' 7"	"Classicism" Satin Special Veneers	97,298.
168 K	5' 7"	"Classicism" Polished Special Veneers	108,136.
168 S	5' 7"	"Studio" Polished Ebony	68,558.
205 N	6' 9"	Polished Ebony	96,868.
205 N	6' 9"	Polished Ebony with Wood Accents	105,252.
205 N	6' 9"	Polished Sapeli Mahogany	107,624.
205 N	6' 9"	Satin Special Veneers	109,808.
205 N	6' 9"	Polished Special Veneers	121,380.
205 K	6' 9"	"Classicism" Polished Ebony	107,842.
205 K	6' 9"	"Classicism" Polished Ebony w/Wood Accents	116,116.
205 K	6' 9"	"Classicism" Polished Sapeli Mahogany	118,490.

*For explanation of terms and prices, please see pages 113–117.

Model	Size	Style and Finish	Price*

Steingraeber & Söhne (continued)

205 K	6' 9"	"Classicism" Satin Special Veneers	120,566.
205 K	6' 9"	"Classicism" Polished Special Veneers	131,322.
205 S	6' 9"	"Studio" Polished Ebony	93,820.
E-272	8' 11"	Polished Ebony	188,614.

Steinway & Sons

These are the prices at the Steinway retail store in New York City, often used as a "benchmark" for Steinway prices throughout the country. Model K-52 in ebony; model 1098 in ebony, mahogany, and walnut; and grand models in ebony, mahogany, and walnut include adjustable artist bench. Other models include regular wood bench. Ebony models are in a satin finish; all other models are in a semi-gloss finish called "satin lustre."

Verticals

4510	45"	Sheraton Satin Ebony	20,600.
4510	45"	Sheraton Mahogany	22,900.
4510	45"	Sheraton Walnut	23,900.
4510	45"	Sheraton Dark Cherry	25,400.
4510	45"	Sheraton Macassar Ebony	30,300.
4510	45"	Sheraton Marbelized	29,200.
1098	46½"	Satin Ebony	19,300.
1098	46½"	Mahogany	21,100.
1098	46½"	Walnut	21,900.
1098	46½"	Dark Cherry	22,900.
1098	46½"	Marbelized	27,100.
K-52	52"	Satin Ebony	25,300.
K-52	52"	Mahogany	28,700.
K-52	52"	Walnut	29,700.
K-52	52"	East Indian Rosewood	37,100.
K-52	52"	Marbelized	35,100.

Grands

S	5' 1"	Satin Ebony	42,100.
S	5' 1"	Mahogany	47,200.
S	5' 1"	Walnut	49,100.
S	5' 1"	Figured Sapele	51,600.
S	5' 1"	Dark Cherry	52,100.
S	5' 1"	Kewazinga Bubinga	53,700.
S	5' 1"	Santos Rosewood	59,700.
S	5' 1"	East Indian Rosewood	60,300.
S	5' 1"	African Pommele	60,700.
S	5' 1"	Macassar Ebony	66,400.
S	5' 1"	Marbelized	59,700.
S	5' 1"	Chinoiserie	57,700.

Model	Size	Style and Finish	Price*
S	5' 1"	Hepplewhite Dark Cherry	54,700.
M	5' 7"	Satin Ebony	48,300.
M	5' 7"	Mahogany	54,100.
M	5' 7"	Walnut	56,100.
M	5' 7"	Figured Sapele	57,800.
M	5' 7"	Dark Cherry	59,400.
M	5' 7"	Kewazinga Bubinga	60,700.
M	5' 7"	Santos Rosewood	66,400.
M	5' 7"	East Indian Rosewood	67,400.
M	5' 7"	African Pommele	67,900.
M	5' 7"	Macassar Ebony	74,500.
M	5' 7"	Marbelized	67,100.
M	5' 7"	Chinoiserie	63,900.
M	5' 7"	Hepplewhite Dark Cherry	62,100.
M 1014A	5' 7"	Chippendale Mahogany	67,800.
M 1014A	5' 7"	Chippendale Walnut	69,500.
M 501A	5' 7"	Louis XV Walnut	87,400.
M 501A	5' 7"	Louis XV East Indian Rosewood	101,800.
O	5' 10½"	Satin Ebony	54,600.
O	5' 10½"	Mahogany	60,800.
O	5' 10½"	Walnut	62,900.
O	5' 10½"	Figured Sapele	65,200.
O	5' 10½"	Dark Cherry	66,100.
O	5' 10½"	Kewazinga Bubinga	68,100.
O	5' 10½"	Santos Rosewood	74,900.
O	5' 10½"	East Indian Rosewood	76,200.
O	5' 10½"	African Pommele	76,400.
O	5' 10½"	Macassar Ebony	84,500.
O	5' 10½"	Marbelized	75,800.
O	5' 10½"	Chinoiserie	70,200.
O	5' 10½"	Hepplewhite Dark Cherry	69,500.
O	5' 10½"	Henry Z. Steinway Limited Edition Ebony	71,100.
O	5' 10½"	Henry Z. Steinway Ltd. Edition Rosewood	99,100.
A	6' 2"	Satin Ebony	62,800.
A	6' 2"	Mahogany	69,500.
A	6' 2"	Walnut	71,600.
A	6' 2"	Figured Sapele	74,400.
A	6' 2"	Dark Cherry	75,400.
A	6' 2"	Kewazinga Bubinga	77,700.
A	6' 2"	Santos Rosewood	85,100.
A	6' 2"	East Indian Rosewood	85,600.
A	6' 2"	African Pommele	86,700.
A	6' 2"	Macassar Ebony	95,900.
A	6' 2"	Marbelized	85,100.
A	6' 2"	Chinoiserie	81,100.

*For explanation of terms and prices, please see pages 113–117.

Model	Size	Style and Finish	Price*

Steinway & Sons (continued)

Model	Size	Style and Finish	Price*
A	6' 2"	Limited Edition Lagerfield Ebony	85,000.
B	6' 10½"	Satin Ebony	70,700.
B	6' 10½"	Mahogany	77,900.
B	6' 10½"	Walnut	80,300.
B	6' 10½"	Figured Sapele	83,500.
B	6' 10½"	Dark Cherry	84,600.
B	6' 10½"	Kewazinga Bubinga	87,200.
B	6' 10½"	Santos Rosewood	95,500.
B	6' 10½"	East Indian Rosewood	96,400.
B	6' 10½"	African Pommele	96,700.
B	6' 10½"	Macassar Ebony	107,100.
B	6' 10½"	Marbelized	94,100.
B	6' 10½"	Chinoiserie	88,900.
B	6' 10½"	Hepplewhite Dark Cherry	89,500.
B	6' 10½"	Henry Z. Steinway Limited Edition Ebony	92,100.
B	6' 10½"	Henry Z. Steinway Ltd. Edition Rosewood	125,400.
D	8' 11¾"	Satin Ebony	107,100.
D	8' 11¾"	Mahogany	119,200.
D	8' 11¾"	Walnut	122,100.
D	8' 11¾"	Figured Sapele	128,500.
D	8' 11¾"	Dark Cherry	131,900.
D	8' 11¾"	Kewazinga Bubinga	136,700.
D	8' 11¾"	Santos Rosewood	146,600.
D	8' 11¾"	East Indian Rosewood	147,700.
D	8' 11¾"	African Pommele	148,400.
D	8' 11¾"	Macassar Ebony	163,800.
D	8' 11¾"	Chinoiserie	127,800.
D	8' 11¾"	Hepplewhite Dark Cherry	138,500.

Grands (Hamburg)

I frequently get requests for prices of pianos made in Steinway's branch factory in Hamburg, Germany. Officially, these pianos are not sold in North America, but it is possible to order one through an American Steinway dealer, or to go to Europe and purchase one there. The following list shows approximately how much it would cost to purchase a Hamburg Steinway in Europe and have it shipped to the United States. The list was derived by taking the published retail price in Europe, subtracting the value-added tax not applicable to foreign purchasers, converting to U.S. dollars (the rate used here is 1 Euro = $1.35, but is obviously subject to change), and adding approximate charges for duty, air freight, crating, insurance, brokerage fees, and delivery. Only prices for grands in polished ebony are shown here. *Caution:* This list is published for general informational purposes only. The price that Steinway would charge for a piano ordered through an American Steinway dealer may be different. (Also, the cost of a trip to Europe to purchase the piano is not included!)

Model	Size	Style and Finish	Price*
S-155	5' 1"	Polished Ebony	63,900.
M-170	5' 7"	Polished Ebony	69,900.
O-180	5' 10½"	Polished Ebony	74,000.
A-188	6' 2"	Polished Ebony	78,900.
B-211	6' 11"	Polished Ebony	91,700.
C-227	7' 5½"	Polished Ebony	107,400.
D-274	8' 11¾"	Polished Ebony	138,400.

Story & Clark

Verticals

Model	Size	Style and Finish	Price
111	45"	Continental Polished Ebony/Mahogany	3,590.
112	45"	"Arlington Fluted" Satin Cherry/Oak	4,790.
113	45"	"Charleston" Satin Fruitwood/Cherry/Oak	4,790.
114	45"	Institutional Satin Ebony/Oak	4,490.
114	45"	Institutional Polished Ebony	4,290.
115	45"	Queen Anne Polished Ebony	3,790.
115	45"	Queen Anne Polished Mahogany	3,990.
120	47"	"Deluxe" Polished Ebony/Mahogany	5,290.
123	48"	"Cosmopolitan" Polished Ebony	5,390.
140	53"	Polished Mahogany	6,790.

Grands

Model	Size	Style and Finish	Price
146	4' 9"	"Prelude" Polished Ebony	8,390.
152	5'	"Prelude" Satin Ebony/Mahogany	9,990.
152	5'	"Prelude" Polished Ebony	9,190.
152	5'	"Prelude" Polished Mahogany/White	9,990.
152 I	5'	"Imperial" Satin Ebony/Mahogany	12,190.
152 I	5'	"Imperial" Polished Ebony	11,790.
152 M	5'	"Cosmopolitan" Satin Ebony	11,990.
152 M	5'	"Cosmopolitan" Polished Ebony	11,790.
152 S	5'	French Provincial Polished Ebony	9,990.
152 S	5'	French Provincial Satin Mahogany	10,990.
152 S	5'	French Provincial Polished Mahogany/White	10,590.
165	5' 5"	"Prelude" Satin Ebony	11,390.
165	5' 5"	"Prelude" Polished Ebony	10,790.
165	5' 5"	"Prelude" Polished Mahogany	11,390.
165 V	5' 5"	"Victorian" Polished Ebony w/Bubinga	12,790.
185	6'	"Prelude" Polished Ebony	13,390.
185	6'	"Prelude" Polished Mahogany	13,990.
215	7'	"Prelude" Polished Ebony	19,190.
All grands		With Pianomation 2000CD+ Installed, add'l	3,300.
All grands		With Pianomation Petine Installed, add'l	4,100.
All grands		With Pianomation Ancho Installed, add'l	4,500.

*For explanation of terms and prices, please see pages 113–117.

Model	Size	Style and Finish	Price*

Suzuki

The models and prices below are the ones listed on Suzuki's web site.

Verticals

Model	Size	Style and Finish	Price
T-43C	43"	Continental Polished Ebony	2,587.
T-43C	43"	Continental Polished Mahogany	2,697.
T-43	43"	Polished Ebony	2,687.
T-43	43"	Polished Mahogany	2,797.
T-45	45"	Polished Ebony	2,887.
T-45	45"	Polished Mahogany	2,997.
T-48	48"	Polished Ebony	3,087.
T-48	48"	Polished Mahogany	3,197.

Grands

Model	Size	Style and Finish	Price
F-410	4' 10"	Polished Ebony	5,887.
F-410	4' 10"	Polished Mahogany	6,097.
F-52	5' 2"	Polished Ebony	6,487.
F-52	5' 2"	Polished Mahogany	6,697.
F-58	5' 8"	Polished Ebony	7,487.
F-58	5' 8"	Polished Mahogany	7,697.
F-62	6' 2"	Polished Ebony	8,487.
F-70	7'	Polished Ebony	10,287.

Vogel

Verticals

Model	Size	Style and Finish	Price
V-115 M	45"	Continental Polished Ebony	11,180.
V-115 M	45"	Continental Wood Finish	11,980.
V-115 T	45"	Polished Ebony	11,180.
V-115 T	45"	Polished Mahogany/White	11,980.
V-121 T	48"	Polished Ebony	12,580.
V-121 T	48"	Polished Mahogany	12,980.

Grands

Model	Size	Style and Finish	Price
V-160 C	5' 3"	Chippendale Polished Ebony	26,180.
V-160 C	5' 3"	Chippendale Polished Mahogany/Walnut/White	28,180.
V-160 R	5' 3"	"Royal" Polished Ebony	26,780.
V-160 R	5' 3"	"Royal" Polished Mahogany/Walnut/White	28,180.
V-160 RIO	5' 3"	"Royal" Polished Mahogany Intarsia Oval	30,780.
V-160 RM	5' 3"	"Royal" Polished Flame Mahogany Coffer	30,780.
V-160 T	5' 3"	Polished Ebony	23,580.
V-160 T	5' 3"	Polished Mahogany/Walnut/White	24,980.
V-160 TI	5' 3"	Polished Mahogany Intarsia	32,780.
V-177 C	5' 11"	Chippendale Polished Ebony	26,980.
V-177 C	5' 11"	Chippendale Polished Mahogany/Walnut/White	28,780.
V-177 R	5' 11"	"Royal" Polished Ebony	28,780.

Model	Size	Style and Finish	Price*
V-177 R	5' 11"	"Royal" Polished Mahogany/Walnut/White	28,980.
V-177 RI	5' 11"	"Royal" Polished Mahogany Intarsia	30,780.
V-177 RM	5' 11"	"Royal" Polished Flame Mahogany Coffer	30,780.
V-177 T	5' 11"	Polished Ebony	24,380.
V-177 T	5' 11"	Polished Mahogany/Walnut/White	25,780.
V-177 TI	5' 11"	Polished Mahogany Intarsia	32,780.

Vose & Sons

Verticals

113	45"	Polished Ebony	3,590.
113	45"	Polished Mahogany	3,690.

Grands

147	4' 10"	Polished Ebony	7,990.
147	4' 10"	Polished Mahogany	8,390.

Walter, Charles R.

Verticals

1520	43"	Satin Ebony	11,720.
1520	43"	Semi-Gloss Ebony	11,820.
1520	43"	Polished Ebony	11,960.
1520	43"	Satin Walnut	11,400.
1520	43"	Satin Cherry	11,370.
1520	43"	Satin Oak	11,040.
1520	43"	Satin Mahogany	11,580.
1520	43"	Italian Provincial Satin Ebony	11,720.
1520	43"	Italian Provincial Semi-Gloss Ebony	11,820.
1520	43"	Italian Provincial Polished Ebony	11,960.
1520	43"	Italian Provincial Satin Walnut	11,420.
1520	43"	Italian Provincial Satin Mahogany	11,600.
1520	43"	Italian Provincial Satin Oak	11,050.
1520	43"	Country Classic Satin Cherry	11,280.
1520	43"	Country Classic Satin Oak	11,100.
1520	43"	French Provincial Satin Oak	11,420.
1520	43"	French Prov. Satin Cherry/Walnut/Mahogany	11,720.
1520	43"	Riviera Satin Oak	11,010.
1520	43"	Queen Anne Satin Oak	11,500.
1520	43"	Queen Anne Satin Mahogany/Cherry	11,720.
1500	45"	Satin Ebony	10,700.
1500	45"	Semi-Gloss Ebony	10,880.
1500	45"	Polished Ebony	10,990.
1500	45"	Satin Oak	10,250.
1500	45"	Satin Walnut	10,800.
1500	45"	Satin Mahogany	10,940.

*For explanation of terms and prices, please see pages 113–117.

Model	Size	Style and Finish	Price*

Walter, Charles R. (continued)

Model	Size	Style and Finish	Price*
1500	45"	Gothic Satin Oak/Cherry	10,910.
All Verticals		Chinese-made action instead of Renner, less	1,200.

Grands

Model	Size	Style and Finish	Price*
W-175	5' 9"	Satin Ebony	43,010.
W-175	5' 9"	Semi-Polished and Polished Ebony	44,120.
W-175	5' 9"	Satin Mahogany/Walnut/Cherry	44,930.
W-175	5' 9"	Semi-Polished & Pol. Mahogany/Walnut/Cherry	46,070.
W-175	5' 9"	Open-Pore Walnut	43,850.
W-175	5' 9"	Satin Oak	41,340.
W-175	5' 9"	Chippendale Satin Mahogany/Cherry	46,340.
W-175	5' 9"	Chip. Semi-Polished & Pol. Mahogany/Cherry	47,440.
W-190	6' 4"	Satin Ebony	44,130.
W-190	6' 4"	Semi-Polished and Polished Ebony	45,240.
W-190	6' 4"	Satin Mahogany/Walnut/Cherry	46,050.
W-190	6' 4"	Semi-Polished & Pol. Mahogany/Walnut/Cherry	47,190.
W-190	6' 4"	Open-Pore Walnut	44,970.
W-190	6' 4"	Satin Oak	42,460.
W-190	6' 4"	Chippendale Satin Mahogany/Cherry	47,460.
W-190	6' 4"	Chip. Semi-Polished & Pol. Mahogany/Cherry	48,560.

Weber

"Legend" Verticals

Model	Size	Style and Finish	Price*
WLE 410	43"	Continental Polished Ebony/Ivory	3,680.
WLE 410	43"	Continental Polished Mahogany	3,760.
WLF 430	43"	French Provincial Satin Cherry	4,160.
WLF 430	43"	Mediterranean Satin Oak	4,160.
WLF 430	43"	Queen Anne Satin Cherry/Oak	4,160.
WLF 430	43"	Satin Mahogany	4,160.
WLE 460	46½"	Polished Ebony/Mahogany	4,360.
WLE 460	46½"	Satin Oak/Walnut	4,390.
WLE 480	48"	Polished Ebony	4,320.
WLE 480	48"	Polished Mahogany/Walnut/Bubinga	4,440.
WLE 520	52"	Polished Ebony	4,560.
WLE 520	52"	Polished Mahogany	4,680.

"Sovereign" Verticals

Model	Size	Style and Finish	Price*
WSF 44	43½"	French Provincial Satin Cherry	6,360.
WSF 44	43½"	Mediterranean Satin Oak	6,160.
WSF 44	43½"	Queen Anne Satin Cherry/Oak	6,560.
WSF 44	43½"	Satin Mahogany	6,160.
WSE 46	46½"	Satin Ebony	6,160.
WSE 46	46½"	American Satin Oak/Walnut	6,360.
WSE 47	47"	Satin and Polished Ebony	5,960.

Model	Size	Style and Finish	Price*
WSE 47	47"	Polished Mahogany	6,160.
WSE 48	48"	Satin and Polished Ebony	6,160.
WSE 48	48"	Satin Mahogany/Walnut	6,560.
WSE 48	48"	Polished Mahogany	6,360.
WSE 52	52"	Satin and Polished Ebony	7,080.
"Albert Weber" Verticals			
AW 48	48"	Polished Ebony	8,160.
AW 48	48"	Satin Satin Mahogany/Cherry	8,560.
AW 48	48"	Satin Bubinga/Rosewood	8,760.
AW 52	52"	Polished Ebony	10,160.
AW 52	52"	Satin Bubinga/Rosewood	10,760.
"Legend" Grands			
WLG 50	4' 11"	Polished Ebony/Ivory	9,600.
WLG 50	4' 11"	Satin Walnut/Cherry	9,800.
WLG 50	4' 11"	Polished Mahogany	9,800.
WLG 50C	4' 11"	French Provincial Cherry	9,900.
WLG 51	5' 2"	Polished Ebony/Ivory	10,640.
WLG 51	5' 2"	Polished Mahogany	10,760.
WLG 57	5' 9"	Polished Ebony	11,880.
WLG 57	5' 9"	Polished Mahogany	12,080.
WLG 60	6' 1"	Polished Ebony	12,760.
WLG 60	6' 1"	Polished Mahogany	13,080.
"Sovereign" Grands			
WSG 51	5' 1"	Satin and Polished Ebony	15,160.
WSG 51	5' 1"	Polished Mahogany	15,760.
WSG 51	5' 1"	Satin Walnut	15,960.
WSG 51	5' 1"	Satin Cherry	16,360.
WSG 51	5' 1"	Polished Ivory/White	15,360.
WSG 51D	5' 1"	Queen Anne Satin Mahogany	18,760.
WSG 51D	5' 1"	Queen Anne Satin Cherry	18,960.
WSG 51D	5' 1"	Country French Satin Cherry	18,960.
WSG 51D	5' 1"	Empire Satin Brown Mahogany	19,560.
WSG 57	5' 9"	Satin and Polished Ebony	16,960.
WSG 57	5' 9"	Satin Walnut	17,760.
WSG 57	5' 9"	Satin Cherry	17,960.
WSG 57	5' 9"	Polished Mahogany	17,560.
WSG 57D	5' 9"	Empire Polished Mahogany	21,120.
WSG 60	6' 1"	Satin and Polished Ebony	18,560.
WSG 60	6' 1"	Satin Walnut	19,760.
WSG 60	6' 1"	Polished Mahogany	19,560.
"Albert Weber" Grands			
AW 57	5' 9"	Satin Ebony	20,760.
AW 57	5' 9"	Polished Ebony	20,560.
AW 57	5' 9"	Polished Mahogany	21,160.

*For explanation of terms and prices, please see pages 113–117.

Model	Size	Style and Finish	Price*

Weber (continued)

Model	Size	Style and Finish	Price
AW 57	5' 9"	Satin Cherry	21,160.
AW 60	6' 1"	Satin Ebony	24,160.
AW 60	6' 1"	Polished Ebony	23,960.
AW 60	6' 1"	Polished Mahogany	24,760.
AW 60	6' 1"	Satin Cherry/Walnut	24,760.
AW 60	6' 1"	Polished Bubinga	26,760.
AW 69	6' 10"	Satin Ebony	28,960.
AW 69	6' 10"	Polished Ebony	28,760.
AW 76	7' 6"	Satin Ebony	37,360.
AW 76	7' 6"	Polished Ebony	37,160.
AW 90	9'	Polished Ebony	46,790.

Weinbach

Grands

Model	Size	Style and Finish	Price
Estate 50	5'	Polished Ebony	11,790.
Estate 50	5'	Polished Walnut/Mahogany	12,390.
Estate 50 DC	5'	Demi-Chippendale Polished Ebony	12,790.
Estate 50 DC	5'	Demi-Chippendale Polished Walnut/Mahogany	13,390.
Manor 55	5' 5"	Polished Ebony	12,990.
Manor 55	5' 5"	Polished Walnut/Mahogany	13,590.
Manor 55 DC	5' 5"	Demi-Chippendale Polished Ebony	13,990.
Manor 55 DC	5' 5"	Demi-Chippendale Polished Walnut/Mahogany	14,590.
Chateau 60	6'	Polished Ebony	14,790.
Chateau 60	6'	Polished Walnut/Mahogany	15,390.

Weinberger

Prices do not include bench. Euro=$1.35

Verticals

Model	Size	Style and Finish	Price
Friend	45"	Polished Ebony	15,100.
Friend	45"	Polished Mahogany/Dark Walnut	16,300.
Friend	45"	Satin Walnut	15,220.
Friend	45"	Satin Cherry	15,450.
Friend	45"	Polished Cherry	16,650.
Friend	45"	Cherry Oiled and Waxed	15,790.
Friend	45"	Satin Beech/Alder	14,935.
Friend	45"	Polished White	16,820.
Vision One	47"	Polished Ebony	16,760.
Vision One	47"	Polished Mahogany/Dark Walnut	18,475.
Vision One	47"	Satin Walnut	17,100.
Vision One	47"	Satin Cherry	17,330.
Vision One	47"	Polished Cherry	18,650.

Model	Size	Style and Finish	Price*
Vision One	47"	Cherry Oiled and Waxed	17,700.
Vision One	47"	Satin Beech/Alder	16,760.
Vision One	47"	Polished White	18,650.
Concert	51"	Polished Ebony	23,215.
Concert	51"	Polished Mahogany/Dark Walnut	25,000.
Concert	51"	Satin Walnut	23,725.
Concert	51"	Satin Cherry	24,150.
Concert	51"	Polished Cherry	25,440.
Concert	51"	Polished Rosewood	26,550.
Concert	51"	Polished White	24,925.
All models		Other Finishes	on request

Grands

Passion	5' 7"	Polished Ebony	62,850.
Passion	5' 7"	Polished Mahogany/Dark Walnut	69,700.
Passion	5' 7"	Polished White	64,550.
Chamber	6' 3"	Polished Ebony	71,200.
All models		Other Finishes	on request

Wurlitzer

Grands

C143	4' 7"	Polished Ebony/White	9,828.
C143	4' 7"	Polished Mahogany/Oak	10,098.
C153	5' 1"	Satin and Polished Ebony	11,240.
C153	5' 1"	Polished Mahogany	11,600.
C153	5' 1"	Satin Oak/Walnut	11,600.
C153	5' 1"	Polished Ivory	11,240.
C153QA	5' 1"	Queen Anne Polished Mahogany	13,400.
C153QA	5' 1"	Queen Anne Satin Oak/Cherry	13,400.
C173	5' 8"	Satin and Polished Ebony	12,320.
C173	5' 8"	Polished Mahogany	12,672.
C173	5' 8"	Polished White	12,320.
C203	6' 9"	Satin and Polished Ebony	16,510.
C203QA	6' 9"	Queen Anne Polished Cherry	17,510.
C223	7' 5"	Satin and Polished Ebony	20,544.
C273	9'	Satin and Polished Ebony	48,778.

Wyman

Verticals

WV108	42½"	Continental Polished Ebony	3,590.
WV108	42½"	Continental Polished Mahogany/Cherry	3,650.
WV110	43"	Polished Ebony	3,990.
WV110	43"	Polished Mahogany/Cherry	4,050.
WV110	43"	American Country Satin Gallery Oak	4,590.

*For explanation of terms and prices, please see pages 113–117.

Model	Size	Style and Finish	Price*

Wyman (continued)

Model	Size	Style and Finish	Price
WV110	43"	Satin Sable Brown Mahogany	4,590.
WV110	43"	French Provincial Satin Sable Cherry	4,650.
WV110	43"	Country French Satin Oak	4,650.
WV115	45"	Polished Ebony	4,190.
WV115	45"	Polished Mahgoany/Cherry	4,250.
WV118	46"	Polished Ebony	4,790.
WV118	46"	Satin Walnut	4,850.
WV118DL	46"	Polished Ebony w/Chrome Trim (double leg)	4,850.
WV120	48"	Polished Ebony	4,590.
WV120	48"	Polished Mahogany	4,650.
WV127	50"	Polished Ebony w/Mahog. Trim (straight leg)	6,790.
WV127	50"	Polished Ebony w/Mahog. Trim (curved leg)	6,850.
WV132	52"	Polished Ebony	5,590.

Grands

Model	Size	Style and Finish	Price
WG145	4' 9"	Satin Ebony/Mahogany/Cherry	8,690.
WG145	4' 9"	Polished Ebony	8,390.
WG145	4' 9"	Polished Mahogany/Cherry/White	8,990.
WG160	5' 3"	Satin Ebony/Mahogany/Cherry	10,290.
WG160	5' 3"	Polished Ebony	9,990.
WG160	5' 3"	Polished Mahogany/Cherry/White	10,390.
GP160	5' 3"	Polished Ebony	9,950.
GP160	5' 3"	Polished Mahogany/Cherry/White	10,550.
WG170	5' 7"	Satin Ebony/Mahogany/Cherry	11,090.
WG170	5' 7"	Polished Ebony	10,790.
WG170	5' 7"	Polished Mahogany/Cherry/White	11,390.
GP175	5' 8"	Polished Ebony	11,950.
GP175	5' 8"	Polished Mahogany/Cherry/White	12,550.
WG185	6' 1"	Satin Ebony/Mahogany/Cherry	13,090.
WG185	6' 1"	Polished Ebony	12,790.
WG185	6' 1"	Polished Mahogany/Cherry/White	13,390.
GP190	6' 3"	Polished Ebony	13,950.
GP190	6' 3"	Polished Mahogany/Cherry/White	14,550.
GP215	7'	Polished Ebony	20,750.
GP215	7'	Polished Mahogany/Cherry/White	21,350.
All models		Empire or French, add'l	200.
All models		CD Player System, add'l	4,200.

Yamaha

Verticals

Model	Size	Style and Finish	Price
M112	44"	Continental Satin Ebony	5,890.
M112	44"	Continental Polished Ebony	5,990.
M112	44"	Continental Satin American Walnut	6,090.

Model	Size	Style and Finish	Price*
M112	44"	Continental Polished Mahogany	7,190.
M112	44"	Continental Polished Ivory/White	7,090.
M425	44"	Satin Mahogany/Cherry	4,190.
M450	44"	Satin Cherry	4,590.
M450	44"	Satin Brown Cherry	4,700.
M475	44"	Satin Mahogany	5,090.
M475	44"	Italian Provincial Satin Dark Cherry	5,090.
M500	44"	Chippendale Satin Brown Mahogany	6,790.
M500	44"	Florentine Satin Light Oak	5,690.
M500	44"	Georgian Satin Mahogany	6,790.
M500	44"	Hancock Satin Brown Cherry	5,090.
M500	44"	Milano Satin Dark Oak	5,690.
M500	44"	Parisian Satin Cherry/Dark Cherry	6,990.
M500	44"	Queen Anne Satin Cherry/Dark Cherry	5,890.
M500	44"	Sheraton Satin Mahogany	5,090.
P22	45"	Satin Ebony/Walnut/Cherry/Oak	5,990.
T116	45"	Satin Ebony	4,790.
T116	45"	Polished Ebony	6,190.
T116S	45"	Polished Ebony with Silver Hardware	6,590.
T116	45"	Polished Mahogany	7,190.
P600	45"	Sheraton Satin Brown Mahogany	6,790.
P600	45"	Queen Anne Satin Brown Cherry	6,790.
P600	45"	Tuscan Satin Ash	6,990.
T118	46"	Polished Ebony	5,190.
T118	46"	Polished Mahogany	5,590.
T121	48"	Polished Ebony	7,390.
U1	48"	Satin Ebony	9,250.
U1	48"	Polished Ebony	8,990.
U1	48"	Satin American Walnut	9,790.
U1	48"	Polished American Walnut/Mahogany	10,390.
U1	48"	Polished White	10,490.
YUS1	48"	Satin Ebony	11,250.
YUS1	48"	Polished Ebony	10,990.
YUS1	48"	Satin American Walnut	11,790.
YUS1	48"	Polished American Walnut/Mahogany	13,390.
U3	52"	Polished Ebony	12,490.
U3	52"	Satin American Walnut	12,690.
U3	52"	Polished Mahogany	13,690.
YUS3	52"	Polished Ebony	13,590.
YUS3	52"	Polished Mahogany	15,790.
YUS5	52"	Polished Ebony	15,790.
Disklavier Verticals			
MX500	44"	Chippendale Satin Brown Mahogany	11,790.
MX500	44"	Florentine Satin Light Oak	10,590.

*For explanation of terms and prices, please see pages 113–117.

Model	Size	Style and Finish	Price*
Yamaha (continued)			
MX500	44"	Georgian Satin Mahogany	11,590.
MX500	44"	Milano Satin Dark Oak	10,590.
MX500	44"	Parisian Satin Cherry/Dark Cherry	11,790.
MX500	44"	Queen Anne Satin Cherry/Dark Cherry	10,790.
MX22	45"	Satin American Walnut/Oak/Ebony	10,990.
MX116	45"	Polished Ebony	11,190.
MX116	45"	Polished Mahogany	12,190.
MX600	45"	Sheraton Satin Brown Mahogany	11,790.
MX600	45"	Queen Anne Satin Dark Cherry	11,790.
MX600	45"	Tuscan Satin Ash	11,990.
MIDIPiano (Silent) Verticals			
MP500	44"	Florentine Satin Light Oak	8,390.
MP500	44"	Georgian Satin Mahogany	9,390.
MP500	44"	Hancock Satin Brown Cherry	7,890.
MP500	44"	Milano Satin Dark Oak	8,390.
MP500	44"	Parisian Satin Cherry	9,590.
MP500	44"	Queen Anne Satin Cherry/Dark Cherry	8,590.
MP500	44"	Sheraton Satin Mahogany	7,890.
MP22	45"	Satin American Walnut	8,590.
MPU1	48"	Polished Ebony	11,700.
Disklavier Verticals with Silent Feature			
DU1A	48"	Polished Ebony	16,790.
DU1A	48"	Satin American Walnut	17,590.
DU1A	48"	Polished Mahogany	18,190.
DU1A	48"	Polished White	18,290.
Grands			
GB1	4' 11"	Polished Ebony	11,300.
GB1	4' 11"	Polished American Walnut/Mahogany	12,900.
GC1	5' 3"	Satin Ebony	17,300.
GC1	5' 3"	Polished Ebony	16,790.
GC1	5' 3"	Satin American Walnut	18,790.
GC1	5' 3"	Polished Mahogany/American Walnut	18,790.
GC1	5' 3"	Polished Ivory/White	18,390.
GC1FP	5' 3"	French Provincial Satin Brown Cherry	19,900.
GC1G	5' 3"	Georgian Satin Brown Mahogany	19,900.
C1	5' 3"	Satin Ebony	22,190.
C1	5' 3"	Polished Ebony	21,790.
C1	5' 3"	Satin American Walnut	24,590.
C1	5' 3"	Polished American Walnut	25,500.
C1	5' 3"	Satin and Polished Mahogany	25,500.
C1	5' 3"	Polished White	24,590.
C2	5' 8"	Satin Ebony	24,990.

Model	Size	Style and Finish	Price*
C2	5' 8"	Polished Ebony	24,500.
C2	5' 8"	Satin American Walnut	27,990.
C2	5' 8"	Polished American Walnut/Mahogany	28,790.
C2	5' 8"	Satin Light American Oak	27,990.
C2	5' 8"	Polished White	26,390.
C3	6' 1"	Satin Ebony	33,790.
C3	6' 1"	Polished Ebony	32,990.
C3	6' 1"	Satin American Walnut	36,590.
C3	6' 1"	Polished Mahogany/American Walnut	38,590.
C3	6' 1"	Polished White	37,300.
S4B	6' 3"	Polished Ebony	59,190.
C5	6' 7"	Satin Ebony	36,390.
C5	6' 7"	Polished Ebony	35,790.
C5	6' 7"	Polished Mahogany	45,590.
C6	6' 11"	Satin Ebony	40,500.
C6	6' 11"	Polished Ebony	39,790.
C6	6' 11"	Polished Mahogany	47,790.
S6B	6' 11"	Polished Ebony	66,990.
C7	7' 6"	Satin Ebony	45,990.
C7	7' 6"	Polished Ebony	45,590.
C7	7' 6"	Polished Mahogany	52,190.
CFIIIS	9'	Satin Ebony	121,790.
CFIIIS	9'	Polished Ebony	120,300.
Disklavier Grands			
DGB1CD	4' 11"	Polished Ebony (playback only)	19,870.
DGB1CD	4' 11"	Polished Mahogany/Walnut (playback only)	21,470.
DGC1B	5' 3"	Polished Ebony (playback only)	25,990.
DGC1B	5' 3"	Polished Mahogany/Walnut (playback only)	27,990.
DGC1M4	5' 3"	Satin Ebony	34,442.
DGC1M4	5' 3"	Polished Ebony	33,932.
DGC1M4	5' 3"	Satin American Walnut	35,932.
DGC1M4	5' 3"	Polished American Walnut/Mahogany	35,932.
DGC1M4	5' 3"	Polished Ivory/White	35,532.
DC1M4	5' 3"	Satin Ebony	39,332.
DC1M4	5' 3"	Polished Ebony	38,932.
DC1M4	5' 3"	Satin American Walnut	41,732.
DC1M4	5' 3"	Polished American Walnut	42,642.
DC1M4	5' 3"	Satin and Polished Mahogany	42,642.
DC1M4	5' 3"	Polished White	41,732.
DC2M4	5' 8"	Satin Ebony	42,132.
DC2M4	5' 8"	Polished Ebony	41,642.
DC2M4	5' 8"	Satin American Walnut	45,132.
DC2M4	5' 8"	Polished American Walnut/Mahogany	45,932.
DC2M4	5' 8"	Polished White	43,532.

*For explanation of terms and prices, please see pages 113–117.

Model	Size	Style and Finish	Price*

Yamaha (continued)

Model	Size	Style and Finish	Price*
DC3M4T	6' 1"	Satin Ebony	59,490.
DC3M4T	6' 1"	Polished Ebony	58,690.
DC3M4T	6' 1"	Satin American Walnut	62,290.
DC3M4T	6' 1"	Polished Mahogany	64,290.
DC3M4T	6' 1"	Polished White	63,000.
DC5M4T	6' 7"	Satin Ebony	62,090.
DC5M4T	6' 7"	Polished Ebony	60,890.
DC5M4T	6' 7"	Polished Mahogany	71,290.
DC6M4T	6' 11"	Satin Ebony	66,200.
DC6M4T	6' 11"	Polished Ebony	65,490.
DC6M4T	6' 11"	Polished Mahogany	73,490.
DC7M4T	7' 6"	Satin Ebony	71,690.
DC7M4T	7' 6"	Polished Ebony	71,290.
DC7M4T	7' 6"	Polished Mahogany	77,890.

Disklavier Pro Grands

Model	Size	Style and Finish	Price*
DC3M4PRO	6' 1"	Polished Ebony	58,990.
DS4M4PROB	6' 3"	Polished Ebony	85,190.
DC5M4PRO	6' 7"	Polished Ebony	61,790.
DC6M4PRO	6' 11"	Polished Ebony	65,790.
DS6M4PROB	6' 11"	Polished Ebony	92,990.
DC7M4PRO	7' 6"	Polished Ebony	71,590.
DCFIIISM4PRO	9'	Polished Ebony	150,300.

MIDIPiano (Silent) Grands

Model	Size	Style and Finish	Price*
MPC1	5' 3"	Polished Ebony	26,100.
MPC2	5' 8"	Polished Ebony	28,700.
MPC3	6' 1"	Polished Ebony	36,790.
MPC6	6' 11"	Polished Ebony	42,900.
MPC7	7' 6"	Polished Ebony	48,190.

Young Chang

Verticals

Model	Size	Style and Finish	Price*
PF-110	43½"	Satin Mahogany	6,190.
PF-110	43½"	Satin Queen Anne Oak/Cherry	6,590.
PF-110	43½"	Mediterranean Satin Oak	6,190.
PF-110	43½"	French Provincial Satin Cherry	6,390.
PE-116S	46½"	Satin Ebony	6,190.
PE-116S	46½"	Satin American Walnut/Oak	6,390.
PE-116S	46½"	Satin American Cherry	6,590.
PE-118	47"	Satin and Polished Ebony	5,990.
PE-118	47"	Polished Mahogany	6,190.
PE-121	48"	Satin and Polished Ebony	6,190.
PE-121	48"	Satin Mahogany/Walnut/Oak	6,590.

Model	Size	Style and Finish	Price*
PE-121	48"	Polished Mahogany/Walnut/Oak	6,390.
P-121SE	48"	50th Anniversary Polished Ebony	8,190.
YP-48	48"	Polished Ebony	8,190.
YP-48	48"	Satin Mahogany/Cherry	8,590.
YP-48	48"	Satin Bubinga/Rosewood	8,790.
YP-49	49"	Polished Ebony w/Chrome	9,790.
YP-49	49"	Satin Mahogany	9,790.
YP-49	49"	Satin Bubinga	9,990.
PE-131	52"	Satin and Polished Ebony	7,110.
YP-52	52"	Polished Ebony	10,190.
YP-52	52"	Satin Bubinga/Rosewood	10,790.
Grands			
PG-157	5' 1"	Satin and Polished Ebony	15,190.
PG-157	5' 1"	Satin Walnut	15,990.
PG-157	5' 1"	Satin Cherry	16,390.
PG-157	5' 1"	Polished Mahogany/Walnut	15,790.
PG-157	5' 1"	Polished Ivory/White	15,390.
PG-157D	5' 1"	Country French Satin Cherry	18,990.
PG-157D	5' 1"	Queen Anne Satin Mahogany	18,790.
PG-157D	5' 1"	Queen Anne Satin Cherry	18,990.
PG-157D	5' 1"	Empire Polished Mahogany	19,590.
PG-175	5' 9"	Satin and Polished Ebony	16,990.
PG-175	5' 9"	Satin Walnut	17,790.
PG-175	5' 9"	Satin Cherry	17,990.
PG-175	5' 9"	Polished Mahogany/Walnut	17,590.
PG-175	5' 9"	Polished Ivory/White	17,190.
PG-175D	5' 9"	Empire Polished Mahogany	21,150.
YP-175	5' 9"	Satin Ebony	20,790.
YP-175	5' 9"	Polished Ebony	20,590.
YP-175	5' 9"	Polished Ebony with Pommele Inlay	21,190.
YP-175	5' 9"	Polished Mahogany/Rosewood	21,190.
YP-175SE	5' 9"	50th Anniversary Polished Ebony w/Chrome	20,590.
PG-185	6' 1"	Satin and Polished Ebony	18,590.
PG-185	6' 1"	Satin Walnut	19,790.
PG-185	6' 1"	Satin Cherry	20,190.
PG-185	6' 1"	Polished Mahogany/Walnut	19,590.
PG-185	6' 1"	Polished Ivory	18,790.
YP-185	6' 1"	Satin Ebony	24,190.
YP-185	6' 1"	Polished Ebony	23,990.
YP-185	6' 1"	Polished Ebony with Pommele Inlay	24,790.
YP-185	6' 1"	Polished Mahogany	24,790.
YP-185	6' 1"	Polished Bubinga	26,790.
YP-185	6' 1"	Polished African Pommele	27,190.
YP-185	6' 1"	Polished Rosewood	27,990.
YP-208	6' 10"	Satin Ebony	28,990.

*For explanation of terms and prices, please see pages 113–117.

Model	Size	Style and Finish	Price*

Young Chang (continued)

YP-208	6' 10"	Polished Ebony	28,790.
YP-208	6' 10"	Polished Pommele/Rosewood	35,190.
YP-228	7' 6"	Satin Ebony	37,390.
YP-228	7' 6"	Polished Ebony	37,190.
YP-275	9'	Polished Ebony	46,790.